Bourdieu and Educ

Bourdieu and Education:
Acts of Practical Theory

Michael Grenfell and David James
with Philip Hodkinson, Diane Reay and Derek Robbins

FALMER PRESS
Taylor & Francis Group

UK   Falmer Press, 1 Gunpowder Square, London, EC4A 3DE
USA   Falmer Press, Taylor & Francis Inc., 1900 Frost Road, Suite 101, Bristol, PA 19007

First published in 1998

A catalogue record for this book is available from the British Library

ISBN 0 7507 0887 5 cased
ISBN 0 7507 0886 7 paper

Library of Congress Cataloging-in-Publication Data are available on request

Jacket design by Caroline Archer

Typeset in 10/12pt Times by
Graphicraft Typesetters Limited, Hong Kong

Printed in Great Britain by Biddles Ltd., Guildford and King's Lynn on paper which has a specified pH value on final paper manufacture of not less than 7.5 and is therefore 'acid free'.

Contents

Chapter 1

Introduction

The work of the French social theorist, Pierre Bourdieu, has attracted increasing interest in recent years. Since initial publications in the late 1950s and early 1960s he has demonstrated considerable intellectual rigour and insight in engaging with the main social science debates of the day. The list of topics and themes he has covered takes in most of the major fields of study. However, it is education to which his attention has repeatedly turned, and it is probably in education that his ideas have had the greatest impact. Much of his early work dealt with educational issues, topics and themes and appeared in two major books: *Les Héritiers* (Bourdieu and Passeron, 1964) and *La Reproduction. Eléments pour une théorie du système d'enseignement* (Bourdieu and Passeron, 1970). The latter was published in English in 1977 and quickly became a classic text in the sociology of education canon. Bourdieu also contributed two chapters to the seminal book, *Knowledge and Control* (1971), which was edited by Michael Young and represented a new sociological direction in the study of the processes of classroom knowledge construction.

Since these early works, Bourdieu has offered a number of articles on topics related to aspects of education and pedagogy. Other major books have dealt with his own French academic field and the training of the national bureaucratic elites: *Homo Academicus* (1984) and *La Noblesse d'Etat* (1989a). In 1993, he published a large collection entitled *La Misère du Monde* (1993b), which chronicles the social production of the 'poverty' of experience, including that of the classroom, teacher and staffroom. And, in perhaps his most philosophical discussion to date, he has returned to the notion of the scholastic view in *Méditations Pascaliennes* (1997).

Interest in Bourdieu has meant that all but the most recent of these books are now available in English, and it is common to find reference to one or two of his works across the expanse of research and literature in education. Bourdieu is a social theorist whose work has addressed a wide range of contemporary topics and themes, including art, the media, language, sport, politics and other socio-cultural issues. His ideas have long been used by sociologists of education to develop their explanations of class, status and power in pedagogic contexts. Much of his work has been developed in a French academic field which has included the principal instigators of post-modernism; namely, Foucault, Derrida, Lacan, Lyotard. Bourdieu has worked to differentiate himself from this trend. At the same time, he has taken on, and argued against, much of the approach and method that goes under the title of objectivity in the social sciences, and which he sees as being so prevalent in an Anglo-Saxon academic world. At the base of this work, therefore, is both a philosophical perspective and practical methodology which have attempted to establish an alternative to the extremes of post-modernist subjectivity and positivist objectivity. Both traditions have deeply marked research and writing on education. The principal *point de départ* in this book is, consequently, the view that Bourdieu's ideas offer an epistemological and methodological third way, which has implications for the way we approach enquiry into educational phenomena; for example, how we carry out research, analyse data and present results. Although there are exceptions, discussion of his work so far amongst western educationalists has tended to consider it mainly in terms of theoretical concepts rather than its practical applications. Such theoretical discussion has often carried an explicit critical objective. Whilst it cannot be said that we are uncritical in this book, our purpose of considering the practical application of Bourdieu's ideas in educational research requires a generally positive engagement with those ideas.

Our main aims are two-fold: firstly, to present the main components of Bourdieu's theoretical position in a way which highlights its implications for education; secondly, to offer examples of individuals using the approach in educational research so as to indicate how the ideas might be employed in practical situations. The book is a fully integrated text but not of the kind written by a single author. Nor does it present an exclusively linear narrative structure. There are many voices throughout the ten chapters. One of them is Bourdieu's own, and we have made use of the available publications as a way of indicating his main theoretical arguments. We have also included contributions from researchers who have drawn extensively on Bourdieu's ideas in their own work. Some of these accounts report the words, opinions, and experiences of others in a range of educational contexts. However, the book is not simply an edited collection of papers. It seeks instead to approach Bourdieu's work from directions that are distinct, but which, when read together, make up a composite picture of what it is to use these ideas in practice and of the nature of our understandings arising from such an undertaking.

Our project is both modest and ambitious. It is modest in that it recognizes that what we offer can hardly do justice to Bourdieu's voluminous writings and the very many sophisticated points of detail he has made regarding education over almost four decades of writing about it. Moreover, the practical examples we include can also only be considered as a small beginning to the type of research that is possible from this perspective. Yet whilst we do not wish to insist that a Bourdieuian approach is always or automatically the best way to research educational phenomena, our project is an ambitious one because it is based on a particular conviction. Put simply, this is that research in terms of Bourdieu's theory of practice offers insights and understandings not readily visible in other approaches.

We recognize that what we present goes beyond a simple replication of Bourdieu's own work. The practical case examples we include are very different from Bourdieu's. Nevertheless, we believe that many of the issues he explores in an explicit fashion, and the connected issues he raises, have direct and generally applicable implications for numerous aspects of educational research. The book includes contributions from those researching language, relations between school and the family, young people's career choices and elements within the academic discourse in higher education. These accounts demonstrate the way others have drawn on Bourdieu's ideas and felt, as a consequence, that they have been able to enrich their own thematic explorations. The underlying invitation in the book is for others to apply the approach to particular research areas in similar ways in order to assess its ultimate worth. The book is aimed at students at a variety of levels, both graduate and post-graduate, as well as academics and researchers working in education. The issues raised and approaches adopted will also be of interest to teachers and others working at what is still often called 'the chalk face'.

The main themes of the book are both theoretical and practical, and these preoccupations are reflected in its structure. Early chapters set out the basic theoretical position and the central terms of analysis. This coverage is treated from a socio-cultural perspective in order to indicate when and how the ideas arose and their relevance to the contemporary debates of the day. We also look at the philosophical justifications for Bourdieu's theory of practice.

The core of the book contains detail of the practical applications of Bourdieu's theories to a series of specific pedagogic studies, with the intention of showing how the ideas have been used in practice. Diane Reay examines the relationship between home and the school in terms of gender differences. Michael Grenfell reviews approaches to analysing classroom language from a Bourdieuian perspective. Philip Hodkinson offers a critique of representations of young people's career decision making, whilst David James looks at elements of the academic discourse in higher education. Some aspects of these applications are much as we would expect from a conventional sociological treatment. In each of these cases, particular dimensions and elements of educational processes are discussed from a perspective provided by Bourdieu's work, and it is shown how these ideas shaped the approach taken and the conclusions drawn. As a follow up to these chapters, the writers involved are invited to reflect on their own experience of using the approach. Here, elements of the relationship between the researcher and the researched are rendered visible in a way that is not common in discussion on education. The nature of the various dimensions of reflexivity available in the research process is discussed across these accounts rather than in terms of each of their particular characteristics; for example, the relationship between the researcher and the researched and the way that theoretical perspectives develop during research.

Reflexivity will be a principal concept throughout the book, and, at key points in the text, people appear as individuals. However, this heightened profile of the writer should not be mistaken for a fascination with their personality. Rather, the issue at stake is the understanding of the social world as an engagement of individuals with it in practical situations. We see this to be no less true for the processes and techniques undertaken in social science and educational research than in other topics of investigation. The theory of practice outlined will hence be discussed and applied to the activities involved in carrying out research as much as to the object of the research itself.

A detailed discussion of what it is to conduct research within a Bourdieuian framework is set out as a way of suggesting to others how they might go about thinking through their own research projects in these terms. The intention here is to be suggestive rather than prescriptive. We do not want to appear to be telling other educational researchers how they should be conducting research. At the same time, we do not want to be overly tentative, *laissez-faire*, or methodologically timid. Our intention is to offer a range of case examples of research undertaken in Britain in the 1990s in a way which is suggestive of how similar research might be carried out. What these examples show is the same basic structures in operation in different contexts.

The book will be of interest to those new to research as well as those familiar with Bourdieu's work but who have not applied it in any direct way to particular educational contexts. Different readers may want to approach the book in different ways. Those interested primarily in a discussion of the basic theoretical position will find this in Chapter 2. After this, practical issues of research methodology are included in Parts II and IV. The four key pedagogic topics are dealt with individually in Part II. Alternatively, those seeking a more philosophical account of Bourdieu's main theoretical position may well wish to start with Chapter 3, where details of the various writings in the light of major themes in educational research are also given. Other readers who are mainly interested in questions of reflexivity may turn first to Parts III and IV. There are, then, at least four ways of reading this book.

As a final point of introduction, we would wish to emphasize one aspect of Bourdieu's work which is perhaps so obvious that it is sometimes overlooked. We refer to Bourdieu's own socio-cultural context. Bourdieu works in a French academic field. Most of his work is written first in French. Much of this writing is necessarily shaped by the thematic preoccupations of his home field. There is, of course, rivalry between competing factions within it. We can only ever view these ongoing intellectual battles from a distance, and only ever take partial account of them in our own uses and potential misuses of the ideas generated within such struggles to establish the dominant arguments. As shall become evident later in the book, the use of language itself also renders problematic the terms of the discussion; it is certainly not true that translated text can always capture the full sense of the originally intended meaning. Here we aim to render as accessible some of the principal ideas in Bourdieu's work. Whenever possible we have indicated where the more obvious misunderstandings may lie, and have illustrated major ideas with reference to familiar educational contexts. Different contributors to the book have also chosen to work from either French or English versions of Bourdieu's texts, or to use both. There are often important differences between the two, and we would not wish to suppress the possibilities offered by working with originals. However, for the purposes of this book, quotations are offered uniquely in English; either according to published translations or our contributors' own interpretations of the French texts. We feel this is preferable to insisting on only using the English versions. Readers should note that unless indicated 'own translation', the reference is to the published English text.

Part I

Bourdieu in Education

Anyone encountering Bourdieu's work is immediately struck by the range of theoretical concepts he employs; for example, field, habitus capital, etc. What is the meaning of these terms and why are they necessary? This part of the book answers these questions, but it does so in two ways as represented by its two separate chapters.

Chapter 2 sets out to define the basic terms and to explain the issues of theory and practice underlying them. Bourdieu is a sociologist with sociological preoccupations. However, the themes raised in his methodological discussions have implications for the whole of social science research in general and education in particular. This chapter shows how this is so. The intention is to provide a theoretical and conceptual map within which the practical applications in later chapters can be located.

Chapter 3 approaches these theoretical and practical issues from a more philosophical direction. Again, the accent is on showing the way Bourdieu's ideas have developed in response to a range of key epistemological issues. This discussion is set in a historical context. What the various issues meant for educationalists and the way they responded to Bourdieu's work is also discussed. The points raised are thus connected to the hot debates of the day. The term epistemology is adopted to indicate the way knowledge is used in and gained from educational research. This knowledge has a different character and status according to the type of approach adopted. The 'break' mentioned in the chapter title refers to the attempt to move away from pre-established methodological positions. Why this should be necessary is the central purpose of this chapter. Bourdieu's own background is also referred to in order to indicate the roots of his main theoretical position. Similar accounts are used later in the book in order to highlight the relationship between the researcher and their research.

Chapter 2

Theory, Practice and Pedagogic Research

Introduction

In this chapter, Bourdieu's basic terms of analysis will be described and explained; for example, *field*, *capital*, *habitus*. We begin the chapter with a broader discussion of prevailing approaches to educational research, and then connect these approaches with Bourdieu's own theory of practice in order to show up the relevance of the connecting themes. The structure of the chapter seeks to place Bourdieu's terms of analysis within the context of British educational research and its struggles with such notions as theory and practice; objectivity and subjectivity; and the various paradigmatic approaches to these.

Theory and the Idea of Paradigms in Educational Research

As any field of social science, educational research has undergone enormous changes in the course of its post-war development. For the most part, this development can be seen as a gradual move away from semi-experimental investigations based on the statistical analysis of empirical data to more qualitative approaches aimed at naturalistic enquiries into a range of educational contexts. Throughout these changes, the role, form and status of theory and practice in educational research have been continuously debated. What is the nature of theory? How is it represented? Is it prior to or arising from analysis of the world? What methods are used to conduct this analysis? How do the outcomes of research relate to the shaping of educational policy and practice? Bourdieu's major statement on these issues is his *Outline of a Theory of Practice*, which was published in 1972 in France and in English translation in 1977. It is worth spending a little time considering the title of this book, as it does give us some clue as to the intention behind it. Firstly, it is an 'outline'; in other words, a basic structure only — there is much detail to fill in. Secondly, it is 'a' theory — one synthetic description. An element of post-modernist contingency and doubt is therefore retained. Thirdly, theory is enjoined to practice. It is not theory for its own sake in some idealistic, platonic realm, but is intricately linked to practical activity. Before looking at the detail behind this theory *of* practice, it might be helpful to consider how issues of theory *and* practice have been represented in education in recent decades.

An Early View

Up until the 1950s, theory in educational research was regarded in much the same way as theory in the physical, normative sciences. For example, the educational philosopher O'Connor (1957) saw educational theory as a way of developing, connecting and evaluating hypotheses in order to understand particular educational phenomena. As education is a practical activity, theory is often seen as a means to forming or justifying certain forms of methodology or pedagogy. The normative, scientific view of theory might see it as improving teaching and learning by directly applying theoretical findings to classroom practices.

In the 1960s, however, a major shift took place. The British philosopher Paul Hirst argued that an applied 'science' view of educational theory and practice misrepresented the nature of theory in an educational context. For him, educational theory was distinct from theories derived from the normative sciences:

> the word theory is used as it occurs in the natural sciences where it refers to a single hypothesis or a logically interconnected set of hypotheses that have been confirmed by observation. It is this sense of the word that is said to provide us with standards by which we can assess the values and use of any claimant to the title theory. (Hirst, 1966, p. 38)

Hirst pointed out that if we judge educational theory by these standards it comes off very badly. We had to find new ways to connect theory and 'facts' in educational contexts. Teaching and learning take place in highly complex, context-dependent sites, where unpredictability and individual idiosyncrasy are the norm rather than the exception. A different way of thinking is needed which will better represent the reality of education. Hirst subsequently attempted to redefine educational theory as 'the essential background to rational educational practice, not as a limited would-be scientific pursuit' (*ibid.*, p. 40). Educational theory for Hirst was less knowledge for its own sake than 'knowledge that is organized for determining some practical activity' (*ibid.*). Theory, in this sense, is not so much the means by which we can understand and explain practical educational activity, as the way we might make choices to effect and determine that activity in the first place. As Hilliard puts it: 'scientific theory is descriptive, educational theory is predictive' (1971, p. 42). The word predictive is used in the sense of individuals being seen to master educational practice by working with its theoretical, multi-dimensional aspects: 'It could be argued that just as physics uses mathematics but results in distinctive, validated scientific statements, so educational theory uses philosophy, psychology, sociology, etc., and issues in distinctive, validated educational practice' (Hirst, 1966, p. 49).

The foundations for educational knowledge were therefore based on the human science disciplines of sociology, psychology, history, and philosophy. These arguments concerning theory formation are epistemological; in other words, they pertain to the way knowledge is formed, organized and represented.

The Idea of Paradigm

It can be seen that those working within the various traditions of the 1950s and 1960s were doing so from vastly different standpoints; making different assumptions to guide their research activities. Those within each shared commonalities of approach, epistemology and ways of formulating problematizations. The word *paradigm* has been employed to refer to these commonalities, to the knowledge that is shared in a typical patterning. The term came into general use after Thomas Kuhn (1962/1970) used it to describe the complex interplay of a scientific community and its set of assumptions, usually within a particular period of time. A paradigm ends in a 'revolution', an abrupt shift in perspective, and is replaced by a new paradigm. Thomas Kuhn also suggests paradigms are by nature socially derivative and thus are characteristic in many ways of the predominant intellectual conventions of the day. We therefore have the notion of the paradigm itself being another area of activity within society shaped by socio-historical forces. The post-war evolution in thinking about educational theory and research practice may be understood in terms of shifts of paradigms. Indeed, it might be argued that Bourdieu's own approach should also be regarded as a new paradigm, or at least an attempt to bring one about. Behind all these paradigms, ways of constructing and understanding the world are at issue, and it is not simply coincidental that considerable competition exists between them. Crucial issues of approach, technique, method, reliability and validity are at stake.

Various writers (e.g., Phillips, 1987; Carr and Kemmis, 1986) have attempted to classify research paradigms in the social sciences in terms of distinctions between their characteristic 'foundations'. For example, a frequent distinction is that between a *positivist, empirical*, 'scientific' approach and *hermeneutics*. Generally speaking, the empirical-analytic paradigm, which is often referred to as nomothetic since the prefix 'nomo' means lawful, is concerned with the natural sciences; the search for universal laws and explanations through the objective study of the world. This tradition implies a degree of 'scientific' neutrality, the control of experimental variables and the application of human reasoning.

Seemingly opposed to this is the hermeneutic paradigm, a term deriving from the Greek god Hermes, whose job it was to interpret and communicate the ideas of the gods to mankind. Key notions here are individual understanding, subjective interpretation and the acceptance of multiple realities in the world. Latter day versions of this might include the fragmentation of research practice apparent in post-modernist and post-structuralist approaches.

Both paradigms imply a specific character to knowledge, and ultimately theory, deriving from activity in each of them: the hermeneutic is concerned with the role that language plays in interpreting the world and with methodological pluralism in studying it; the empirical-analytic stands for the experimental, the controlled and instrumentality in research method. Moreover, the status of knowledge consequently gained from research is implicated: the empirical-analytic viewed as publicly accountable and giving rise to theories that are predictively robust; hermeneutic knowledge being expressed best as *verstehen*, a concept employed by Weber and philosophers of the neo-Kantian school such as Dilthey and Rickert to denote understanding from within, or empathy. This implies an affective as well as a rational involvement with the object of study.

Confronted by a large and expanding range of research literature, the new-comer to educational research could be forgiven for thinking that their first task is to make a choice between paradigms. Furthermore, they are quite likely to have gained the impression that a whole web of complex methodological and epistemological issues are set at the very point where they make a decision, or that all such choices can be *reduced* to a paradigm choice. Some of the literature which aims to help the educational researcher gives a clear map of the paradigmatic territory; for example, the first edition of a widely used text for teachers-as-researchers, Hitchcock and Hughes (1989). This account suggests that there may be two ways of making sense of social reality, and that these give rise to two opposing models, the positivist and the interpretive/ethnographic. A further example can be found in a series of three short articles by Bassey (1990a, 1990b, 1990c) in which it is claimed that there are in fact three paradigms — the positivist, the interpretive and action research — the latter referring to a practitioner-based, developmental approach to research. 'Some-times the network of a paradigm is so strong in the minds of its practitioners' it is argued 'that they may deny the validity of other paradigms. Because of this denial it becomes problematic to try and discuss the different paradigms to which different researchers conform' (1990b, p. 40).

Of course these paradigms offer us ideal types, and it is arguable that they can never exist in a pure form. In educational research, it would be a gross over-simplification to attribute the empirical-analytic paradigm solely to research prior to the 1960s, and the hermeneutic paradigm to research since then. Although the former has been waning, it is not yet clear that there is a credible replacement, and there now exist all manner of interpretative approaches to conducting educational research. Following on from Hirst's work in the 1960s, and the prominence sub-sequently given to sociological, philosophical and historical analyses of learning contexts, educational research mirrored the type of qualitative, naturalistic approaches used in these social sciences. In particular, ethnography has become a popular means of representing the pedagogic context. Ethnography has been described as a 'culture studying culture' (Spradley, 1980, p. 13), which pertains to its anthropo-logical origins; that is the study of human activity in terms of context, relations, and belief systems. The ways of doing this are numerous and hotly disputed, and we consider them in more detail in Chapter 9, where we discuss how to conduct educational research from a Bourdieuian perspective. Issues of theory and practice do remain, however. Do we bring theory to the context in order to explain what is going on, or do we 'ground' it in observation? Do we form mini-hypotheses which are tested out in a range of situations en route to producing something that is more generalizable and rigorous? Does theory represent reality, or is reality so relative to context that any formal description of its base actuality is bound to fail to capture its rationale? Theory pretends in some ways to explain reality, but how does it do this? To what extent does it represent what actually occurs? On what evidence is it based? How far can we generalize from the particular context? These issues are often expressed in terms of *representationalism* and *relativism* and are fraught with contradictions. A leading writer on ethnography has put it as follows: 'The first (representationalism) involves unacceptable assumptions about the asymmetry of explanations of true and false beliefs and of actions based on them; the second (relativism) leads to all those problems that usually follow from the adoption of a relative epistemology, notably internal inconsistency' (Hammersley, 1992, p. 54).

The fact that we might not regard knowledge as uni-dimensional but as multi-faceted has long been recognized. Two important ideal types in social science research express the extremes of this plurality of view; namely, *subjectivity* and *objectivity*. Subjectivity refers to individual knowledge. It is personal; partly intuitive; affective; and may not have any direct relevance outside of the person who holds it. Hermeneutic approaches are a characteristic version of this. Objectivity refers to the contrary. It is 'knowledge without a knowing subject', to adopt a phrase coined by a modern day founder of scientific theory, Karl Popper. It transcends the individual and has general, if not universal, applicability. The natural, normative sciences aspire to this form of knowledge.

Clearly, both forms of knowledge have their place; both must exist. However, a crucial issue is at stake here, in that social science and educational research very often define themselves in terms of objectivity and generalizability, even when more qualitative approaches are employed or when those researched are described as operating in terms of individual subjectivities. Indeed, issues of objectivity and subjectivity seem to haunt educational research. There is often the feeling that researchers are either being too personal and context-dependent, or conversely, too general and too distant from the people and situations they study.

Bourdieu's theory of practice attempts to go beyond this dichotomy. His intent is to find a theory which is robust enough to be objective and generalizable, and yet accounts for individual, subjective thought and action. Moreover, the intention is to do so in a way that not only explains the logic of a range of social activities, including education, but also guides the practice of research into such activities. To show how he does this, and to illustrate it with examples, is the purpose of this book. Bourdieu's theory of practice rests on his understanding of culture; i.e., the way the organization of society gives rise to ideas which in turn shapes the organization of society. In his use of culture, Bourdieu attempts to reconcile dichotomies like the one referred to above and to offer a synthesis of existing paradigms. The next section shows how he does this.

Culture and the Idea of a Theory of Practice

Culture is a key word as it refers to the world of knowledge, ideas, objects which are the product of human activity. Education is part of culture; so is educational research. Indeed, ethnography was earlier referred to as a 'culture studying culture'. Understanding the processes and products of culture should therefore give insight into education and research into it. How has culture been dealt with in the social sciences? What does Bourdieu understand by the term?

Bourdieu identifies two traditions in the study of culture: the structural tradition, which sees culture as an instrument of communication and knowledge, as a '*structured structure*' made up of signs based on shared consensus of world meanings; and the functionalist tradition, which sees culture as an ideological force or political power for imposing social order (cf. Bourdieu, 1968). The first tradition is probably best represented by Levi-Strauss, who, throughout the 1960s sought to uncover the universal structures of culture inherent in such products as language and myth, where the meaning of any unit is defined through a system of contrasts with other units. For the second, functionalist, tradition, human knowledge is the product of the social infrastructure: material relations organized along class and economic lines. This functionalism can take two principal forms: positivist and critical radical. Bourdieu criticizes both the structural and the functionalist traditions: the first for its overemphasis on primitive societies and its tendency to describe cultural relations as structured structure in synchronic, anthropological terms. The second tradition is criticized for reifying ideology: as a pervasive force in maintaining social control, in the positivist tradition; as a way of imposing the ideas of the dominant class, in the radical one. Bourdieu attempts to reconcile these two traditions; to use what has been learnt from the: 'analysis of structures of symbolic systems (particularly language and myth) so as to arrive at the basic principle behind the efficacy of symbols, that is the structured structure which confers upon symbolic systems their structuring power' (Bourdieu, 1971a, p. 1255).

This proposition is seen as representing an initial 'break' with objectivism, particularly anthropology. Objective structures are not only identifiably *structured*: they are identifiably *structuring*. In other words, observed structures can and should be seen as constituting and dynamic, not static.

It is important to acknowledge what Bourdieu calls the 'socio-genesis' of his argument, or the cultural context in which it arose. He developed his main theoretical approach during the 1960s in a French academic field which was dominated by the structuralism of Levi-Strauss and the existentialism of Sartre. The 'objectivism' to which he refers in the above context did not at the time refer directly to the empirical-analytic, scientific paradigm. Indeed, Bourdieu himself made extensive use of statistics in his earliest writings. He has also claimed to be the most 'empirical' of French sociologists and philosophers. Many of his books are peppered with the kind of data and analysis characteristic of the 'objectivist paradigm'. The way he reconciles this use with his own methodological approach is detailed in Chapter 9. For the moment, it is important to state that as his work developed, Bourdieu broadened out his main argument in terms of a 'reflexive objectivity'. Such objectivity directly opposes the identification of static rules based on pseudo-experimental analyses, as in the 'scientific theory' of Popper. Indeed, Bourdieu's notion of reflexive objectivity opposes any research which reduces its object to an undynamic 'thing'. For Bourdieu, knowledge without a knowing subject would be anathema (cf. Bourdieu, 1979, p. 252).

A second break with overt objectivism, however, is required to restore the notion of practice to human activity. This argument involves the whole objectivist/subjectivist debate, at the interface of which Bourdieu constructs his theory. Indeed, he calls the traditional opposition between these in the social sciences 'most artificial, fundamental and ruinous' (1980a, p. 43, own translation). For him, if culture and material relations form a state of objective reality, this latter is only expressed and reproduced in 'practice'; through a practical sense. He begins his book, *Outline of a Theory of Practice* with a famous quote from Marx criticizing any materialism (objectivism) that does not take account of human activity as 'sense' activity:

> The principal defect of all materialism up to now — including that of Feuerbach — is that the external object, reality, the sensible world, is grasped in the form of *an object or an intuition*; but not as *concrete human activity*, as *practice*, in a subjective way. This is why the active aspect was developed by idealism, in opposition to materialism — but only in an abstract way, since idealism naturally does not know real concrete activity as such. (Marx; *Theses on Feuerbach*, quoted in Bourdieu, 1977a, p. vi)

Here, Bourdieu is arguing that objectivity can only be revealed in the nature of individuals' practice. Objective structures are not simply inculcated as a reflection of material relations. Such human sense activity as social products arise historically in time but are revealed in individual action.

The debate focusing on the relationship between material, objective structures and individual agents' mental activity is central to the social theoretical tradition, echoing the paradigms referred to previously. Bourdieu aims to avoid overt objectivism and subjectivism by making: 'a science of dialectical relations between objective structures . . . and the subjective dispositions within which these structures are actualised and which tend to reproduce them' (1977a, p. 3).

Bourdieu calls this 'science' the dialectic of 'the internalisation of externality and the externalisation of internality', or simply incorporation and objectification. This interplay seeks to go beyond what he calls the *opus operatum* (structured structure) to emphasize the importance of the *modus operandi* (the productive activity of consciousness): 'one must remember that ultimately objective relations do not exist and do not realize themselves except in and through the systems of dispositions of agents, produced by the internalizing of objective conditions' (1968, p. 105).

There is a continual dialectic between objectivity and subjectivity. Social agents are incorporated bodies who possess, indeed, are *possessed by* structural, generative schemes which operate by orientating social practice. This, in a nutshell, is Bourdieu's theory of practice. Practice, the dynamic of which is probably better captured by the word praxis, is a cognitive operation; it is structured and tends to reproduce structures of which it is a product. We are, of course, not simply repeating actions endlessly. Evolution and change *in practice* do occur. However, it comes about, not so much through the replication of action but its reproduction. Reproduction implies both variation and limitation in what is and is not possible in the behaviour, thought and physical action of people.

Following through this argument, Bourdieu eventually refers to his method and approach as 'constructivist structuralism' or 'structural constructivism' (1989b,

p. 14): Constructivist pertaining to the dynamic reproduction of human activity in ever-changing contexts; structuralist to refer to the relations of those involved.

It is worth saying something more about structure since, although Bourdieu's approach is launched from his attack on traditional structuralism, he also seems to be using the term extensively himself. How are these different uses of the term structure distinct?

Structure has clearly been at the base of the dominant philosophical paradigms of the post-war period. But structure is often a vague and amorphous term. Piaget (1968) claims that structures are 'observed identities' that embody the idea of wholeness, transformation and self-regulation. Here wholeness is in terms of internal coherence, transformation refers to a generative quality, and self-regulation is meant in the sense of being closed to external reference. Such a definition would not contradict Bourdieu's own. However, structuralism can subsequently be seen as 'a way of thinking about the world that is predominantly concerned with the perception and description of structures' (Hawkes, 1977, p. 17). As previously alluded to, structuralism, in its most overt form, for example in the work of Levi-Strauss, becomes a method for the synchronic description of language, myths and legends, and the illustration of slow structural transformations. Such structures are foundational and transcendent. They cross time and cultures and are seen as being innate to the human mind. This is in part the structuralism against which Bourdieu is reacting. For him, structure is dynamic and dialectical, is manifest in links at and between the objective and subjective levels of human contingency; links which are structural *and* structuring.

For Bourdieu, structure is not only objective in a Levi-Straussian sense. Structures can also be highly subjective. Indeed, the individual 'sense activity' which Bourdieu alludes to in his 'second break' with objectivism can be seen in terms of relations between individual (subjectivities) and object phenomena. Structure then is also to be viewed as a phenomenological occurrence. Indeed, it is possible to connect Bourdieu's understanding of structure with the phenomenology of Husserl, for whom being in the world needs to be understood as a *differential* event. This differentiation implies a structural relationship. For Husserl (1982), differentiation is characterized by two structural forms of consciousness: noematic and noetic. The 'noema' is everything that one knows about an object of thought. The noesis represents individuals 'moments' of perception, where not everything is brought into being, is brought to mind. What is known at any one instant is the product of the relationship between what is already known and new sense data. There is a constant interplay between the noematic and the noetic: but this does not take place in a neutral realm of platonic ideals or individual freedom. Indeed, the constituent knowledge is also the product of 'doxa'; i.e., the sense of reality which is orthodox. Bourdieu pushes this line of thought to its logical, sociological conclusion in seeing 'doxa' as a social derivative. What Bourdieu has done is to make these phenomenological acts essentially social. Structures are based on differing, differential principles. The purpose of social science research is to uncover such principles. So far, we have an epistemology, not a method; indeed, an *outline* of a theory of practice. Before turning to what this theory looks like *in* practice, it is necessary to consider further theoretical concepts which Bourdieu uses in his approach. The two most fundamental are *Habitus* and *Field*, which are dealt with next.

Habitus and Field

In the discussion above, we have seen how, in Bourdieu's theory of practice, human action is constituted through a dialectical relationship between individuals' thought and activity and the objective world. Bourdieu further represents these two as habitus and field respectively. Habitus 'ensures the active presence of past experiences, which, deposited in each organism in the form of schemes of perception, thought and action, tend to guarantee the 'correctness' of practices and their constancy over time, more reliably than all formal rules and explicit norms ... habitus makes possible the free production of all the thoughts, perceptions and actions inherent in the particular conditions of its production — and only those' (Bourdieu quoted by Harker, 1992, p. 16).

Habitus, most succinctly, is therefore 'an acquired system of generative schemes objectively adjusted to the particular conditions in which it is constituted' (Bourdieu, 1977a, p. 95). Its original Latin meaning is close to that of a Greek word, *hexis*, also used by Bourdieu, and again links with phenomenology. Bourdieu was a former student of Merleau-Ponty, the leading French phenomenologist, who saw 'phenomenal' structures as being 'embodied' in individuals. A strong sense of the embodiment of social and cultural messages is therefore created; including how people carry themselves as well as the (slightly) more metaphorical carrying of thoughts and feelings.

Structure is still at the heart of this concept. Structure mediates between objectivity and subjectivity. Structures remain the final methodological unit of analysis; but not structure in the traditional structuralist intent of uncovering transcultural patterns, but structure as a dynamic cause and effect; as a structured structure *and* a structuring structure. Habitus is best understood as the operational site of this dual sense of structure:

> The notion of habitus ... is relational in that it designates a mediation between objective structures and practices. First and foremost, habitus has the function of overcoming the alternative between consciousness and unconsciousness ... Social reality exists, so to speak, twice, in things and in minds, in fields and in habitus, outside and inside agents. And when habitus encounters a social world of which it is the product, it finds itself 'as a fish in water', it does not feel the weight of the water and takes the world about itself for granted. (Bourdieu in interview with Wacquant, in Bourdieu, 1989c, p. 43)

The concept of habitus derives from an effort to create a methodological construct that will give sufficient representation to the dynamic of structure in social reality as expressed through human knowledge and action. In one sense, habitus is social inheritance (cf. Robbins, 1993a) but it also implies habit, or unthinking-ness in actions, and 'disposition'. Some dispositions are transferable; for example, a practical taxonomy can be utilized to find relevance in a new situation. Habitus also has a role in the production of practices by individuals. This works through 'the subjective expectation of objective probabilities'. It is the structural view that postulates 'practice provoking dispositions', or the dispositions to act in a certain way, to grasp experience in a certain way, to think in a certain way. Habitus goes beyond a simple formulation of biographical determinism. If habitus is ontologically specific, epistemologically universal, it is only actualized through individuals, and individual instances. In other words, social action always has a time and a place:

> The structures constitutive of a particular type of environment (e.g., the material conditions of existence characteristic of class condition) produce *habitus*, systems of durable, transposable dispositions, structured structures predisposed to function as structuring structures, that is principles of the generation and structuring of practices and representations which can be objectively 'regulated' and 'regular' without in any way being the product of obedience to rules, objectively adapted to their goals without presupposing a conscious aiming at ends or an express mastery of the operations necessary to attain them and, being all this, collectively orchestrated without being the product of the orchestrating action of a conductor. (Bourdieu, 1977a, p. 72)

Habitus is not necessarily a unique or original concept. Commentators and critics have pointed out its near omnipresence over the centuries, and it is a term which has been linked to such writers as Aristotle, Thomas Aquinas, Husserl, Merleau-Ponty, and Elias. However, the concept of habitus has been present in Bourdieu's work from the very beginning; especially in his writing on education. In *Les Héritiers*, habitus appeared as 'habitat' (p. 23), as the conditions of life that conferred on individuals the necessary culture. In *Reproduction* (1977) habitus is more formally developed as a medium of inculcation and production of the cultural arbitrary (pp. 31–2); as the way the products of pedagogic action and work are durable sociogenerative dispositions which guide and perpetuate practice. From *Outline* onwards, however, Bourdieu develops the concept as an epistemologically grounded analytic tool, as central to his theory of practice and thus as a way of comprehending social activity. We shall see how habitus has implications not only for understanding educational practice but the practical activity of research into it. *Outline* is peppered with passages concerning habitus and education:

> The habitus acquired in the family underlines the structuring of school experiences (in particular the reception and assimilation of the specifically pedagogic message), and the habitus transformed by schooling, itself diversified, in turn underlies the structuring of all subsequent experiences (e.g., the reception and assimilation of the message of the culture industry or work experiences) and so on, from restructuring to restructuring. (p. 87)

However, for Bourdieu, if individual aspects of habitus lay in individual consciousnesses and unconsciousnesses, the constituent effect of these in and through human practice is actualized in an objectively defined *field*. If habitus brings into focus the subjective end of the equation, *field* focuses on the objective:

I define field as a network, or a configuration, of objective relations between positions objectively defined, in their existence and in the determinations they impose
upon their occupants, agents or institutions, by their present and potential situation
(situs) in the structure of the distribution of species of power (or capital) whose
possession commands access to the specific profits that are at stake in the field, as
well as by their objective relation to other positions (domination, subordination,
homology, etc.). (Bourdieu and Wacquant, 1992a, pp. 72–3, own translation)

Field is therefore a structured system of social relations at a micro and macro
level. In other words, individuals, institutions and groupings, both large and small,
all exist in structural relation to each other in some way. These relations determine
and reproduce social activity in its multifarious forms. Moreover, because they are
structural, positions (of individuals, between individuals, between individuals and
institutions, and between institutions and institutions) can be mapped or located,
and the generating principles behind their relations ascertained.

Bourdieu has referred to the relationship between field and habitus as one of
'ontological complicity' (1982a, p. 47). Ontology can be defined as the nature of
being or the essence of things. For Bourdieu, such things are the product of habitus
and field and between habitus and field:

the relation between habitus and field operates in two ways. On the one side, it is
a relation of conditioning: the field structures the habitus, which is the product of
the embodiment of immanent necessity of a field (or of a hierarchically intersect-
ing sets of fields). On the other side, it is a relation of knowledge or cognitive
construction: habitus contributes to constituting the field as a meaningful world, a
world endowed with sense and with value, in which it is worth investing one's
practice. (1989c, p. 44)

This argument means that field and habitus are mutually constituting. They are
based on identical generating principles and there are structural homologies between the two.

Bourdieu has been variously accused of excessive materialism and idealism,
not to mention determinism, in this approach. His theory of practice is constituted
by a theory of knowledge that seeks to build a dialectical relationship between
human thought, action and objective surroundings; except that these latter will also
include social 'things' expressed in a cultural, ideational sense.

Bourdieu's work first came to be known to many educationalists in the
English-speaking world via the publication of the translation of his 1970 book
(with Passeron) *Reproduction in Education, Society and Culture* in 1977. One result
of this was the rapid spread of the use of his concepts, such as Habitus and Field,
often without reference to their theoretical basis and sometimes in ways which indicated misunderstanding (cf. Nash, 1990). However, the work also attracted fierce
criticism for apparently mechanistic notions of power and domination; an overly
determined view of human agency; and the over-simplification of class cultures and
their relationships to each other (Giroux, 1983, p. 271). The theory seemed to leave

no room for notions like resistance, incorporation and accommodation, which had by that time come to be common features of a new sociology of education which had broken free of the shackles of structural-functionalism. Yet, as Harker observes (1990), it is inappropriate to extrapolate Bourdieu's theoretical framework from such writings on education, since these predate the period in which he developed his theoretical writing most intensively. Furthermore, to take *Reproduction* as his *magnum opus* is to mistake the working out of a method in a French context for an attempt to produce universal laws of pedagogic practices, a point taken up by Derek Robbins in Chapter 3 of this book. Some will feel that Bourdieu's formalistic presentation of variables in this particular work suggests he is indeed attempting a universal theory of pedagogic practices. Nevertheless, the point about the timing of development still holds, and it is no longer possible to criticize Bourdieu for being a 'structural determinist' in quite the same way (cf. May, 1994).

A criticism with perhaps more tenacity relates to Bourdieu's use of the concept of habitus. Nash (*op cit.*) has argued that behind this notion is an inadequately precise concept of structure, in that a wide variety of social arrangements can count as 'structure', from small regularities through to massive institutions. With regard to habitus itself, Nash acknowledges the useful work this concept does in mediating agency and structure in various ways, but finds it wanting when he uses it as a theory of socialization. Nash writes that it often seems to exclude ideas like 'self' 'choice' and 'action', by virtue of its emphasis on practices arising from the group's relation to culture. This problem is revealed clearly when Bourdieu '. . . even suggests that people are only rational when they step out of the automatic responses prompted by their habitus' (*ibid.*, p. 434).

Nash could be overstating the case here, and in Part II we shall see work which employs habitus precisely in ways which he feels are lacking. However, the point he makes is an important one for anyone wishing to draw on Bourdieu's conceptual tools in empirical work. In a similar vein, Jenkins (1992) objects to Bourdieu's seeming subordination of calculated and rational action to the generative schemes of the habitus, and suggests that there are difficulties in Bourdieu's reliance on the term *disposition* within the general concept of habitus. Sometimes the term implies conscious action, whilst at other times, it indicates unconscious action (cf. Jenkins, p. 77).

These concerns about Bourdieu's theory of practice will be developed later in the book in the light of discussion of its application to the research case examples. For the moment, it is worth stating that Bourdieu seems to have had two intentions. Firstly, to found a 'scientific' theory of social praxis as a research epistemology, which goes beyond traditional dichotomies, paradigms and consequent oppositions — for example, conscious–unconscious, structure–agency, theory–practice, objectivity–subjectivity. Secondly, to use this epistemology to study the manifestations and processes of social distinction and differentiation. Thus, the principle he focuses on as being behind habitus as a structuring structure is the same as that behind the division of social groups into socio-economically based classes:

(As a) structuring structure which organises practice and perception of practice, the habitus is also a structured structure; the principle of the division into logical classes which organises the perception of the social world is itself the product of the incorporation of the division in social classes. (1979, p. 191 own translation)

Because the principle of social action, and the meaning we give to it, is the same as that behind the division of labour in society, such action is liable to the same processes toward hierarchy formation. This means that knowledge and action have objective value subjectively perceived in the course of human activity. As culture is a product of mental activity, and this latter is in some way shaped by objective relations, then it follows that culture contains symbolic systems which have value because they are valued according to the same underlying principle as that of social differentiation. Bourdieu uses the word *capital* to describe the social products of a field or system of relations through which individuals carry out social intercourse. Social products in this sense include the material and the ideational: thoughts, actions, objects, any product of human activity. Capital can be seen as another concept used to give 'a material base to an ideational reading of social action' (1980b, pp. 2–3). It is useful as a concept because it allows us to think about social action in terms of varying degrees of capital; to this extent, it is sometimes quantifiable. Moreover, capital is not readily available to everyone on the same basis: scarcity of social resource is the lubricant of social systems. In order to address the concept of capital in more detail, let us look at further examples and analogies from Bourdieu's own writings.

Symbolic Action and Capital

Bourdieu often writes about social activity as a sort of game. There is the same sense of being in or out of the game. As we have already noted, social activity occupies specific time and space. There are good and poor players, winners and losers; although why this should be the case is never absolutely clear. There are rules which govern how the game is played, what is and is not allowed and how deviancy is dealt with. However, play seems to depend on intuition and game-sense as much as mastery of explicit procedures. By entering the game, individuals implicitly agree to be ruled by it and immediately set up personal relations with it, as well as with other players.

The 'gift exchange' is a good example of how this looks in practice. The gift exchange refers to the meanings, both explicit and implicit, of offering and receiving gifts. On the surface, one gives and receives gifts for mainly altruistic purposes. Below the surface, gifts seem to have a number of underlying functions which have frequently been studied by social scientists. In *Outline*, Bourdieu draws on the contrast between two approaches to this issue. The first is the structuralist (objectivist) approach of Levi-Strauss and the second is the phenomenological ('subjectivist') one of Mauss. Bourdieu argues that the two approaches lead to mutually '. . . antagonistic principles of gift exchange: the gift as experienced, or, at least, meant to be experienced, and the gift as seen from outside' (1977, p. 5). It is again the space between these two types of account which yields a 'sort of third order knowledge' (*ibid.*, p. 4), in that whilst both provide accounts which are in their own way truthful and complete, it is in the interaction between them that social practices are to be understood, again pertaining to the synthesis between objective and subjective views of the phenomenon. The argument in sociology goes that in order for gift exchanges to 'work', the individuals involved must experience them as irreversible, that is, without a subjective expectation of reciprocal giving. Yet objectively, most gift exchange *is* 'reciprocal'. Bourdieu's approach promises to show us what is really going on:

> the operation of gift exchange presupposes (individual and collective) misrecognition of the reality of the objective 'mechanism' of the exchange, a reality which an immediate response brutally exposes: the *interval* between gift and counter-gift is what allows a pattern of exchange that is always liable to strike the observer and also the participants as *reversible*, i.e., both forced and interested, to be experienced as irreversible. (*ibid.*, p. 6)

And:

> If the system is to work, the agents must not be entirely unaware of the truth of their exchanges, which is made explicit in the anthropologist's model, while at the same time they must refuse to know and above all recognise it. In short, everything takes place as if agents' practice, and in particular their manipulation of time, were organized exclusively with a view to concealing from themselves and from others the truth of their practice . . . (*ibid.*, p. 6)

For present purposes, this example illustrates an important point: the conception of the individual in social practices and the way they orientate their practice. Individuals have (effectively boundless) opportunities for employing *strategy* in this context; especially with the controlling of the interval between gift and counter-gift and the 'tempo' of the next event in the sequence. Clearly, volition is limited in one sense, but virtually limitless in another. In other words, there is a degree of space 'to play with', so to speak, within which the eventual reciprocity eventually occurs. It is in this space that individual strategy is employed. Bourdieu uses the term 'strategy' in a rather unusual way. The term is usually employed to imply fully conscious and rational calculation of risks or resource deployment. However, Bourdieu insists that strategy rests on a practical 'feel for the game', allowing any number of possible and original 'moves' within the general 'sense of limits, commonly called the sense of reality' (Bourdieu, 1977a, p. 164). One of Bourdieu's major publications is entitled *Le Sens Pratique*: practical sense as affective, intuitive as well as 'good sense'. The analogy to the 'rules' of a game, given earlier in this section, is therefore a little misleading. It is wrong to think of strategies as solely the objective, or conscious, following of prescribed rules. Strategies are rather the result of combining practical good sense and commonly accepted practices, often in an implicit, semi-automatic manner. Exchanging gifts is a sort of game in which a number of assumptions are made and strategies employed, and it has social functions in addition to its common sense one. The game needs also to be understood as a *field* site, the structurally identifiable space which marks out the sphere of social activity.

Education is a *field*, made up of identifiable interconnecting relations. It also involves 'gifts', this time scholastic. It is governed by overarching principles; for example those to do with its purposes, or equality of access. These principles possess power which arises from the interplay between individual authorities who articulate them in an explicit manner (in this case, educational agents and agencies designated by the state) and the resultant acceptance and recognition conferred on them by educationalists both within and outside of the field. But no field ever exists in isolation, and there is the sense of fields within fields within fields. So, if education is a field, primary, secondary and higher education might be regarded as subfields. They connect with and partially share the principles of the superordinate field, all whilst having their own particular context characteristics; for example, the shifting aims and objectives of different phases of education, the ways they are organized and who is involved. Moreover, these fields within fields connect with other fields outside of education: the health service, industry and the media. These are structural relationships, which constitute the nature and mechanisms of each separate field. Each subfield will have its own orthodoxy, its own way of doing things, rules, assumptions and beliefs; in sum, its own legitimate means. Indeed, at a micro level, a particular deviant subculture evident amongst pupils will have its own orthodox ways of being in relation to the official fields which surround it.

However, just as in the gift example, we all know that in any sphere of activity the defining principles are only ever partially articulated, and much of the orthodox way of thinking and acting passes in an implicit, tacit manner. Thus, the legitimate is never made fully explicit: 'What does legitimate mean? . . . An instruction, or an action, or a usage is legitimate when it is dominant and misrecognised as such, that is to say tacitly recognised' (Bourdieu, 1980c, p. 110, own translation).

In other words, many of the rules and principles of the game go on in a way that is not consciously held in the heads of those playing it. It is played out in terms of forces of supply and demand, of the 'products' of the field — the *symbolic capital*.

Given the use of such terms as capital and supply and demand, it is unsurprising if Bourdieu has also referred to social activity as a *market*. The analogy is a telling one. As a market, social activity is governed by individuals competing for its products. There is a sense of 'purchasing power', on the basis of personal resources, of gain and loss, of winners and losers. There is a price to pay, inflation and a constant 'renegotiation' of the values of market products. Again, this approach may sound very mechanistic and deterministic, but it is actually quite the opposite. Just as structures arise from differentiation, and this differentiation is grounded in a defining principle, so ultimately value is assigned according to a base rate; expressed on the basis of the proximity to and distance from the present orthodoxy or the legitimate. All 'products' and actions within a field therefore have value: but this value is not a neutral, passive feature of the field. It is value which buys other products of the field. It therefore has power. It is *capital*.

In Bourdieu's scheme there are three forms of capital: Economic, Social and Cultural. Economic Capital is literally money wealth: it can be 'cashed' in any part of society. Social Capital exists as a 'network of lasting social relations'; in other words, an individual's or individual group's sphere of contacts. Cultural Capital is the product of education, which Bourdieu also often refers to as an 'academic market', and exists in three distinct forms: connected to individuals in their general educated character — accent, dispositions, learning, etc.; connected to objects — books, qualifications, machines, dictionaries, etc.; and connected to institutions — places of learning, universities, libraries, etc.

Bourdieu reasons that capital attracts capital, as like attracts like, and the various forms are, in many ways, interconvertible. So, for example, high academic qualifications traditionally tend to 'buy' good jobs with good salaries. Yet, at the same time, as 'players' in the market acquire more capital, so it becomes devalued. For example, there is *qualification inflation*, where over time, a given level of certification no longer guarantees the same prestigious jobs. Capital exists in ever changing configurations in relation to the fields which generate it, and, the values of its three forms are constantly being renegotiated in implicit and explicit ways.

Capital attracts capital, but, as in the case of education, we do not enter fields with equal amounts, or identical configurations, of capital. Some have inherited wealth, cultural distinctions from up-bringing and family connections. Some individuals, therefore, already possess quantities of relevant capital bestowed on them in the process of habitus formation, which makes them better players than others in certain field games. Conversely, some are disadvantaged. However, it is crucial that we do not get carried away by the apparent determinism of this type of argument. There is always choice; indeed, the system can only function because there is readily apparent choice; there is, so to speak, everything to play for. For example, in education, it is important that the school should be seen to be free from direct influence and coercion in its professional activity. Pupils constantly have choice about what they do, how they act and think in response to the pedagogic opportunities that are offered. However, those pupils with habitus which most resembles the structural dispositions, and hence, values through which the school seeks to work (the legitimate), are more likely to be disposed to a certain type of practice through a process of *elective affinities* (Bourdieu, 1973). Here, Bourdieu is employing a term used by the German sociologist Max Weber to describe how the ideas and values (symbolic) which individuals possess have consequences for social action, and vice versa, by processes of convergence and divergence from like and non-like values and ideas. This understanding of thought and action again recalls Husserl's relational structures with the objects of thought in terms of a socially given orthodoxy. Proximity to this orthodoxy at birth has a determinate effect on habitus not only in ways of thinking which more closely approximate that of schools but in terms of a whole cultural disposition: 'The most privileged students do not only owe the habits, behaviour and attitudes which help them directly in pedagogic tasks to their social origins; they also inherit from their knowledge and *savoir-faire*, tastes and a 'good taste' (Bourdieu and Passeron, 1964, p. 30, own translation).

Such social privilege passes as a natural fact or given state of affairs because the founding principle of equality of aspiration and achievement is made legitimate by common tacit agreement. In fact, parents are also unknowing collaborators in the process of legitimizing social distinction as 'natural' differences:

When a pupil's mother says of her son, often in front of him, that 'he is not strong in French', she makes herself an accomplice of three forms of unfavourable influence: firstly, ignoring that her son's results are a direct function of the family's cultural atmosphere, she transforms into individual destiny all that which is only the product of an education and which still might be corrected, at least partly, by educational activity; secondly, through lack of information on school matters, due sometimes to having nothing with which to oppose teachers' authority, she draws final and premature conclusions from a single school report; finally, by sanctioning this type of judgment, she reinforces for the child the feeling of being such and such by nature. Therefore, the legitimizing authority of school can redouble social inequalities because the least favoured classes, too aware of their future and yet too unaware of the routes by which it happens, contribute in this way to its realization. (*ibid.*, p. 109, own translation)

In this case, parents' own judgments are made by recognizing what is legitimate and thus misrecognizing which fundamental processes of social differentiation are being operationalized. As in the case of the gift exchange, there is the issue of what is knowingly or unknowingly brought into being in such decision, thoughts and actions. Bourdieu's whole mission seems to be to render visible these invisible operations as a way of making available the possibility at least of democratizing the product and processes of the field.

If education is a sort of 'gift exchange', a game where social inequalities are reproduced in ways that are systematically misrecognized, it also operates through individuals' strategic positioning. Some strategies operate to maintain or improve positioning in the symbolic field by increasing capital. Other strategies convert one form of capital to another; again in order to improve on personal worth through social valuing. It is Bourdieu's contention that these processes are the unrecognized, or misrecognized, generating structures of social, in this case, educational practice: 'The whole trick of pedagogic reason lies precisely in the way it extorts the essential while seeming to demand the insignificant' (Bourdieu, 1977a, p. 95).

Thus *misrecognition* is at the heart of the efficiency and power of education:

It must be asserted . . . that capital (or power) becomes symbolic capital, that is capital endowed with a specific efficacy, only when it is *misrecognised* in its arbitrary truth as capital and *recognised* as legitimate and, on the other hand, that this act of (false) knowledge and recognition is an act of *practical* knowledge which in no way implies that the object known and recognised be posited as an object. (Bourdieu, 1990b, p. 112 emphasis in original)

In other words, capital should be understood in terms of its practical consequences, not objectified as a static product of the system. Knowledge is capital because, as a symbolic product of social fields, it has consequences which are more than simply symbolic; it 'buys' prestige, power and consequent economic positioning. In this context, it is worth saying a little more about 'knowledge' and Bourdieu.

Knowledge is a translation of the French word '*connaissance*'. However, *connaissance* in French implies familiarity at an implicit, tacit level as much as knowledge of facts and things. Its practical power is only ever partly objectifiable by those who hold it. Furthermore, knowledge is rarely only knowledge *about* something, but includes knowledge of how to do things. This latter, practical, procedural knowledge is not only pragmatically based, for example how to drive a car or make a cup of tea, but includes how to act, think and talk in relation to social orthodoxies and heterodoxies. Related to this word, are two others: '*reconnaissance*' (recognition) and '*méconnaissance*' (misrecognition). We have already referred to the second of these. Misrecognition relates to the ways these underlying processes and generating structures of fields are not consciously acknowledged in terms of the social differentiation they perpetuate, often in the name of democracy and equality. Ruling principles are accepted as one thing, while the operations of the field are another. Legitimate norms maintain their defining hold on the systems or fields in what is or is not thinkable and 'do-able' by the values they attribute to different forms and types of action.

Reconnaissance implies acknowledged value–status as well as an identified feature — be it accent, qualification, social position, cultural authority — as licensed by the field. We shall keep these words in French in this book in order to draw attention to these various dimensions. Bourdieu argues that the value of capital is dependent on the degree of reconnaissance attributed to it, and: 'agents possess power in proportion to their symbolic capital, i.e., in proportion to the recognition they receive from a group' (Bourdieu, 1991, p. 106).

The ultimate source of valuing is, then, the field or group in which individuals are placed. Knowledge can only receive value and power by being recognized as legitimate: but it is a recognition which maintains and reproduces a strict hierarchy to the advantage, and disadvantage, of factions within it. Paradoxically, many in the field recognize the legitimate without having practical knowledge of it themselves: 'the dominated classes, and in particular the petit-bourgeois' says Bourdieu, 'are condemned to reconnaissance without connaissance' (Bourdieu and Boltanski, 1975, p. 8, own translation).

The example of gift-giving cited earlier is a good illustration of these elements. On the surface, there is the social altruism of offering gifts, as a way of honouring another. This is real enough, yet beneath this apparent generosity lies an altogether different function, one which involves the establishing of status and power relations which binds exchanging parties together. This operation is played out in the strategies individuals adopt over time in positioning themselves with regard to the giving and receiving of gifts, and is concealed so as not to challenge other media of exchange with their own currency of, say, symbolic capital (e.g., honour). This is an example of the misrecognition of underlying processes. As a translation of *méconnaissance*, however, *misrecognition* does not quite place the necessary emphasis on how a practice might be made '. . . invisible through a displacement of understanding and a reconstrual as part of other aspects of the habitus that "go without saying"' (Mahar *et al.*, 1990, p. 19). Such misrecognition operates in the education system, Bourdieu argues, through an arbitrary curriculum that is 'naturalized' so that social classifications are transformed into academic ones. The result is that instead of being experienced for what they are (i.e., partial and technical hierarchies), such social classifications become 'total' hierarchies, experienced as if they were grounded in nature. For example,

> Misrecognition of the social determinants of the educational career — and therefore of the social trajectory it helps to determine — gives the educational certificate the value of a natural right and makes the educational system one of the fundamental agencies of the maintenance of the social order. (Bourdieu, 1984a, p. 387)

The processes of values and valuing described earlier therefore give rise to differentiated responses from individuals who are significantly advantaged or disadvantaged in their handling of the 'field game' in which they are involved. The fact that inequality of resources and access is at the base of field operations, and that this automatically and tacitly favours and disfavours individuals according to their socio-cognitive background, leads Bourdieu to refer to such symbolic capital as a form of *violence*, which is: 'the struggle between different specialists in symbolic production (full-time producers), a struggle over the monopoly of legitimate symbolic violence (cf. Weber), that is, of the power to impose (or even inculcate) the arbitrary instruments of knowledge and expression (taxonomies) of social reality' (Bourdieu, 1991, p. 168).

The legitimate is accepted as open to debate. However, the outcome of such a debate is not arbitrary. One form of knowledge, one way of doing things, has to be imposed and accepted, mostly with the tacit and conscious acceptance of those imposed upon. Consequently, some factions of a group are dominated by others, who in turn may be dominated, within and between fields. Because one group's legitimacy rules another, a 'violence' has been and continues to be done.

Conclusion

Bourdieu's world is a highly symbolic one because it is based on values which arise from structured relations. These relations are multifarious and can be imagined as an interconnecting network which stretches from the individual to and from the macro level of society. *Fields* are bounded spheres identifiable in terms of shared areas of activities and contain and connect with other fields and various levels. Each is lubricated by forms of knowledge which are only partially consciously known, have their own self-referential legitimacy, and, to a large extent, operate in a tacit manner. Such knowledge forms conform to orthodox ways of viewing and being in the world, but equally, may exist as deviant opposition to such. Whether orthodox or non-orthodox, the mechanisms of reproduction are the same.

These structural relations and the forms of knowledge to which they give rise are a social given at any one time but are not static. Rather, they are in flux; are constantly in movement, forming and reforming themselves. Such restructuring also implies a revaluing of the 'products' of these relations: knowledge, taste, ways of thinking and acting — in a word, *capital*. Individuals, by existing in social space, encounter fields but come with their own generating structures, inculcated in the process of their own development in the world. This *habitus* forms affinities and disaffinities with the structural relations, or fields, which surround them. As such, individuals may be in, or out, of the game, and may or may not have the necessary pre-existing capital to play it to their advantage.

We have seen that a common criticism of Bourdieu is that this makes for a deterministic theoretical approach. However, this is not the case. Rather, everything is up for grabs. It appears as if everyone is free to play, everything is negotiable. If it were not, the 'rules' of the games themselves would not be accepted. Everyone plays, but differential structures ensure that not everyone is equal. This *misrecognition* is an essential component of the legitimate and the social processes described. Moreover, one should avoid reifying *capital*, the product and process of the fields, as a quantifiable object. Although, conceptually it is quantifiable, there is an extent to which we all possess capital to a greater or lesser extent. Ultimately the form it takes is arbitrary and only receives its value from that ascribed to it by field operations. We do not know we have capital until we enter a field where it is valued, where it buys something. Linguistic theory has, for a long time, recognized that the link between objects and words is not a natural given, is quite arbitrary. In other words, any sound or word may be used to designate an object or germ of meaning. What is important is that the words and objects which are linked are socially sanctioned, so that we share a common means of communication and 'value' meaning in the same way. Similarly, capital is arbitrary but has power through the recognized value field participants give it. Indeed, it is precisely the question of what capital is at stake and how it is valued which is constantly at issue in social interactions.

Bourdieu uses complex and sophisticated language. But, of course, language itself is a social product, arises from particular, in this case, intellectual, academic fields. It is important to keep in mind that behind such concepts as *habitus*, *field*, *capital* and *symbolic violence* lies a theory of knowledge which has two principal objectives: firstly, to go beyond traditional subjective and objective philosophies; secondly, to do so in a way which provides a theory of practice that is indeed of practical use. At the outset of this chapter, we discussed the place of theory and practice in education and educational research. Clearly, Bourdieu's theory of practice is very different in expression and intent from traditional approaches to educational theory and its relationship to practice; both in pedagogy and research. The remainder of this book illustrates and discusses how his approach can be used in practice. The content of Parts II and III show others working with Bourdieu's tools, both in their research and in their own reflexivity in conducting it. We have noted that Bourdieu is a sociologist, and his concerns, consequently, are with social differentiation, which implies a preoccupation with analyses of class reproduction. The illustrative examples in the present chapter have covered much the same ground. However, class itself is manifested in a multitude of ways and includes macro issues of gender, race and age as well as multiple micro aspects. Differentiation within fields may not always be directly about opposition between the popular classes and the bourgeoisie. It could, for example, be about the way classroom discourse operates, or the way students and staff experience higher education, or the way career choices are made, or the relations between school and the family.

These are the topics of Part II. However, in order to further justify this extension of Bourdieu's work, the next chapter considers in detail the philosophical issues at stake in conducting social science and educational research in the light of Bourdieu's theory of practice. It shows why it is that an 'epistemological break' with established approaches was and is needed.

Chapter 3

The Need for an Epistemological 'Break'

Derek Robbins

Introduction

In considering Bourdieu's contribution to thinking about education and in recommending his research practice to those involved in education, we are confronted by the complicated task of unravelling the contexts of the production and consumption of his works. This is a necessary task and one which leads to an identification of the coherent purpose in Bourdieu's work which has not often been clearly revealed through the piecemeal interpretations of only partial aspects. The two texts which first introduced the work of Bourdieu to English readers in the educational context were the two essays included in 1971 by Michael Young in *Knowledge and Control: New Directions for the Sociology of Education*. These essays were entitled 'Intellectual field and creative project' and 'Systems of education and systems of thought'. Subsequently, Bourdieu's reputation as a 'sociologist of education' was established as a result of the publication, in 1977, of *Reproduction in Education, Society and Culture*. That reputation was consolidated by the publication in the States of *The Inheritors* (1979) which had, in fact, originally been published in French as *Les Héritiers* in 1964 — before either of the articles which were included in *Knowledge and Control*. By the time these two translations of the late 1970s were receiving critical attention, Bourdieu was concluding a major research project on the educational and cultural characteristics of the captains of French industry — 'le patronat' — and was beginning to become preoccupied with the significance of educational institutions *as institutions* at the time of his appointment to the Chair of Sociology at the Collège de France, Paris, in the autumn of 1981. The publications of *Homo Academicus* — the English translation in 1988 of a text of 1984 — and, of *State Nobility* — the English translation in 1996 of *La Noblesse d'Etat* of 1989, have, perhaps, had less *educational* impact than the re-issue, in 1990 of *Reproduction in Education, Society and Culture* — nominated as a 'citation classic' by the Institute for Scientific Information Social Science Citation Index in 1988.

This chapter attempts, first of all, to give an account of the early reception of Bourdieu's work within the educational sphere. It then argues that this reception within an exclusively educational framework led to misconception or misrepresentation as a result of neglect or ignorance of both the philosophy of knowledge underpinning Bourdieu's prior social anthropology and the philosophy of science underlying his research methodology. The chapter proceeds to offer an account of the progression of Bourdieu's thinking about education in the light of these important factors. It then suggests that, consistent with his philosophical position, by continually *practising* sociological method Bourdieu has, over 35 years, generated descriptions of education and society which, although tentative, partial, or exploratory, have acquired prescriptive, objective status. Many of his analyses of the forces in social relations which underlie behavioural appearances have seemed to be manifested in subsequent, actual occurrences. Those theoretical models of the social world produced by Bourdieu during the time span of a generation seem now adequately to represent the actuality of the facts and events which we currently observe. In this situation, the chapter concludes by recommending that the appropriate way to emulate Bourdieu, therefore, is to follow the procedures whereby his research detected social tendencies in such a way as to anticipate or actualize future developments. The inappropriate response to Bourdieu's work is to treat it essentially as the object of exegesis and discipline-constrained criticism. In Bourdieu's own terms, his work has to be understood as an *opus operandum* rather than an *opus operatum*. Much of the discussion that follows is philosophical but it does not contribute to the 'philosophy of education', nor does it seek to imply that Bourdieu's contribution to thinking in the field of education is essentially to that academic subdiscipline. He was trained as a philosopher and, from the beginning, he was preoccupied with the problems of knowledge and of the knowledge of other selves. Influenced by Bachelard, Bourdieu adopted the view that epistemological difficulties could be resolved by requiring knowers deliberately to construct an alternative perspective on 'common-sense' knowledge or 'everyday' events. Hence, as the chapter title suggests, the need for an epistemological break. Bourdieu's attempt to carry out philosophically motivated research on education has been an attempt to rethink our everyday assumptions about educational practices. This chapter tries to show how the responses of educationists almost succeeded in concealing those insights which were derived from Bourdieu's philosophical approach towards educational issues. In doing so, it necessarily involves some clarification of the philosophical position that Bourdieu holds and recommends.

The Early Educational Reception: Presentation and Misrepresentation

As Michael Young admitted in the Preface to *Knowledge and Control*: 'The idea of this book was first conceived in a discussion between Pierre Bourdieu, Basil Bernstein and myself after the Durham Conference of the British Sociological Association, of April 1970' (Young, 1971, p. vi).

It rapidly became a very influential book. Already by 1974, one observer commented that the development of the new perspective on education contained within the book had affected, '...the assumptions in terms of which this activity of thinking sociologically about education has been embraced. There is hardly a lecture course in the land unaffected by it' (W. Williamson in Flude and Ahier, 1974, p. 3).

Young was pleased to be able to harness the two Bourdieu texts included in *Knowledge and Control* in support of the main emphasis of his collection — that the sociology of education should shift emphasis so as to become concerned with the construction and transmission of curriculum content — so as, in fact, to become a subcomponent of a larger sociology of knowledge. Young deliberately challenged the dominant forms of 'sociology of education' in the UK and in the States, arguing, for instance, that, for the UK, recent texts such as O. Banks: *The Sociology of Education* (1968); P. Musgrave: *The Sociology of Education* (1966); and D. Swift: *The Sociology of Education* (1968) all conspicuously failed to pay adequate attention to the sociological theorizing of Durkheim, Weber, and Marx. Young wanted to shift attention away, for instance, from discussion of the performance of working-class children to a consideration, instead, of the social construction of the curriculum that was imposed upon those children. The collection of essays attempted to hold together different notions of 'construction'. Nell Keddie's 'Classroom Knowledge' preceded Bourdieu's 'Intellectual Field and Creative Project' in the section devoted to 'Social Definitions of Knowledge'. Keddie's contribution sought to analyse the ways in which, amongst other things, 'subject' orientation or 'pupil' orientation in teaching were dependent on the perceived capacities of the pupils. There was no reference to the prior, objective status of the knowledge to be transmitted but, instead, only analytical attention to the classroom transactions which determined the balance of emphasis between transmission and reception. The approach was phenomenological or ethnomethodological. Young argued that, by contrast, Bourdieu was primarily interested in the question of 'content'. For Young, both of the contributions made by Bourdieu offered 'essentially a structural analysis' by which, he claimed, the mutual reinforcement of the interrelations between curricular practice and patterns of thought embedded in French culture were exposed. If Keddie emphasized 'agency', Bourdieu was represented as emphasizing the wider social pre-existence of cognitive structures.

In fact, as discussed in Chapter 2, Bourdieu was continuing to struggle in both articles to liberate himself from the 'objectivist' structural anthropology, which, consequent on the dominating influence of Lévi-Strauss, had been the prevailing paradigm when he had been carrying out his ethnographic fieldwork in Algeria at the end of the 1950s. In organizing *Knowledge and Control* as a collection of essays, Young sought to reconcile articles which appeared to emphasize agency with ones which appeared to emphasize structure. This textual strategy resulted in a slight caricature of Bourdieu's position, for Bourdieu was himself already seeking to develop a theory which would integrate agency with structure. 'Champ intellectuel et projet créateur' had been first published in 1966 in a number of *Les Temps Modernes* devoted to 'The Problems of Structuralism' whilst 'Systèmes d'enseignement et systèmes de pensée' had been first published in 1967 and was a spin-off from Bourdieu's translation of and commentary on Panofsky's *Gothic Architecture and Scholastic Thought* which was published in the same year. 'Intellectual Field and Creative Project' argued that, depending on their social positions, artists and intellectuals possess the varying capacity to construct the 'field' in which their works or ideas will be well received. A key factor in the way in which an artist may acquire a reputation is his capacity to construct a 'field' or market in which his work will be valued objectively. This had two consequences. Firstly, it was assumed that the valuation of art products and, for that matter, intellectual products must always be internal to the field in which they are produced and consumed. Secondly, it was argued that the important relationship was between social agents and the structures which they themselves generated. The so-called explanatory structural analysis practised by structuralist anthropologists or sociologists might have value within the fields of anthropology and sociology and could be appreciated in those contexts but it did not explain the practice of the agents.

'Systems of education and systems of thought' has to be seen in relation to the work of Panofsky. The art critic and historian identified a homology between the structure of scholastic thinking and the structure of Gothic architecture, but he was not prepared to wheel in the notion of a *Zeitgeist* to account for the affinity between structures. Instead, he suggested that the structure of scholastic thinking constituted a kind of generative grammar for all other contemporary cultural forms. The architecture was a physical embodiment of the forms of thinking transmitted in the few important cathedral schools.

Bourdieu took this idea and added it to his thinking about creative projects and intellectual fields. What emerged was the notion that schools are the socially objectified structures which generate all other social practices. The field of institutionalized education is a highly influential one but its current form is the consequence of earlier social agency. Its values are internal to itself and the purpose of the system is to reproduce those values.

It is now possible to see that Bourdieu was not to be located on either side of the structure/agency divide. In a still tentative, exploratory fashion Bourdieu was seeking to articulate the view that social and cultural reproduction occurs by means of a constant reciprocity or dialectic between agency and structure. Within societies, educational institutions embody forms of knowledge which are the legacy of the construction of earlier generations. Within these institutions teachers possess the delegated authority to transmit those forms. They also have the capacity to transmit those forms because, as themselves learners, they once, in part, constituted them. In teaching those forms to their pupils, teachers are engaged in a process by which future forms are constituted for future transmission by their pupils. Classroom interaction occurs in the context of the prior cognitive structures of both teachers and learners. Later in this book, Chapter 5 continues this discussion of the way teaching and learning is not to be reduced to spontaneous interaction but neither is it to be seen as the transmission and reception of absolutely structured knowledge. As Bourdieu was to clarify in a paper entitled 'On Symbolic Power' given in 1973 (published in 1977) and made more generally accessible through inclusion in *Language and Symbolic Power* (1991), we need to understand both the process of 'structuring structures' and the nature of 'structured structures'.

'On Symbolic Power' is not an essay which featured in the 'canon' of Bourdieu educational texts which gradually became established by the end of the 1970s. If it had been more generally known, misreadings of Bourdieu might have been avoided. In that essay, Bourdieu makes it clear that the interest in 'structuring structures' arises from a neo-Kantian tradition that was concerned with the *generation* of systems of thought by which the external world is conceptually organized. He traces the progression from Kantian epistemology in terms of 'categories' of the mind through to the historical relativism of neo-Kantians such as Cassirer and Panofsky and on to the sociologized epistemology of Durkheim. Following Durkheim, Bourdieu accepts the view that 'reality' is the product of social consensus within any given society. At the same time, however, Bourdieu argues that the structuralist approach characteristic of Lévi-Strauss is also to be upheld as a way of ensuring that forms of knowledge receive some attention in themselves and are not reduced simply to social function. Bourdieu tabulates the two approaches in two vertical tables, but, importantly, he adds a third table by which he tries to suggest that the insights of Marxism help us to understand that the consensual structuring of structures is really a competition for domination amongst groups within society possessing different degrees of economic power. 'On Symbolic Power' proposes, therefore, a synthesis whereby agents compete with each other to create new structures in terms of the inherited structures which are isolable as transitory, free-standing entities, unsubmerged by the process of change. At the same time, agents compete in terms of existing structures on the basis of their differential economic capacities.

For Bourdieu, in other words, structures have autonomous but transient life. They exist to be deployed and adapted by agents seeking to establish their social position within the possibilities offered to them as a result of the prior social and economic position that is their inheritance. Bourdieu's view has to be put cautiously in this way because he clearly argues that his 'structured structures' do not correspond, as 'superstructure' with any economic base, and because he is equally clear that the structuring capacity of agents is not economically determined. In a sense, Bourdieu's concept of 'structure' mediates formally between base and superstructure, but it has to be remembered that Bourdieu does not suppose that there is any superstructure and, equally, supposes that the base is not an economic fixture but, rather, one which is a consequence of continuous processes of social exchange.

These conceptual positions were not at all clear to the first readers of Bourdieu's early texts. In an article which was generally perceptive and, indeed, prescient about the fundamental importance of Bourdieu's epistemological position, John Kennett commented:

> Of course, Bourdieu is a marxist, but we must see how he proceeds from the marxist theory of the ideological function of culture into a deeper awareness of the peculiar efficacy of culture in that culture is seen as structuring the system of social relations by its own functioning. (Kennett, 1973, pp. 238–9)

There are no grounds for considering that Bourdieu was ever a Marxist, but Kennett was right to see that Bourdieu had adapted the form of Marxist thinking to come to terms with the way in which culture — and, therefore, education — might function as an independent force to be manipulated by agents to secure social position. Others were more inclined simply to welcome Bourdieu as a Marxist. Flude and Ahier's *Educability, Schools and Ideology* (1974) expressed concern at the phenomenological tendency of *Knowledge and Control*. There was a call for 'a return to the work of Marxist-oriented writers' so as to avoid 'celebrating the act of "doing knowledge" at the expense of any consideration of the created product' (Whitty in Flude and Ahier, 1974, p. 127) and *Schooling and Capitalism* (1976), edited by Roger Dale, obliged. This was a collection of papers which was 'assembled to show how the capitalist mode of production influences one social institution, schooling' (Dale *et al.*, 1976, p. 1). Within this general intention, the editor had no problem in including Bourdieu's 'Systems of Education and Systems of Thought' as well as his 'The School as a Conservative Force: Scholastic and Cultural Inequalities'.

The validity of this appropriation of Bourdieu's texts by the anti-phenomenological, Marxist-structuralist wing of the 'new directions in the sociology of education' movement in the 1970s seemed to be confirmed by the appearance of the first reporting of Bourdieu's empirical research. 'Scholastic excellence and the values of the educational system' — which had appeared in French in 1970 — was published in English in 1974 in *Contemporary Research in the Sociology of Education*, edited by John Eggleston. It reported the findings of a survey carried out by correspondence by Bourdieu and Monique de Saint Martin with successful candidates of the *concours générale* from 1966, 1967, and 1968. It was, in other words, a report on the social backgrounds of those pupils who had performed well in the standardized national examination equivalent to A-level. A footnote commented that 'The distribution of successful candidates by *lycée* and *département* remained more or less constant throughout the period' (Bourdieu and de Saint Martin in Eggleston, 1974, p. 359), suggesting, in other words, that performance in the examination was not the consequence of individual student capacity so much as a reflection of the homology between the values of certain schools and regions and the values of the national examiners. The article was primarily designed to expose the fallacy of supposing that individuals possess innate intelligence or 'giftedness' but it also analysed mechanisms of selection and elimination which could be taken to be the devices adopted by capitalism to exclude the working class from power.

In the United Kingdom, the publication of a collection of essays edited by Denis Gleeson under the title: *Identity and Structure: Issues in the Sociology of Education*, can be said to mark, in 1977, the end of the 'new directions' movement. The collection ends with an essay by Brian Davies in which he lampoons the intellectual trajectory of his fellow sociologists of education in the previous decade. He argues that philosophical allegiance to interactionism and phenomenology did little for the reform of educational practice and that, equally, the rediscovery of 'early' Marx did not alter the fact that Marxist explanation can 'find no place for education except as mechanical reproducer of social relations' (Davies in Gleeson, 1977, p. 200). As the new intellectual fashions had become moribund, Davies argued that there had developed a new, doom-laden form of Marxist resignation and a return to 'sloganized appeals to the inevitability of class warfare' (*ibid.*). As evidence of this trend, Davies cited S. Bowles and H. Gintis: *Schooling in Capitalist America* that was published in the United States in 1976. This was the text against which American critics tested Bourdieu as *Reproduction* and *The Inheritors* became known in the States in the last few years of the 1970s.

The Fundamental 'Educational' Misconceptions

The period between 1971 and 1977 was one in which, in the UK, attempts were made to harness Bourdieu's work in support of a movement for educational change which can be seen as an extension of the impulse that generated the student revolts of 1968. The appropriation was as much political as intellectual. The political movement had lost momentum by the time of the publication of *Reproduction* in English in 1977. Not only had there been the devastating intellectual exposé given by Davies, but 1977 was the year of Callaghan's Green Paper on Education which anticipated the kind of subjugation of education to the economy that characterized the eighteen years of Tory hegemony that commenced in May, 1979. There was, suddenly, no space for radical educational action. The first significant British consideration of *Reproduction* came in Margaret Archer's 'Process without System' (1983), but even this article was published in the *Archives Européennes de Sociologie*. It was a lecturer in the education department of a New Zealand university — Richard Harker — who provided, in 1984, the first article on Bourdieu in the *British Journal of the Sociology of Education* — the journal which, it might be added, had been established in 1980 precisely so as to sustain intellectually the debate about those ideas which had been politically unsuccessful in the previous decade.

By contrast, Bourdieu's early educational work had never been appropriated in the States during the 1970s with a view to giving support to any radical movement for educational reform. The first important American considerations of Bourdieu's educational work appeared in the well-established *Harvard Educational Review* and the *Journal of Curriculum Studies*. Whereas, in the UK, Bourdieu's work was used through the 1970s in collections of texts and 'readers' which sought to mobilize radical educational opinion, in the United States, the intellectual reception was, from the outset, circumscribed by institutionalized intellectual compartments, embodied in specialist 'discipline' journals.

In singling out two articles for particular attention, I am seeking to substantiate, in turn, the claims that the American academic and educational response to Bourdieu's educational research and findings was misconceived: firstly, because there was little appreciation of Bourdieu's philosophy of knowledge; secondly, because there was equally little sympathy for his philosophy of science.

The 'Philosophy of Knowledge' Misconception

The article on Bourdieu contained in the *Harvard Educational Review* was David Swartz's: 'Pierre Bourdieu: The Cultural Transmission of Social Inequality' (1977). Swartz acknowledges in his first footnote that, 'the sociology of education represents only one dimension of Bourdieu's highly varied work.' But, he suggests that a common orientation has led Bourdieu, '. . . to write on a variety of subjects, ranging from cultural practices, such as museum attendance and photography, to the sociology of intellectuals and of science.'

This common 'orientation' that is thought to steer Bourdieu's enquiries is defined as a concern, '. . . with exploring and explaining the multitude of ways in which cultural phenomena and practices relate social structure to power' (Swartz, 1977, p. 545).

At first sight, this seems an adequate paraphrase of Bourdieu's project. There is, however, something wrong about the tone or the emphasis. Swartz imposes a sense of externality or detachment and, along with this, he implies that the object of Bourdieu's work is to observe the static relations between hypostatized elements of all social systems — 'cultural phenomena', 'social structure' and 'power'. It is because Swartz assumes that Bourdieu is engaged in a systematic testing of the same abstracted hypothesis in respect of a range of aspects of society that he feels justified in evaluating Bourdieu's work in relation to just one of those aspects — the education system. Swartz is clearly aware, in other words, of *Un Art Moyen* (1965), *L'Amour de l'Art* (1966), and, probably, of 'The specificity of the scientific field and the social conditions of the progress of reason' (1975), but he restricts his discussion to what he describes as the five of Bourdieu's articles which have recently been translated into English, and appear in several readers on the sociology of education, and to *Reproduction*, the forthcoming translation of *Les Héritiers* (1964), and 'Les stratégies de reconversion: les classes sociales et le système d'enseignement' (Bourdieu, Boltanski and de Saint Martin, 1973).

What is conspicuously missing from this clear statement of textual sources is any reference whatsoever to the anthropological fieldwork which pre-dated Bourdieu's educational researches. Swartz makes one footnote reference to *Outline of a Theory of Practice* but he makes no attempt to accommodate the perspective of that book in his representation of Bourdieu's educational work. The consequence of this exclusion is that Swartz has no access to the philosophy of knowledge which Bourdieu developed academically as a philosophy student and which he tested in the ethnographic research that he has since characterized as being motivated by a desire to produce a 'phenomenology of emotional life' (Bourdieu, 1990b, pp. 6–7).

Later in this chapter I shall consider further the precise implications of understanding Bourdieu's philosophy of knowledge for using his thoughts on education, but, for the moment, I want to concentrate on the negative effects of misunderstanding. Swartz sought to give 'a descriptive overview of salient features of Bourdieu's approach to educational institutions; . . .' (Swartz, 1977, p. 546). Below are a few of the representations of Bourdieu's position which are slightly off target as a result of Swartz's blinkered perspective.

Swartz offers the general, initial statement that: 'the central thrust of Bourdieu's work in education is its exploration of the relationship between the higher-education system and social-class structure.' This is quickly followed by the comment that, 'The system of higher education, according to Bourdieu, functions to transmit privilege, allocate status, and instill respect for the existing social order' (*ibid.*).

Still 'summarizing' Bourdieu's position, Swartz continues: 'Through socialization and education, relatively permanent cultural dispositions are internalized; these, in turn, structure individual and group behaviour in ways that tend to reproduce existing class relations' (p. 547).

The main problem with these representations is that Swartz does not appreciate the significance of the distinction between the first two modes of theoretical knowledge, as sketched by Bourdieu in the revaluation of his early ethnographic research that he offered in *Esquisse d'une Théorie de la Pratique* (1972). Social agents possess primary, unreflecting knowledge of their situations. This is the initial point from which they develop in their lives. It is the *habitus* which is their inheritance of the accumulated experiences of their antecedents. The manifestation of the *habitus* of some agents is that they have acquired the capacity to reflect systematically on their own situations and on those of others. Detached discourses for talking about primary experience have developed historically and, by virtue of becoming initiated into these discourses, some social agents have gained the power to superimpose their conceptualizations of the experiences of others on thoughts and actions which may be lived pre-conceptually or less conceptually by those others. For Bourdieu, people live within two competing kinds of culture. Corporally transmitted cultures are constantly invaded and modified by historically objectified cultures. Social classes and educational institutions are both examples of objectification. To talk in terms of 'classes' is to consolidate the social differentiation constructed by some agents to impose their dominance over others. The transmission of knowledge in educational institutions doubly imposes artificially constructed objectifications because both the abstracted knowledge that is taught and the institutions themselves within which it is taught are products of the basic inclination to achieve distinction by imposing dominant conceptualizations ('symbolic violence').

This should all have been clear from a reading of *Reproduction*, but it is the progression of Bourdieu's rejection of structuralism in the anthropological context that clarifies absolutely the extent to which his analytical orientation is towards an understanding of *agents* rather than structures. It becomes apparent, in this perspective, why Swartz's emphasis is wrong. Bourdieu was not interested in the relationship between the 'higher-education system' and 'social-class structure' in abstract or as such but, instead, in the constantly changing ways in which social agents and societies play with institutions and with class classifications. In each of his statements, Swartz seemed to read Bourdieu in terms of a set of given, functional, systemic relations, whereas the essence of Bourdieu's position was that *all* of the relational variables are historically contingent — manifestations of the unending process of ontological adaptation that is the history of humankind.

The 'Philosophy of Science' Misconception

The second American critical response to Bourdieu's work is Bredo and Feinberg's 'Meaning, Power and Pedagogy' (1979) which was explicitly an 'essay review' of the recently published translation of *La Reproduction*. The authors painstakingly seek to subject to a 'non-ideological' reading a text which they suspect is actually laden with ideology or normative values. They are eager, in other words, to evaluate the work of Bourdieu and Passeron as science. In making this attempt, however, they fail to recognize that Bourdieu and Passeron were operating with a different conception of science — one which they had fully articulated in *Le Métier de Sociologue* (1968: with Chamboredon and Passeron) which was published whilst they were revising the data of *Les Héritiers* for systematic presentation in *La Reproduction*. Bredo and Feinberg distinguish between 'the first part, a theoretical essay, entitled "Foundations of a theory of symbolic violence"' and the 'second "empirical" part of the book' (Bredo and Feinberg, 1979, p. 316) but they do not seek to understand the purpose of the mode of presentation chosen by Bourdieu and Passeron. It seems clear that Bourdieu and Passeron were experimenting with a mode of sociological writing that was derived from the presentational procedures of the rationalist philosophers — either Leibniz or Spinoza or both. In Leibnizian terminology, they were clearly differentiating between matters of reason and matters of fact and were seeking to articulate logical propositions which did not universally explain 'facts' but which could be deployed in particular situations to construct testable facts from phenomena. Bredo and Feinberg missed this crucial methodological point. By describing the first part as 'a series of propositions and sub-propositions with some logical ordering among them' (Bredo and Feinberg, 1979, p. 316) they make it abundantly obvious that they do not appreciate the fundamental point that the propositions are themselves logical rather than simply logically connected. The misunderstanding is apparent again when Bredo and Feinberg comment on the second part of the book. Bourdieu and Passeron, they say, '. . . actually use rather less in the way of systematic data than is claimed and are empirical primarily in that they consider a particular historic case, France, in an interpretative fashion' (p. 317).

Although they seek to maintain a generous, dispassionate, 'scientific' procedure in their analysis, it is evident that Bredo and Feinberg do not consider the 'interpretation' of a 'particular' geographic and 'historic' case really to be empirical in their meaning of the word. It follows, therefore, that a genuinely sympathetic critical review inevitably proceeds to find the work of Bourdieu and Passeron wanting by reference to the unquestioned norms of positivist science. Again, I shall move towards a positive statement of the development of Bourdieu's methodological position shortly, but, for the moment, several further examples demonstrate the way in which criticism within the field of American social and educational science 'talked past' Bourdieu's work. Bredo and Feinberg give proper coverage of the view of Bourdieu and Passeron that much conventional research 'serves to further reify objective social "facts"' (p. 321) and they go on to state that:

> The authors are particularly critical of research such as that on college effects, educational production functions, and cost-benefit analyses that attempt to explore optimization of returns on investment in education. Research such as the Coleman Report and most contemporary studies of educational and occupational attainment would similarly fall within their criticism. (pp. 321–2)

In the quest for precision and scientificity, however, Bredo and Feinberg seek to evaluate these criticisms. They appear to work on the assumption that Bourdieu and Passeron were saying that conventional, positivist research was methodologically inadequate or underdeveloped whereas, on the contrary, they were saying that it was fundamentally misconceived. Bredo and Feinberg appreciate that Bourdieu and Passeron were arguing that, for instance, the effects of different kinds of college majors have been treated by positivists as absolute whereas they should be understood to be relative to changing historical conditions, but they do not realize that the purpose of the propositional style adopted by Bourdieu and Passeron is to locate possible explanation within contingency rather than to aspire to more sophisticated, absolute knowledge. In summarizing Bourdieu and Passeron's critique of positivism as that 'it takes these facts as given rather than as products of the relation between different power and cultural groups' (p. 322), Bredo and Feinberg keep open the hope that Bourdieu and Passeron's relationalism can be absorbed into a 'better' understanding of objective reality. They fight back against Bourdieu and Passeron's exposé of limitations in positivist methodology: 'Yet multivariate studies can include larger social structural variables (with cross-national data), utilize longitudinal or time-series data, and can be used to study interaction effects' (p. 323).

They do not, however, realize that, for Bourdieu, such absorption of the strategic perceptions of particular social scientific agents into the universalizing maelstrom of impersonal data-sets would simply cause him to find a new 'field' or interpretative framework within which to sustain freedom of thought and action in opposition to the oppressive totalization of the dominant number crunchers.

Towards a Proper Contextualization of Bourdieu's Educational Work

I am suggesting that Bourdieu's work on education was received in contexts which were institutionally and intellectually framed in such a way that misrepresentation was inevitable. Equally, it was an inevitability that Bourdieu could not resist if he was to acquire reputation and power — both of which could then be deployed to make clear what he really wanted to say. It is significant that, in discussing in 1967 the fate of Durkheim within the French university system, Bourdieu (with Passeron) wrote:

> The records of the discussions of the French Philosophical Society reveal how Durkheim had to fight on his opponents' ground, accepting the role of defendant by the very fact of offering a defense and in the end yielding to his opponents by explaining the reasons for his action in terms of the reasoning of his opponents. (Bourdieu and Passeron, 1967, p. 170)

This was the game that Bourdieu was having to play — not with university officials but, certainly, in relation to his critics. What now follows, therefore, is an attempt to reconstruct or retrieve what Bourdieu has always been saying. This account suggests that Bourdieu has only gradually acquired the capacity to speak out clearly as, recently, in his *Méditations Pascaliennes* (1997). His complex analyses of education were parts of the process by which he has acquired the legitimate authority to speak clearly and simply on educational and other matters. Similarly, Bourdieu's discussions of knowledge and scientific method have been elements of a strategy to give himself the power to practise what he has preached. This intention of offering a 'proper' contextualization of Bourdieu's educational work, therefore, is subordinate to the intention of liberating those fundamental aspects of Bourdieu's effort that deserve to be used and imitated.

Bourdieu's methodological endeavour has always been to offer his particular analyses as *potentially* rather than actually universal. It is helpful to place Bourdieu's educational work in the context of his own particular educational experience. What follows is not an exercise in biography for its own sake but, rather, an introduction to reflection on the general relevance of Bourdieu's attempt to offer the objectification of personal experience as science. In other words the starting point in considering Bourdieu's contribution to the science of education must be an examination of his upbringing and early experience of education.

He has recollected that, like Flaubert, he attended a boarding school from an early age: 'Reading Flaubert, I found out that I had also been profoundly marked by another social experience, that of life as a boarder in a public school (*internat*)' (Bourdieu and Wacquant, 1992b, p. 205).

In providing the background to the politics of educational reform in France between 1918 and 1940, J.E. Talbott has traced the origin of the tradition of French secondary education back to the law of 1 Floréal, An X (May 1, 1802) which laid down that secondary education would be given in, '. . . lycées and special schools maintained at the expense of the public treasury' (Talbott, 1969, p. 8). He continued to suggest that the development of the lycées 'marked a return to the principles of education laid down by the Jesuits' (p. 8) such that:

> The atmosphere of the lycée was both military and monastic. The Jesuits constructed an extremely sophisticated educational philosophy based on the *internat*, or boarding school, in which they kept their students under constant surveillance, sealed off from the cares and temptations of the world. (p. 9)

In the early 1880s, a series of laws had established the free, compulsory and secular primary schools in which children could qualify for a *certificat des études primaires* and, if they wished to continue beyond obligatory schooling, might proceed to *écoles primaires supérieures* after the age of 13. But there were no connections between this universal provision and privileged progression through public secondary education. As Talbott comments: 'Primary and secondary education were under separate administrations that jealously guarded their every prerogative. The lycées operated their own elementary classes whose program differed markedly from that of the public primary schools' (p. 29).

He concludes:

> The futures of the overwhelming majority of children were likely to be determined at the age of six, when they entered either the public primary school or the elementary class of the lycée. For the bright primary school pupil of limited means,

one narrow and uncertain path to the university was open; he might obtain a scholarship to the lycée that would enable him to acquire the indispensable baccalaureate.
(p. 32)

This was the situation prior to the period covered by Talbott's study. He
remarks that, in 1911, '. . . there were only some 100 lycées and 240 collèges in all
of France' (p. 19) offering public secondary education. This was elitist provision
and Talbott's book examines the political machinations which led to the gradual
introduction of free secondary education so that, by 1933, charges were abolished
for attendance at all seven classes of the lycée. The impact of the new funding
arrangements was likely to have been slow and it is safe to assume, therefore, that
Bourdieu's education took place within a system that was still radically divided.

This point is not made in order to recriminate or to seek to invalidate Bourdieu's
subsequent analyses of education. What is important is that, growing up in a context in which the liberalization of the schooling system was a matter of constant
political debate, Bourdieu seems to have felt strongly the ambivalence of his position. As Michelet had put it in the mid-Nineteenth Century: 'The difficult thing is
not to rise in the world, but, while rising, to remain oneself' (quoted in Talbott,
1969, p. 132).

In *Homo Academicus*, Bourdieu implied that many professors were conservative in 1968 because they were *oblates*. This was a term which Bourdieu borrowed,
'. . . to suggest the intensity of institutional loyalty felt by the teacher of humble
origins who owes his whole education, culture, training and career to the state
educational system' (Bourdieu, 1988, p. 291).

There is the strong sense that Bourdieu considers that he was himself an *oblate*
who was able to resist conservatism as a result of his capacity to understand his
situation. This is the general significance of Bourdieu's educational experience. It is
not that his work has been adversely affected by his privileged schooling but,
rather, that it enabled him to conceptualize the ambivalence of his personal experience in such a way that his concepts have related pertinently to the objective
phenomena of divided educational social systems.

The distinction of Bourdieu's educational career continued in the 1950s in
Paris. I have discussed elsewhere (Robbins, forthcoming) the likely characteristics
of the *Ecole Normale Supérieure* during the period in which Bourdieu studied there
from 1950 to 1954. Bourdieu has, of course, himself — subsequently and indirectly
— analysed his own experience of the social construction of the *normalien* ethos
in 'Les catégories de l'entendement professoral' (1975: with de Saint Martin) and
in *La Noblesse d'État* (1989a). Since the 1970s, in other words, Bourdieu has been
prepared to turn his intellectual training against itself. Before that time, however,
he appears to have struggled to come to terms with his cultural ambivalence. By
all accounts, he was a troubled student at the *Ecole Normale Supérieure*, kicking
against the pricks of privilege. He produced an academic dissertation for a *diplôme
d'études supérieures* but he did not proceed to study for a *doctorat*. He taught at a
provincial lycée for several years before being conscripted to fight in Algeria.
Bourdieu's Algerian experience offered an objective correlative of his own cultural

ambivalence. He used the period of enforced military service to embark upon a process of social observation of indigenous Algerians which, methodologically, sought to apply a phenomenological approach derived from his Parisian studies in philosophy. Partly influenced by the 'acculturation' studies of American ethnographers, Bourdieu sought to analyse the phenomena of cultural adjustment which were apparent in the transitions of Algerian tribespeople from 'traditional' to 'modern' or from 'rural' to 'urban' values. He did this as a self-taught anthropologist, or as a generally well-educated graduate, who acquired his tools of analysis as he practised his observation. The object of his study was the process of cultural encounter and change within Algeria, but, equally, Bourdieu was aware that the study was itself a process of encounter between the observed indigenous population and the observing, colonial intellectual — a process which, in turn, was an objectification of the tension in his own personality between the man of traditional, rural Gascon origins and the intellectual constructed by a privileged educational experience.

Bourdieu struggled with these tensions in the early 1960s and his analysis of his home region in 'Célibat et condition paysanne' (1962) is the main illustration of his attempt to use his educationally acquired capacity to objectify — to be scientifically detached — to analyse the very social conditions which generated those values of modern, rational objectivity. Apart from a few comments in the closing paragraphs of *Le Déracinement* (1964: with Sayad), Bourdieu seems at first to have ignored the effects of schooling in the acculturation process. It was only after he began to teach at the University of Lille that he began to make the experience of students one of the objects of his enquiries. Here, again, Bourdieu's analyses had a reflexive, or self-regarding dimension. The motive behind the enquiry which was to lead to the publication, firstly, of a working-paper entitled 'Les étudiants et leurs études', and, then, in revised form, of *Les Héritiers* (1964) was to understand the process of 'being a student' as one of cultural adaptation rather than of learning. It is significant that, as a provincial person who had studied in Paris and as someone who had studied philosophy and was beginning to practise as a sociologist, Bourdieu's research findings were based on a sample of philosophy and sociology students and emphasized the comparative trajectories of students of provincial or Parisian origins. The concept of 'cultural capital' which began to emerge at this time was one which helped to universalize Bourdieu's particular experience — that 'scholastic' culture was separate from indigenous culture. It is precisely because scholastic culture is an artificial acquisition presenting itself as absolutely valid that it constructs and legitimates divisions and differences.

In no sense was Bourdieu offering a 'sociology of education' in *Les Héritiers* nor a theory of learning, and, certainly, in no sense was he attempting to present a static correlation between the social class of students and their educational performance. Equally, in no sense was Bourdieu idealizing indigenous culture. Rather, he was attempting to find a way of describing the dynamics of cultural adaptation in operation within the system of education that he observed. The problems of describing the behaviour of Kabyle tribespeople, celibate men of the Béarn, and students at Lille were, methodologically, the same. For this reason, the consequences of Bourdieu's dissociation from structuralism were not confined to the anthropological sphere.

The philosophy of knowledge which Bourdieu eventually articulated in *Esquisse d'une Théorie de la Pratique* (1972) derived from the philosophical orientation that he had acquired prior to his engagement with anthropology, and that prior philosophical position provided him with a basis for criticizing structuralist anthropology. Bourdieu took from Leibniz the view that reality takes the form of a logical proposition. Just as all predicates are logically contained within their subjects, so all possible actual worlds are contained potentially within the originating divine creation. As Bertrand Russell sought to summarize:

> Every proposition is ultimately reducible to one which attributes a predicate to a subject . . . The subject is defined by its predicates, and would be a different subject if these were different. . . . Every predicate, necessary or contingent, past, present or future, is comprised in the notion of the subject. From this proposition it follows, says Leibniz, that every soul is a world apart; for every soul, as a subject, has eternally, as predicates, all the states which time will bring it; and thus these states follow from its notion alone, without any need of action from without. (Russell, 1990, pp. 9, 10, 11)

Similarly, C.D. Broad sought to explain:

> Each possible world corresponds to certain possible *primary* ends or intentions characteristic of it. If God had decided to actualize a certain possible world, he would have made certain *primary* free decisions, embodying the main ends or intentions characteristic of that world. These would have been the most general principles constituting the ground-plan of that world. The notions of all the individual substances in that world would be determined in view of these primary intentions. (Broad, 1975, p. 9)

Related to this, Bourdieu also derived from Leibniz the view that abstract, analytical propositions are ones which are necessarily true whilst contingent, synthetic propositions are not. Once more, Russell's early book on Leibniz clarifies:

> Leibniz and Kant both held that there is a fundamental distinction between propositions that are necessary, and those that are contingent, or, in Kant's language, empirical. Thus the propositions of mathematics are necessary, while those asserting particular existence are contingent. (Russell, 1990, p. 23)

This meant that Bourdieu was able to operate with two notions of reality. On the one hand, all events in the real world, whether human thoughts or acts, occur in conformity with an undisclosed, pre-ordained harmony. They appear to be free but they automatically actualize a necessary, pre-existent abstract proposition. Nevertheless, on the other hand, when we all think in apparent freedom we do so by generating propositions which relate to (apparently) contingent phenomena. To put this another way, Bourdieu's acquaintance with the philosophy of Leibniz enabled him to argue that the findings of empirical science are, at the same time, contingent and, therefore, secondary or arbitrary in the context of real change in the universe, and also substantive or themselves phenomenally 'real' in that they are manifestations of the real processes which they, inadequately, seek to explain. It is this argument that enables Bourdieu to be sceptical about empirical science, to analyse the *Realpolitik* of its discourses and institutions, and to write within these discourses himself whilst sustaining his scepticism by systematic reflexivity.

The Leibnizian rationalism underlying Bourdieu's work allowed him to assume that a universal history was unfolding by a process of bio-genetic interaction, whether these interactions occurred at the level of unreflecting, primary experience or at the level of objectivist intellectualism. It allowed him to grasp that the patterns of human behaviour in which a structural anthropologist such as Lévi-Strauss sought to detect universal truths could not be accorded that status but, equally, could not be denied. The perceptions of the structuralists were not true but they were real. More generally, the observations of science or the ways in which reality has historically been conceptualized in various disciplines, although not true, are inescapably potent. In relation to Bourdieu's own experience, the learning he had acquired within the educational system in opposition to his indigenous culture was not true but it had had the effect of bestowing social status and power. Its arbitrariness could be analysed, not in relation to an ideal non-arbitrariness but by reference to the causes and effects of the phenomenon, or 'fact of life'.

This combination of fundamental criticism and pragmatic realism informed Bourdieu's educational work in the 1960s. In an ideal world, he implies in 'Langage et rapport au langage dans la situation pédagogique' (1965: with Passeron and de Saint Martin), communication between teachers and learners would be a natural social process and would not be distorted by the language of academic discourse, but, he continues, given that we do have historically constructed 'subjects' and 'disciplines', there is no reason why these constructs should not be efficiently transmitted. The fact that this does not happen leads Bourdieu to suggest that the efficient transmission of information is not really on the agenda within the higher education system. Instead, the artificiality of discourse is used to maintain social distinctions between those who have been initiated into the artificial discourse and those who have not.

Many of the insights derived from Bourdieu's developing philosophical critique of anthropological structuralism were systematically formulated by Bourdieu and Passeron in *La Reproduction* (1970). The book can be read as an experiment in various modes of *formal* presentation. As we have seen from Bredo and Feinberg's review, the text was presented in two parts, but Bourdieu and Passeron were eager to pre-empt the kind of distinction between the parts made by the American reviewers. They began their Foreword with the comment that,

> The arrangement of this work in two books, at first sight very dissimilar in their mode of presentation, should not suggest the common conception of the division of intellectual labour between the piecemeal tasks of empirical inquiry and a self-sufficient theoretical activity. (Bourdieu and Passeron, 1977, p. ix)

They continued:

> Unlike a mere catalogue of actual relations or a summa of theoretical statements, the body of propositions presented in Book I is the outcome of an effort to organize into a system amenable to logical verification on the one hand propositions which were constructed in and for the operation of our research or were seen to be logically required as a ground for its findings, and on the other hand theoretical propositions which enabled us to construct, by deduction or specification, propositions amenable to direct empirical verification. (p. ix)

In other words, the authors were not seeking to offer a set of propositions which would establish universal laws governing the relations between education, culture and society. On the contrary, they were seeking to display to the reader the reciprocal movement between theory and practice that had characterized their research. Book I was an attempt to extrapolate from their empirical engagement and from their prior theoretical dispositions propositional statements which could then be tested. After this process, which they described as one of 'mutual rectification', Bourdieu and Passeron insisted that:

> . . . the analyses in Book II may be seen as the application, to a particular historical case, of principles whose generality would support other applications, although those analyses were in fact the starting point for the construction of the principles stated in Book I.

The contention is that the propositions of *La Reproduction* are generalizable even though they are the product of a dialectical relationship between theory and practice in a specific situation. Because the propositions are conceived to be pragmatically valuable rather than necessary truths, they are presented in such a way that their generalizability may be tested in different contexts. Bourdieu and Passeron were eager to make it clear that their propositions were of the contingent, synthetic kind and that, therefore, their analyses of the educational system possessed, like the system itself, a kind of irreducible arbitrariness.

The fold-out diagrammatic model of the 'educational career and its system of determinations' at the back of *La Reproduction* has to be used with this kind of philosophical scepticism, this sensitivity to the competing claims of particular phenomena and universal explanations. The important point is that Bourdieu and Passeron attempted to represent the progression of people through life trajectories. The concentration is on the progression of agents but the engagement of individuals with the education system is affected by a series of arbitrary pauses or breaks. These are presented as moments of transition from primary to secondary to higher education, and then to employment. The progression through these hoops is not to be measured abstractly and statistically but, instead, is to be understood by gauging the ways in which individuals organize their future aspirations by internalizing what they take to be the objective expectations of all members of the social group to which they think they belong. The objective structures controlling entrance to progressive stages of education and employment have no more absolute validity than the observations of structural anthropologists, but, *de facto*, agents act as if they were true to such an extent that, to varying degrees according to their social position, they acquiesce in making themselves the victims of an apparent social determinism.

This diagrammatic presentation of the educational system is the perception of it of someone who had become socially upwardly mobile as a result of its arbitrary rewards. It is the conceptualization of an *oblate*. But Bourdieu and Passeron accepted methodologically that this was the case. Their model of the educational career was an extrapolation from their own educational experiences but it would become part of the thinking about the system which would modify the aspirations and expectations of future agents moving through it. It was not absolutely true even of the whole French system, let alone of international educational systems, but, as a model, it functioned instrumentally for other participants in the system which had generated it and could be applied hypothetically to other systems.

All objective knowledge can be said, for Bourdieu, to be constantly provisional, subject to ongoing test and reformulation. The confusing factor is that whilst Bourdieu was developing this epistemological position, he was also adopting a particular scientific methodology. As a result of his philosophical position, he was not willing to take the claims of science seriously. Scientific explanation could lay no more claim to truth than literary or artistic expression. Nevertheless, again, since the Scientific Revolution, it has become *de facto* the case that scientific explanation possesses higher truth status than other intellectual practice. In order to diminish the affective force of science, therefore, it became necessary for Bourdieu to appropriate the status of science to expose its limits.

An anti-positivist tradition in the philosophy of the social sciences has been particularly strong in France right from the late nineteenth century origins of social science itself. P.Q. Hirst has analysed this French orientation critically in respect of its early stages in *Durkheim, Bernard and Epistemology* (1975) whilst Dominique Lecourt evaluated its more recent manifestations in his *Marxism and Epistemology: Bachelard, Canguilhem and Foucault* (trans. 1975). In his reflections on his studies as a student in 'Fieldwork in Philosophy', Bourdieu commented, in 1985, that, 'I studied mathematics and the history of the sciences. Men like Georges Canguilhem, and also Jules Vuillemin, were for me, and for a few others, real "exemplary prophets" in Weber's sense' (Bourdieu, 1990b, p. 4).

Evidence of Bourdieu's early sympathy with Claude Bernard is to be found in his short methodological commentary offered in *Travail et Travailleurs en Algérie* (Bourdieu, 1963; trans. Robbins, 1994), whilst his indebtedness to Bachelard and Canguilhem is everywhere apparent in *Le Métier de Sociologue* (Bourdieu, Chamboredon and Passeron, 1968) — now available in translation with an added, up-to-date interview with Bourdieu, as *The Craft of Sociology: Epistemological Preliminaries* (ed. Bourdieu, Chamboredon and Passeron, 1991). Although Bourdieu's commitment to Bachelard's philosophy of science was made public in *Le Métier de Sociologue*, it is interesting that he has chosen to reassert this commitment in the late 1980s, explicitly, perhaps, so as to clarify the distinction between his methodology and that of the American positivists, such as Bredo and Feinberg, by whom he had been criticized. In 1989 Bourdieu gave a lecture entitled 'Penser les limites' which was subsequently published as an article entitled 'Thinking about Limits' in *Theory, Culture and Society* in 1992, and then collected in *Cultural Theory and Cultural Change* (ed. M. Featherstone, 1992). Here he gives a brief summary of the essence of Bachelard's philosophy. He writes:

> The French tradition proposes, then, a reflection which is much more general, from which I have drawn an epistemological programme which can be summed up in one statement: 'The scientific fact is conquered, constructed, confirmed'. (Bourdieu, 1992, pp. 41–2)

Bourdieu proceeds to elaborate the initial 'winning' or 'conquest' of scientific facts and, in doing so, seeks to differentiate his approach from the dominant Anglo-Saxon tradition:

> The *conquest* of the given is a central concept in Bachelard's thought, and he sums it up in the term, 'epistemological break'. Why is this phase of scientific research important, and why does it separate, as seems to me to be the case, the tradition I represent from the dominant Anglo-Saxon tradition? It is because to say that the scientific fact has to be fought for is radically to defy, in this regard, all of the 'givens' that social scientific researchers find before them. Researchers in the social sciences have, within arms' reach, just at their fingertips, preconstructed facts which are wholly fabricated: so many terms, so many subjects. At conferences, you can listen to these preconstructed concepts being exchanged, dressed up in theoretical tinsel, and having the air of scientific facts. This is currently how subjects and their limits are defined; the preconstructed appears to be everywhere. ... In a more general way, social problems have tended to be converted too quickly into sociological problems. A 'social problem' ... constituted as such by the fact that it is hotly disputed and fought over, passes lock, stock and barrel into science. Social problems draw attention to critical sociological questions, but they must be approached with a redoubled epistemological vigilance, with a very sharp realization that they must be demolished in order to be reconstructed. (Bourdieu, 1992, p. 42)

Bourdieu next spells out what he means by the *construction* of scientific facts. Having won a problem area for scientific enquiry by making an epistemological break from the dominant way in which the issue is conceptualized in everyday, modish, or popular discourse, the next step for the scientists is to construct the scientific discourse within which they will converse about the problem with other scientists. The scientist has to articulate a methodology which is a response to the object of enquiry and not simply a response to the preconstructed data associated with that object. The scientist has therefore to ensure conceptually that new findings and explanations do not simply reproduce existing 'data' self-fulfillingly. Bourdieu elaborates in the following way:

> Ordinarily, we speak of 'choosing a subject'. There are all sorts of books, a whole Anglo-Saxon literature on 'How to do a thesis', 'How to choose a subject'. In actual fact, the construction of the object is the fundamental operation. For example, when I wanted to study the institutions of higher education, there existed a whole series of monographs, in French and other languages, which bore upon the Grandes

Ecoles. I think that these objects had only been taken because they had offered themselves under the form of already prepared statistics and preselected documents.

My alternative hypothesis was that the truth of what happens in these little enclaves, which is what the Grandes Ecoles are, the truth of these small universes is in their relation with the other universes, in the structure of the relations between the universes. . . . I could, then, have done a beautiful piece of traditional empirical research on the Ecole Normale Supérieure or the Ecole des Hautes Etudes Commerciales. But in this case I would, at bottom, have studied something cut out in such a way that, the lines having been inscribed, what was essential would have remained outside. . . . (Bourdieu, 1992, p. 44)

At first sight there would seem to be an affinity between Bourdieu's philosophy of knowledge and his philosophy of science, so much so that the two are not normally regarded as discrete. I am arguing, however, that they should be kept separate and that, for Bourdieu, science is just one form of knowledge. *Le Métier de Sociologue* performed a necessary function in 1968. It sought to advance an alternative ideology of social science to set against positivism. Given that a form of objectivism is epistemologically unavoidable in observing the actions of others, Bourdieu seemed to be saying, then the best objectivism is that which constantly constructs, de-constructs, and re-constructs objects of enquiry. Methodologically, social scientists should be wary of preconstructions and prenotions. What is described in *Le Métier de Sociologue* as the necessary 'epistemological vigilance' is, however, really a methodological vigilance which is designed to prevent objectivist science from making excessive truth claims. The scientific procedures recommended by Bourdieu in *Le Métier de Sociologue* do not alter the status of science as belonging to the second mode of theoretical knowledge described in *Esquisse d'une Théorie de la Pratique*. Science is *epistemologically* challenged by the systematic reflexivity proposed as the third (sometimes described by Bourdieu as the 'praxeological') mode of knowledge, and not by anti-positivist procedures internal to science.

These are important issues because Bourdieu began to talk about reflexivity at about the same time as he began to reiterate his commitment to an anti-positivist philosophy of science. His *Réponses*, published in 1992, was based on seminars in Chicago and Paris in 1987–8. The French text was subtitled: 'pour une anthropologie réflexive', whereas the English translation of 1992 appeared as *An Invitation to Reflexive Sociology*. This change represents a shift of emphasis from the epistemological in the French to the methodological in the English. Bourdieu's comment early in *La Noblesse d'État* (1989a) is also significant here. Talking of the 'sociology of education', he writes: 'Far from being that kind of applied — and, therefore, inferior — science, only good for pedagogues, that we have come to regard it as, it is situated at the core of a general anthropology of power and legitimacy' (Bourdieu, 1989a, p. 13, own translation).

The point is that Bourdieu has espoused a philosophy of science which is more congenial to him than positivism but, in doing so, he has never relinquished his desire to use science (sociology) to disclose the fundamentals of pre-scientific thought and behaviour (anthropology). At the personal level, he has wanted to use science to detach himself from himself, to analyse fully the nature of the transformations of his *habitus* from its indigenous, inherited state, through stages of cultural accretion, to its present condition. The diagrammatic model annexed to *La Reproduction* is the guiding model by which Bourdieu has conceived his own career. *Homo Academicus* (1984b) and *La Noblesse d'État* (1989a) are both objectivist and scientific in their respective analyses of the structure of Parisian higher education on the eve of 1968 and of the function of the grandes écoles in producing the mandarins of the French state, but their purposes are not just limited scientific purposes. They are not simply offered as sociological analyses but as conscious attempts to expose in a public forum the features of the social trajectory of one private individual — Bourdieu himself. Tacitly, Bourdieu is offering science in order to offer something more fundamentally significant — an autobiography as a kind of archetypal or paradigmatic anthropology of the self. Elements of this are discussed in Chapter 8 of this book, where the meaning of reflexivity is explored.

Bourdieu's Prescriptive Descriptions

Samuel Taylor Coleridge wrote that a symbol, unlike allegory, 'partakes of the reality which it renders intelligible' (Coleridge, ed. White, 1972, p. 30). Elsewhere, he tried to formulate the same thought in the following way:

> The Symbolical cannot, perhaps, be better defined in distinction from the Allegorical, than that it is always itself a part of that, of the whole of which it is the representative. — 'Here comes a sail,' — (that is, a ship) is a symbolic expression. 'Behold our lion!' when we speak of some gallant soldier, is allegorical. (Coleridge, ed. Rhys, 1907, p. 248)

Kierkegaard gave the same kind of insight an existential emphasis. In his *Concluding Unscientific Postscript* he wrote of his own *Either/Or* that,

> There is no didacticism in the book, but from this it does not follow that there is no thought-content; thus it is one thing to think, and another thing to exist in what has been thought. . . . we have here presented to us an existence in thought, and the book or the work has no finite relation to anybody. (Kierkegaard, trans. Swenson and Lowrie, 1941, p. 228)

In these terms, I am suggesting that Bourdieu deploys science symbolically. Without overtly espousing symbolic interactionism, Bourdieu nevertheless deploys as symbolic interaction a conception of science that appears to be inimical to it. Although Bourdieu asserted that he '. . . never really got into the existentialist mood' (Bourdieu, 1990b, p. 5), and also argued that he shared with the structuralists, 'the need to react against what existentialism had represented for them: the flabby "humanism" that was in the air, the complacent appeal to "lived experience" . . .' (Bourdieu, 1990b, pp. 4–5), his project should be seen as an existentialist one. It is not just that his science is symbolic, that it partakes in what it renders intelligible. As such, it is also the manifestation of a continuously reciprocal process of thinking in existence and existing in thought. Bourdieu has tried to secure detachment in engagement, to construct objectivist understanding of social events whilst, in parallel, being socially engaged *and* seeking to understand the ways in which the engagement conditions his objectivism. It is for this reason that Bourdieu's analyses have often seemed to have prescribed reality as much as described it. Bourdieu would, of course, be hostile to the incipient idealism of Shelley's contention that 'poets are the unacknowledged legislators of the world', but there is no reason to suppose that he could not share the view that symbolic statements have the capacity to anticipate reality. As statements participating in the reality which they make intelligible, symbolic statements have the power to extract latent meanings in thoughts and actions which, by the process of extraction, acquire the potential capacity to be actualized. Bourdieu's attitude towards his own social science texts is not dissimilar to the attitude towards novels outlined by Sartre in *What Is Literature* and reiterated in revised form in his *Questions de Méthode*. Bourdieu has criticized Sartre's attempt to marry an existential understanding of the relationship between author and reader with a Marxist/Hegelian view of history — to suppose that authors have a social function in articulating and thus actualizing the latent processes in action in the course of historical progress. But Bourdieu's approach to his own work supposes, nevertheless, a form of embodied exchange between authors and readers which materially or biologically actualizes those events which exist *in potentia* from the Leibnizian beginning of the world.

Bourdieu has discussed these issues in part in his 'Décrire et prescrire. Notes sur les conditions de possibilité et les limites de l'efficacité politique' (1981a). To tease out fully the implications of this convergence between description and prescription for our consideration of the significance of Bourdieu's educational research, I need to revert briefly to the history of the reception of his work with which the chapter began. I argued that the work which Bourdieu had produced in the 1960s, culminating in *La Reproduction*, became known in the UK in a piecemeal fashion and was appropriated by the 'new sociology of education movement' during the 1970s. By the time that *The Inheritors* and *Reproduction* became available in English, the radical moment for their reception in the UK had passed. Instead, the works were evaluated in the United States as contributions to a scientific sociology of education. The debates in the American reviews failed to understand the nature of Bourdieu's descriptive/prescriptive relationship with the particular conditions of reform in French higher education and the particular conditions of his past and present trajectory through the French educational system. I am now arguing that Bourdieu's work of the 1970s developed further the sociological analysis that was incipiently present in *Reproduction*. Writing mainly from within an educational perspective, Bourdieu succeeded, in *Reproduction*, in relativizing the educational system that he had previously regarded as a functionally necessary sector of a socialist state. The analysis in *Reproduction*, expressed, as we have seen, in propositions possessing potential applicability, was not of institutionalized educational practices absolutely but, instead, of those practices as elements in the transmission of values and knowledge in a culturally plural and institutionally diverse society. In the early 1970s, Bourdieu refined conceptually his use of the notion of *field* and applied it empirically to analyse the process of competitive appropriation occurring between the fields of education and employment. This research was undertaken within the *Centre de la Sociologie de l'éducation et de la culture* which Bourdieu had founded in 1968 and for which *Le métier de sociologue* constituted a kind of methodological manifesto. In establishing this Centre and producing the manifesto in 1968 in the year of the May student revolt and the consequent reforms in French higher education, Bourdieu was sensitive to the fact that the autonomy of the educational system within which he had been educated and was now employed was being threatened by the incursions of the 'economic' field. His response was to endeavour to institutionalize an autonomous field of social science which could construct for itself some detachment both from the field of employment and from the field of the conventional higher education system of teaching and learning.

It was from this perspective that Bourdieu carried out the work which led to the publication of *La Distinction* in 1979. It was a text which described/prescribed a commodification of taste and knowledge. It was also a text in which the confusion persisted whether Bourdieu was offering a representational account of objective social reality or simply the account of one person occupying an arbitrary position within what was being described. My contention is that Bourdieu's subsequent work in the 1980s indicated a deliberate retreat from accounts which might be misinterpreted as objective. The objectivities of the accounts in *Homo Academicus* and *La Noblesse d'État* are unashamedly objectifications of Bourdieu's personal position within the plural society which, based on *Distinction*, they are able to presuppose. This shift away from comprehensive objectivity towards a form of special pleading that is seen to be an inescapable consequence of personal *habitus* coincides with Bourdieu's promotion to the Chair in Sociology at the Collège de France in 1981.

The 'objective' description from which Bourdieu has subjectively retreated is, however, one which increasingly had resonances in the situation in the UK in the 1980s. It was as if the latent characteristics in French society which Bourdieu had perceived in the espousal by someone like Michel Crozier of American managerial and entrepreneurial thinking were actualized more quickly in Thatcherite Britain than in France. For those inclined to receive it, Bourdieu's symbolic science that was descriptive of French society in the 1970s became prescriptive or predictive of subsequent British developments. By the end of the 1980s, we were able to turn again to *Reproduction in Education, Society and Culture* to articulate sociologically what had happened and what was continuing to occur. After the collapse of the independent, but State-supported, system of schooling and higher education that had privileged academic learning and had even preferred academically successful students within non-academic vocations, there had developed competition between institutions and values within the educational system — between independent and comprehensive schools, between universities and polytechnics. After 1979, however, that competition was no longer contained within the educational system but was thrown open to the whole of society. The government overtly started to privilege mechanisms for producing and reproducing skilled and competent workers and, in this process, to emphasize the educational input of successful entrepreneurs in business and industry so as to impose values of action rather than of the kind of cognitive reflection that had been the dominant value of traditional educational institutions.

Bourdieu's analyses could readily explain what was happening. If you were disposed to follow him to the limit, you could understand sociologically the way in which those with economic and political power devalue autonomous, meritocratic achievement in the educational field precisely so that there should be no egalitarian threat to the inter-generational reproduction of their economic and political positions. The problem, of course, however, was that, from 1979, sociology was itself systematically discredited. I am suggesting, therefore, that in thinking about Bourdieu's work today we have to accept that traditional sociology of education and traditional sociology are either opposed or, more insidiously, subtly appropriated. As an indication of the process of appropriation by assimilation which we currently perceive, I could refer to an article which I wrote for *The Times Higher Educational Supplement* in September, 1993 (Robbins, 1993b). It was entitled 'A French accent on League tables'. I argued that Bourdieu's *La Noblesse d'État* (1989a) offered a convincing sociological analysis of the hierarchical status of the 84 grandes écoles and that a comparable analysis could be undertaken in the UK with respect to the 100 universities. I suggested that the League Tables produced by Tom Cannon exploited sociology in that they subsumed the findings of the sociology of education in concocting a 'value-added' institutional rating to be placed alongside other institutional performance indicators. I tried to suggest that the managerialist analysis was accommodating sociological insights so as to neutralize them and to construct a non-sociological league table. There was absolutely no comment on my article from any quarter and, of course, the league tables continue to appear, manifesting the same forms of managerial deception.

Bourdieu's emphasis on 'reflexivity' arises from his recognition that the sociological explanation of, amongst other things, the functioning of educational practices, would have to fight for survival in a competitive market in just the same way as those practices themselves. The important thing to be clear about, however, is, again, that Bourdieu recommends 'reflexivity' not as a life-saving approach within sociology but as a research stance from which sociological explanation can be scrutinized as much as any other. What I am leading up to, therefore, is the contention that Bourdieu is important to us now because he has consistently articulated and implemented a reflexive approach.

Pursuing Bourdieu's Procedures

My point, therefore, is that Bourdieu's *practice* is what is important about his work. What is important about his reflexivity is that it enables him to understand the social position from which he constructs the objects of research. He knows that he is someone who came to Paris from a remote provincial region of France and achieved upward mobility by virtue of his capacity to suppress his indigenous culture in order to succeed within the culture of the educational system. He knows that this trajectory, and also his intellectual progression from philosophy to anthropology to sociology, have shaped the self that he presents in society. He knows that his sociological analyses are contaminated both by the agenda of preconstructed social problems prevailing in society and also by the values which he holds as a result of his personal trajectory. In following Bourdieu's practice as a model for our own, there seem to me to be two different strategies to be considered.

Firstly, we can seek to create the social space to practise the kind of scientificity which adequately expresses the commitment to rigour and rationality which are likely to be the legacies, for us, of our educational initiation. Bourdieu argues along these lines in his epilogue to *Social Theory for a Changing Society* (1991b), entitled 'On the Possibility of a Field of World Sociology'. In a market of competing intellectual positions and values, in other words, we can seek to generate a field of enquiry which corresponds with our own value positions and refuses the value positions inherent in the kind of research which, perhaps, is acceptable to funding agencies or sponsors. Of course, this position has to confront the problem of how such intellectual space can be purchased economically.

It probably has to be within this space that we can then, secondly, seek to generate research practice which is different from the kind of sociometric work, plundering of data banks, for instance, which is the 'sociology' that is currently acceptable to what Habermas would call our 'system world'. To generate a sociology which is a form of ethnographic encounter, or, as Bourdieu calls it, socio-analytic encounter, is to perform a political act because the process of research is what Bourdieu, again, calls a 'social maieutics', that is to say, a form of socio-political midwifery. By objectifying the encounter between the researcher and the 'victim' of the research, Bourdieu claims that he is not only giving the victim a 'voice' but, more importantly, making public an encounter between representatives of social groups who might not otherwise, in actuality, ever meet. He is seeking to make manifest the covert tensions in our social relations. The most potent example of this endeavour, of course, is the fairly recent, massive enquiry which led to the publication of *La Misère du Monde* in 1993. Bourdieu represents, amongst other things, his encounters with young people who are drop-outs from the education and training system, who are socially and economically excluded from French society. By articulating their experiences, Bourdieu comments on them from his social position, but juxtaposes his commentary with their verbatim remarks so that, in the publication, both become equally public statements.

However, there is no formula for pursuing Bourdieu's procedures. There are no routines or standardized instruments of enquiry. The blueprint offered in *Le Métier de Sociologue* was one which functioned for him in his situation in 1968. To adhere to the spirit of Bourdieu's work rather than to the letter of his strategic concepts, the essential thing is to deconstruct and reconstruct those concepts in relation to our distinct experiences. Bourdieu's descriptions prescribe our conceptual framework, but if our work is to be sensitive to the latent tendencies in our situations we have to integrate Bourdieu's thoughts critically with other intellectual influences, with our different social conditions and our different experiences. In this way intellectual engagement with Bourdieu's thought constitutes our thinking in its engagement with our experience.

Part II

Practical Applications

The four chapters in this part of the book all deal with the application of Bourdieu's theory of practice to particular educational research projects.

In each case, the key concepts of habitus and field are used in different ways to explore the topics under investigation. In all but one of these examples, the discussion arises from a collection of empirical data in a specific area of the field of education. The other example (Chapter 5) also includes material collected in this way. However, this discussion integrates texts from others who have worked in the area, but who have not explicitly used Bourdieu's theory in their own analyses. The objective, in this case, is to indicate ways in which a Bourdieuian approach differs from and perhaps enhances others.

In order to offer a range of educational subjects and contexts, the four chapters each in turn deal with the four principal phases of education: primary, secondary, post-compulsory and higher education.

Chapter 4 examines the relationship between parents and primary schools. It reveals the inequalities of gender and race which are embedded in the home–school relationships. Such inequalities are expressed in mothers' activities to support their children's schooling, and are discussed in terms of field, habitus, and cultural capital.

Chapter 5 deals with classroom language and the way legitimate discourses are set up in pedagogic exchanges between pupils and teachers. The ways teachers and pupils operate in such exchanges are discussed in terms of the orthodox cognitive processes of the micro-field site and the habitus of those involved. This approach is contrasted with others dealing with language in education, and some reference is made to the ways a Bourdieuian understanding may affect what goes on in pedagogy.

Chapter 6 examines how the concepts of habitus, field and capital might be used to explain the ways in which young people make their career decisions. The story of a small group of young people is told as they chose to leave school and take up Youth Training places. It is shown how various forms of capital together with individual habitus are determinant in decisions which are made and the way in which they are made.

Chapter 7 looks at the experience of mature students in higher education. This is an account of developing academic habitus, and the way it affects those around the students. It describes experiences and feelings of students on entering education, but also considers the activities of academic staff; in particular, the relative value attributed to teaching and research. Students' own changing perceptions of this dichotomy are used as a way of illustrating their changing investments and personal recognition of the legitimate products and processes of higher education.

Each chapter sets out the topic and describes how it has been dealt with in existing literature. There is then discussion of how a Bourdieuian approach differs. Specific reference is made to Bourdieu's writings on the topic. However, extensions are also made from his basic ideas to show how they have relevance to the topic in hand. The context of each individual chapter is set out along with detail of what data was collected and how. Finally, a number of pertinent issues are raised from analysis of data in the light of Bourdieu's theory of practice. The practical implications arising from the conclusions of these analyses are discussed, and some effort is made to explain what a Bourdieuian approach offers which others do not.

Each of the chapters can be read on their own, or together as practical applications of the epistemological approach set out in Chapter 2. The accent in these chapters is on practical exemplification. Questions of reflexivity and more general methodological issues are discussed in Parts III and IV of the book.

Cultural Reproduction: Mothers' Involvement in Their Children's Primary Schooling

Diane Reay

Introduction

There is a long history of sociological writing which sees the educational system as being central to the question of the distribution of advantage and disadvantage within society (see for example, Jackson and Marsden, 1962; Willis, 1977; Halsey *et al.*, 1980; Connell *et al.*, 1982; Gewirtz *et al.*, 1995). However, few studies of cultural reproduction have attempted a 'gendered' analysis of parental involvement in such a process; in other words, examined the differences between men and women in the way they relate to school in their dealings with it as parent. Even fewer have included 'race' within their discussion. This chapter attempts both through a focus on the home–school relationship as a key element to cultural reproduction.

Much recent educational policy in Britain can be interpreted as reconstructing the relationship between home and the primary school; that is breaking down the public/private divide by taking increasing amounts of school work into the home (David, 1993). The rapid growth of workbooks for children to complete in the home and the promotion of supermarket vouchers for parents to collect and exchange for school resources are both examples of this. They offer us an illustration of the increasing commodification of education and the redistribution of responsibility between family and school. During the 1980s and 1990s a new educational agenda developed which offered parents a seemingly powerful role. In public policy discourses parents were increasingly seen as 'consumers' empowered in the educational marketplace through their access to choice. Carol Vincent points out: 'Parents-as-consumers is the mechanism through which disparate elements of Conservative ideology — individualism, freedom, consumer choice, morality, discipline and order — are bound together in the education system' (Vincent, 1996, p. 40).

It is possible to see parental involvement itself in terms of 'discourses', which position mothers as the parent who is either enhancing or holding back children's educational progress (David *et al.*, 1996; Walkerdine and Lucey, 1989). However, at the same time the changing balance between home and school seems to result in an increased differential in responsibilities between mothers and fathers.

The rest of this chapter examines these differential responsibilities in detail and uses Bourdieu's theoretical conceptualization as a way of elucidating its mechanisms and processes.

The Texts on Parental Involvement

When I came to research parental involvement in primary schooling I found myself investigating an area of social practice where the majority of activities are carried out by women. In textbooks, on the other hand, the myriad aspects of mothering work which women undertook was rarely given any recognition. In the place of any such elaboration was an assumption of what we might call 'gender neutrality'; that is, there are no important distinctions between men and women in their dealings with their children's primary schooling. Most of the texts seem to be premised on an implicit and un-examined norm, namely that of the unitary, un-gendered subject. Post-structuralist theory throughout the 1980s and into the 1990s has deconstructed the concept of the unitary individual (Henriques *et al.*, 1984; Kerfoot and Knights, 1994). Yet, the parental involvement debate has been largely immune to its influences. While post-structuralists and feminists, alike, recognize that implicit in modernist conceptions of the unitary (male) self is a denial of the social differences which produce inequalities, there is little evidence of parallel thinking within texts of parental involvement (see David, 1993; David *et al.*, 1996, 1997; Lareau, 1992 for exceptions to this general rule).

The resulting omission of any clear articulation of the place of gender within home–school relationships masks important issues. For example, it serves to hide from the reader's view the differential involvement of mothers and fathers in their children's schooling. It assumes that all parents share an identical experience of involvement in their children's education (cf. Wolfendale, 1989; Topping and Wolfendale, 1986; Bastiani, 1989; Macbeth, 1995). It also renders invisible not only inequalities between the sexes but also those existing between mothers themselves. Structural constraints of gender, 'race', class and marital status become 'problems to be dealt with' rather than inequalities to be challenged.

Pierre Bourdieu: A Useful Starting Point?

Over the 30 years that Bourdieu has been researching and writing, he has continued to recognize the importance of the family as a site of social and cultural reproduction (e.g., Bourdieu, 1972/1977a; 1996b). In recent work he discusses the practical and symbolic work undertaken in families; work which 'falls more particularly to women, who are responsible for maintaining relationships' (1996b, p. 22). The family for Bourdieu is both a habitus generating institution and a key site for the accumulation of cultural capital. In *The Three Forms of Capital* Bourdieu writes:

It is because the cultural capital that is effectively transmitted within the family itself depends not only on the quantity of cultural capital, itself accumulated by spending time, that the domestic group possess, but also on the usable time (particularly in the form of mother's free time) available to it. (Bourdieu, 1986, p. 253)

Bourdieu thus recognizes the pivotal role mothers play in the generation of cultural capital. It is mothers' time that accrues profits. However, once mothers' time is harnessed to the acquisition of cultural capital, it is no longer free time. It becomes mothers' work time. Furthermore, while recognizing the importance of mothers' role, Bourdieu hints at, but does not make explicit, the complexities of contemporary women's lives. It is, for example, not simply a question of time available. In my study, some women receiving financial support from the social services had time on their hands, while a number of more privileged women claimed to have 'no time'. As a result, time can be, and increasingly is being, bought by some middle-class women through, for example, buying into child-care, in order to pursue professional careers. As Bryan Adams suggests it is not so much that 'time is money', rather 'money is time' (Adams, 1990). Time has little value if it is unsupported by resources. As Scott Lash and John Urry point out, 'time varies as to the differential possession of money, as well as to differentials of status and power' (Lash and Urry, 1993, pp. 226–7). Women do need to feel confident about tackling educational work in the home and to have access to material resources to support such work. These are important ingredients of cultural capital: 'and are necessary if mothers' time is going to be valuable and useful'.

Bourdieu writes extensively about the social reproductive nature of the educational system. Much of this work, in particular, his earlier writing, describes a process which is misrecognized (cf. Bourdieu and Passeron, 1977, p. 154). My own research confirms its concealed nature. However, it illustrates in detail how the operationalizing of social differentiation in schooling is tied into individual people's activities. In particular, it is intrinsically present in the work of mothers. Although Bourdieu has not written directly on the home/school relationship, my analysis of the nature of parental involvement in schooling and the processes through which mothers help to reproduce social advantage and disadvantage has been filtered through the lens of Bourdieu's conceptual framework. I have found Bourdieu 'enormously good for thinking with' (Jenkins, 1992, p. 11).

The Research Study: Mothers' Involvement in Children's Primary Schooling

I conducted in-depth interviews with 33 mothers and three of their male partners whose year five children attended two London primary schools. Milner, an inner London primary school, had been designated as an Educational Priority school in the 1970s. 45 per cent of the pupils received free school meals. According to the local authority, unemployment levels in the area in which the school is located stood at 18 per cent. Most of the parents in work, were employed in skilled, semi-skilled or

unskilled manual work. I conducted my research with two classes in their penultim-
ate year of primary education. Over 90 per cent of the children going on school
journeys required local education authority financial support grants because their
parents could not afford to pay the full costs. There had also been a noticeable in-
crease in the admission of children from refugee families and those in homeless
accommodation represented 14 per cent of the roll. Over a third of the children
came from lone mother families.

In contrast, Oak Park was located in one of metropolitan London's most affluent
areas. The parents at Oak Park were predominantly middle-class professionals. The
headteacher told me on my initial visit that the average father was a lawyer, an
accountant or high up in business, and that most of the mothers worked. They could
afford nannies and cleaners. Many of these families were very rich. The relative
affluence of the parental population was reflected in the low percentage (8 per cent)
of pupils who qualified for free school dinners. Only two of the children in the class
I studied were from working-class backgrounds. The pupils were also predominantly
white. 15 per cent of the pupils were Asian, which was the ethnic group with the
largest representation. However, approximately 25 per cent of children in the school
were Jewish.

I spent 18 months from February 1993 until July 1994 participating and
observing in the schools. I carried out research. However, I also taught in the two
schools. My relationships with the mothers of the pupils in the schools either
predated the research period (my own children had attended Milner), or were built
up over the research period. A third of the mothers were interviewed three times
over this period. I had initially intended to interview fathers where the mothers
specified that they were also heavily involved in their children's schooling. I anticipated that I would probably have a sample of approximately 10 fathers (22 of the
mothers were living with male partners). However, I found that lack of paternal
involvement was a feature in many of the women's accounts. This phenomenon
seemed to cross social class differences. Just under half of the 22 women living with
a male partner saw them as uninvolved in their children's education. Of these nine,
five were working-class and four middle-class in terms of conventional socio-
economic categorization. Of the remaining 13 only three described their partner as
equally involved, while four referred to their partners involvement as marginal. The
remaining six mothers talked in terms of fathers 'helping them out from time to time'.

Using Bourdieu's Concepts Empirically

Bourdieu provides a conceptual framework that offers the prospect of developing a
thesis of class formation which suggests other possibilities to those inherent in
conventional stances (I am thinking of those of Goldthorpe, 1980, 1983; Erikson and
Goldthorpe, 1992; Goldthorpe and Marshall, 1992). Bourdieu conceptualizes social
class as social relations in general rather than specifically in terms of relations of
production (cf. Brubaker, 1985). As a result his work would seem to suggest that
social class is just as readily captured by empirical studies of the family as by those

of the market place. For Bourdieu, the family is the site of social reproduction. He claims, for example, that for over 20 years his work has been directed at understanding the specific logic which groups, especially families, use to produce and reproduce themselves (Bourdieu, 1990b, p. 74). However, his concept of habitus permits an analysis of social inequality which is not simply dependent on fixed notions of economic and social location. At the centre of this concept are the social practices which are the outcomes of an interaction between an individual habitus and field. The focus is as much on process as on position. In terms of my own research project, this focus on process allows me to conceptualize mothers' practices in support of their children's education as part of the generation of social class differences.

I have utilized habitus mainly as a way of understanding the impact of women's own past educational experiences on their contemporary activities in support of children's education. However, habitus also provides a mechanism for contextualizing mothers' involvement in primary schooling. At the centre of the concept is the interplay not only between past and present but also between the individual and the forces acting upon them; in other words, agency and structure. The way I have attempted to use habitus stresses the differences as well as the commonalities among mothers and explores their subjective responses to parental involvement. The analysis of habitus is complex. It must recognize both diversity within social groupings and highlight the crucial importance of the context in which actions take place. During the course of my research in the primary schools, I came to perceive habitus as incorporating a tension between what might be termed *possibility* and *constraint*; and between the replication and transformation of social practices. Despite criticisms of the concept for being too deterministic (cf. Jenkins, 1992), I found habitus a useful tool in my own research for focusing on change as well as the continuities of maternal practices.

I have adapted Bourdieu's concept of cultural capital to fit the context of primary schooling. After carrying out a pilot study in one of my two research schools I developed a list of seven main components of cultural capital within the field of home–school relationships. These seven aspects of cultural capital were:

- Material resources;
- Educational qualifications;
- Available time;
- Information about the educational system;
- Social confidence;
- Educational knowledge;
- The extent to which entitlement, assertiveness, aggression or timidity characterized mothers' approaches to teaching staff.

I used Bourdieu's theoretical framework with its organizing concepts of cultural capital, field and habitus as a means of understanding the way in which social structure interweaves with human activity within the sphere of parental involvement in education. As Chapter 2 in this book shows, Bourdieu's concepts locate structure as being 'embodied' and expressed through people's activities and dispositions (see for example, Bourdieu, 1979/1984a; 1980a/1990a). As discussed in Chapter 9, they also provide a means of responding to the constraints operating on researchers carrying out conventional ethnography. Because of the possibilities which terms like cultural capital and habitus offer for 'reading off' structure from people's actions, and, concomitantly, their ability to integrate macro and micro processes, they facilitate a broad focus on the macro relations between education and inequality, while simultaneously allowing for close attention to the micro details of mothering practices.

Gendered Habitus

I have tried to develop understandings of cultural capital and habitus which attempt to extend the concepts to encompass aspects of gender and ethnicity alongside social class. Later, in the section entitled 'The Migrant Experience', I shall examine some of the influences of ethnicity on mothers' efforts to generate cultural capital. Here, I explore the potential for developing our understanding of habitus as gendered. The need to extend such understandings of habitus in terms of gender (argued by Krais (1993) and Reay (1995b, 1997b)) is apparent in the work of a number of writers: 'for example, feminist conceptualisations of parental involvement, understood primarily as mothers' work' (Smith, 1988; Smith and Griffiths, 1990); the importance of parental time devoted to children's education (Brubaker, 1985); and the extension of cultural capital theory to include new aspects, such as emotional capital (Nowotny, 1981; Allatt, 1993). When habitus is viewed from a gender perspective, the institutionalized domination mothers face in the family and school becomes empirically visible. The issue of single parent families is also raised; in particular, lone mothers' relationship to institutional domination and the extent to which it overlaps with, and extends beyond, that of mothers in two parent families.

The concept of 'gendered habitus' shows up a common view of the world in which the division of labour between men and women is seen as 'natural' and much domestic labour is rendered invisible. The 'ontological complicity' (Bourdieu, 1981b, p. 306) of female habitus in this world is expressed in the way mothers feel they were made for their mothering. One consequence is that a majority of women across my sample either take their partners' limited involvement for granted, or reluctantly accept it as inevitable. The division of labour between women and their male partners in relation to parental involvement is rarely problematized in the women's accounts (Reay, 1995c). There seems to be general acceptance of fathers' marginality. Although there is a paucity of research which looks at father's involvement in their children's schooling, what does exist confirms that fathers are often distant from the day to day maintenance of home–school relationships (Lareau, 1989; 1992; Ribbens, 1993). Parental involvement in education for the 33 families in my research study did indeed seem to be powerfully shaped by a gendered division of labour. In such a division, 'parental' became elided with 'maternal' and mothers were to be found undertaking the vast majority of the work involved in supporting children's education.

The most obvious reading of gendered habitus in Bourdieu's own work depicts women as complicit in maintaining male power by viewing gender divisions as natural and universal. However, a second, more feminist reading is possible in which the operations of gendered habitus can also be seen as constitutive of, rather than determined by, social structures (cf. McCall, 1992). In my own research, there were tensions between reinforcing and challenging gender hierarchies as normative in some of the mothers' narratives. Five of the lone mothers told of making a positive decision to leave abusive male partners. A minority of mothers, Dawn, Lelia and Julie, did describe the division of labour between themselves and male partners as inequitable and talked of the techniques used to get their partners to do more. I would suggest that this concept of 'gendered habitus' contains the potential for understanding changes as well as the continuities in gender relationships that Bourdieu outlines in his own work (Bourdieu, 1990c). As such it provides a fruitful area for further research.

Habitus as Gendered History

Bourdieu describes habitus as 'the product of social conditionings, and thus of a history' (Bourdieu, 1987/1990b, p. 116). The amount of cultural capital that mothers are able to draw on in the present is not simply a consequence of their current situation. Women's personal history and their educational experiences have an effect on their propensity for some types of action over others. The research investigated how habitus and educational fields interacted in the past in order to understand maternal activities in the present.

Mothers described their own school days in the 1950s and 1960s as characterized by separation between home and school. However, the nature of that separation was differentiated by social class, as is evident in the accounts of Ann and Alice. Ann, a white working-class Milner mother told me: 'There was a much clearer distinction in those days. You learnt at school, not at home. There was a clear distinction.' Alice, a white middle-class mother at Oak Park also talked of separation between home and school in her own schooling experience, but one that was shaped by a middle-class upbringing. She differentiated between her schooling which was the site of 'repetitious learning' and the home where learning was fun: 'All the creativity went on at home, unlike these days'. It is extremely unlikely that the 'clear distinction' Ann spoke of was premised on a similar dichotomy. She speaks of parents, who were 'particularly hard-up' and relates an occasion when she was given a packet of coloured pencils to take home to complete a piece of homework 'because we didn't have any at home'.

While both mothers define the period of their own schooling as one characterized by separation between home and school, the nature of that separation was powerfully influenced by social class. For working-class mothers, separation in the dual sense of parents not undertaking educational work in the home, either on their own initiative or in response to school demands, was a common feature: 'I can't remember my mother ever once going into my primary school. My mother was never ever there for me. She was too busy working' (Dawn, Milner).

This theme of separation in working-class women's school histories is more analogous to Annette Lareau's description of separation between working-class parents and schooling in the 1980s (Lareau, 1989) than their current reality, which is one of varying degrees of involvement in their children's education.

Unlike Lareau's working-class sample's limited involvement, the working-class mothers I interviewed talked in terms of regular involvement spanning curricular as well as social issues.

Unlike Alice, most middle-class mothers who had attended primary school in the 1950s and 1960s talked in terms of having mothers who had been involved in their primary schooling. In spite of the greater separation between home and school over those decades, there was a submerged text of historical continuity in middle-class women's accounts. In all, over two thirds of the middle-class mothers had been taught by their own mothers. Of the 12 middle-class women who attended state schools, 10 referred to being taught by their mothers. Oya, one of the four women who had attended private schools, detailed the instruction she received from her maternal grandfather. Sonia and Lelia talked about completing homework under their mothers' supervision. In addition, Laura, Linsey, Pamela and Manju all had parents who were involved in either the school's PTA or the governing body. A number of Oak Park mothers, and also Linda at Milner, mentioned regular informal contact between their parents and teachers.

Although primary schools made far fewer educational demands on mothers in the 1950s and 1960s, many middle-class mothers were independently undertaking educational work with their children in the home. This class difference can be understood in terms of differences in cultural capital and time available. It was facilitated by home circumstances and the much greater availability of mothers in middle-class homes. While the vast majority of women from working-class backgrounds had mothers who worked full-time outside the home, over half of the mothers from middle-class backgrounds grew up in households where mothers were full-time housewives. The situation of relative affluence, which most of the Oak Park mothers grew up in, provided material and social conditions under which cultural capital could be generated.

The Influence of Women's Educational Experiences of Involvement in Their Children's Schooling

One consequence of being taught by one's mother, as was the case for 12 of the middle-class women, is that teaching one's own child becomes a process of doing 'what comes naturally' (Bourdieu, 1984a). It is already ingrained in the habitus that a majority of the middle-class women bring to the contemporary educational field. When mothers worked, as most of the middle-class women did, the belief that children needed to be taught in the home did not dissipate. Rather, the situation became one in which mothers' own labour could be substituted for that of hired educational specialists.

For two of the mothers, however, — Clare, a white middle-class mother and Dawn, a white working-class mother — their contemporary mothering practices represented a disjuncture, a break with the past. They were both making a deliberate, conscious effort to ensure their child's educational experience was very different from their own. In Dawn's case, awareness of the negative impact of her own schooling had resulted in a resolve to have a very different relationship to her son's education. Throughout Dawn's account, there runs a very clear theme of repairing the damage of one's own education in interaction with the child's. Dawn's own negative educational experiences have consequences that are played out in the present:

> At my school if you were off for any time they would have chased up. You had to take in a note for a day off or whatever, had to take a note in. I can remember hassling my mum like mad for this note while she was rushing to get ready for work cos we went to school by ourselves and I was saying 'mum write a note please cos I can't go into school without a note', and if she didn't have time to write the note I'd be too frightened to go to school. So it was frightening at primary school.

Dawn decided quite deliberately to be actively involved in Andreas's education on a regular basis, to protect him and act as his advocate in relation to the school because of the consequences of her mother not assuming this role in her own schooling: 'I wasn't going to let what happened to me happen to my kids'. Dawn's account illustrates the powerful push for change that mothers' own educational experience can exert on their involvement in their child's schooling. She is attempting to generate profits of cultural capital but in a situation of little prior investment. Rather than replicating habitus, which was the process most of the middle-class women were involved in, she was attempting 'the transformation of the habitus' (Bourdieu, 1980c/1993a, p. 87).

Clare, despite a privileged background, was one of the few middle-class women to talk about having a very negative experience of schooling:

> It was such a shock when I didn't get into Margaret Macmillan. I suppose I just expected it would happen and when it didn't it was such a shock. I ended up going to Whiteside which was terrible, really terrible and I think that affected my attitude to Sophie's education. I'm determined that isn't going to happen to her.

On being made redundant, she decided not to apply for similar posts to the one she had just left. Instead, she chose to work on a freelance basis from home; 'in order to give Sophie as much time and attention as possible so that there is absolutely no chance of her failing any entrance exam'. Choice on how to act is hence an important generating structure.

As Clare and Dawn's cases illustrate, women's own experience of education informs our understanding of their current involvement in their children's schooling. The influences of the former weave through the latter in myriad ways (cf. Connell *et al.*, 1982; David *et al.*, 1994; Rubin, 1976). It is difficult to assess the repercussions for involvement in their own children's schooling of an education which many of the working-class mothers described in terms of 'nightmare', 'horrible' and 'boring'. It may have contributed to the importance these mothers placed on their children's happiness in school (see also Walkerdine and Lucey, 1989).

However, working-class women's own negative experiences were always there in the background, trammelling mothers' possibilities in relation to their children's schooling. Habitus continued to work long after the objective conditions of its emergence have been dislodged. As Lisa, a white, working class, lone mother, stated passionately: 'God knows, I'm nobody to make those sort of demands on my own daughter'. On the other hand, Denise, a black, working class lone mother, told me: 'I was no good at school, a total failure, didn't get anywhere. How can I tell Rosetta she has to pass all her exams'.

Women were dealing with different layers of continuity and discontinuity between their own and their children's educational experience. The continuity experienced by many of the middle-class mothers was undercut by the discontinuity produced by changing social values. Historical change is key to understanding the current attitudes and actions of these mothers, the majority of whose own primary school experience was in the late 1950s and the 1960s. Often the tension and lack of fit between a habitus, developing in a period when family and school were largely designated as separate spheres, and a contemporary educational field where greater parental involvement is expected, resulted in high levels of resentment among both sets of mothers.

A further commonality across social class was the high value placed on education. In particular, the importance attached to education by working-class mothers was often in spite of their own negative experiences and current misgivings about the specific version of education on offer (cf. Connell *et al.*, 1982). Dawn's experience indicates some of the ways in which working-class women attempted to negotiate the psychological barriers constructed through their own experience of schooling. This process of negotiating and trying to overcome residual negativity illustrates how the work they were undertaking in support of their children's education was of a different scale and level of difficulty to that carried out by most of the middle-class women. Parental involvement neither came naturally nor could be taken for granted. It had to be worked extremely hard for.

The middle-class mothers far less frequently found such powerful barriers impeding their involvement. Apart from Clare and Lelia, they all talked in terms of a reasonable experience of schooling. For the majority, parental involvement was much more an issue of continuity with the past rather than disjuncture. As Stella, one of the middle-class mothers commented: 'My mother always used to sit down and help me with my work after school and now I help Riva'. It was a question of doing more of what one's mother did rather than, as it was for most of the working-class mothers, doing something different. Also, the availability, and resulting involvement, of their own mothers, seemed to bequeath a number of middle-class mothers with a legacy of certainty. Educational problems, when they did arise, were due to deficits in schooling, rather than located in either themselves or their child. Manju's, Clare's, Laura's and Ruth's accounts rested on an unquestioned assumption — that the school was to blame. In contrast, many of the working-class women had learnt from their own experience of schooling that educational difficulties were due to failings in the individual, rather than the system. Although many of them now questioned that message, it continued to influence the present.

The Migrant Experience

Ethnicity and experience of schooling in countries other than Britain also had a powerful impact on mothers' involvement in their children's schooling. For women educated in countries other than Britain the resulting strangeness of their child's educational experiences undermined their ability to mobilize cultural capital with the ease that the middle-class British born mothers did. An experience of attending school overseas and recent migrancy seemed to make it more difficult for these mothers to accrue benefits of cultural capital for their children. This is unsurprising, when as Sonia states, 'your educational experience relates to a completely different cultural experience'. Sharon Gewirtz and her colleagues describe the educational repercussions for recent immigrants to Britain of having a cultural capital which is in the wrong currency (Gewirtz *et al.*, 1994). Nine of the mothers that I interviewed had been born in countries other than Britain: five from Milner and four from Oak Park. Most talked of the resulting erosion of expert status. Yao has written about how the migrant experience can result in parental insecurity and confusion regarding children's education (Yao, 1993). This insecurity and confusion is evident in the accounts of mothers who had not been to school in Britain:

> I have a disadvantage in not knowing the English system. I feel I'm a stranger looking in from the outside rather than having gone through it myself and then comparing it with my daughter's. It's a very different system. (Bo, Milner)

> You see I don't know the system here. (Jalil, Milner)

> You see I find myself coming from a different culture and have a completely, it is worlds apart you see the education I had and the education she is experiencing. The curriculum is so different. I don't know what they teach at school so I have to find out from the teacher what exactly are the things I need to teach her, what books I need to buy. (Sonia, Oak Park)

Submerged rather than articulated in these women's accounts is the vast amount of mothering work necessitated by keeping up with their children's unfamiliar curriculum. This extra work involved in understanding and acclimatizing to an educational system you have had no prior experience of surfaces in what Oya says about the impact Akin's schooling has on her life:

> Akin's education has an enormous effect on my life because I am not used to the system of education here, the nursery rhymes, the fairy stories I have not grown up with. They are not part of my culture. It is fascinating for me to sit here and read with him things I have never heard of. Parents, who are born here automatically fit into the English system whereas for me it's a whole new dimension. I am not automatically able to fit into it. I have to read it up and find out about it with him.

Sharon Gewirtz *et al.* discuss the impact of parents attending schools in other countries on their capacity for engaging productively in the contemporary educational market, irrespective of social class (Gewirtz, Ball and Bowe, 1994). While Manju's and Laura's middle class status seemed to have been a resource in counteracting lack of familiarity with the English system, Stella had enormous problems: 'I don't know about the schools here. It is very difficult for me to find out. The other mothers are, how do you say it, cliquey. They do not really talk to me so it is hard for me to find out.'

Being a recent migrant, plus lack of sufficient language skills, seems to have disadvantaged Stella in relation to other middle-class mothers. She had to deal with a situation in which her cultural capital had been devalued.

Practices varied, however, according to social class even within the group of nine women who were immigrants to Britain. Here we see the influence of working-class habitus. For Maria, in particular, the school had come to be perceived as 'the last and only resort'. Her personal history of immigration, working-class background and academic failure resulted in a sense that there were no other options:

> You need parental involvement. You need parents to be able to complement what you're doing but that's all it should be. It shouldn't be any more. You see not all people speak English, not all parents read and write so how can they help their children at home. They're at a disadvantage anyway so when they come to school they've got to have the help there. You should just be able to say to the teacher 'Look, I can't do it. You're qualified, can you do something about it?' without the teacher getting all upset about it. There's a lot of parents who can't, just can't do it.

In the next section I discuss the myriad aspects of mothering work women are undertaking in relation to their children's schooling. However, the backdrop to these activities is the powerful influence of mothers' own educational experiences which permeates their practices and shapes their responses to the contemporary educational field.

'Complementors, Compensators and Modifiers': Mothers' Relationships to Schooling

Most mothers described their relationship to schooling as a supportive one in which they responded to teachers' requests to hear reading, learn times tables and go over spellings with their children. Working-class mothers like Betty, Rita, Ann and Elaine in Milner, as well as Alice, a middle-class mother in Oak Park talked in terms of 'supporting the school' and 'backing the teacher up' to describe their relationship to schooling. However, a further group, in particular Manju and Clare, saw their role as a compensatory one. Annette Lareau uses this term in relation to her middle-class parents (Lareau, 1989, p. 169). Other mothers, primarily Maria in Milner and Ruth in Oak Park, spoke about their efforts to modify the school provision. These three roles were by no means mutually exclusive. Middle-class mothers like Laura, Judith, Pamela and Linsey moved in and out of different positions with regard to schooling. Laura's preferred practice was to complement her son's learning in the classroom, but she reluctantly compensated when she identified a need and at times intervened on the school site in order to try and modify what the schools offer in her son's favour.

Utilizing a range of different strategies was common in Oak Park where the combination of relative affluence, educational expertise and 'self-certainty' (Bourdieu, 1984a, p. 66) gave mothers options most of the Milner mothers did not have. Middle-class mothers such as Frances, Judith, Ruth and Linsey compensated for what they perceived to be gaps in the state provision through the employment of tutors alongside attempting to modify the provision the school makes for their child, all the while continuing to complement what the school site offers through mothering work in the home. Ruth elaborated two of those strategies very clearly:

> One is the support I give him at home, hearing him read, making him read every night, doing homework with him, trying to get the books he needs for his project. I see that as a support role. The other side, in the particular case of Martin, is where he has had difficulties and finds reading very, very difficult. So a lot of my time has been spent fighting for extra support for him and I mean fighting.

However, later on in the interview she discusses the tuition Martin receives: 'Well he just wasn't making enough progress in school so we decided we'd have to get him a tutor'. Linsey's account provides an example of how a developing sense of dissatisfaction has led to a move over time from complementing to broadening her interventions to include modifying, and compensating for, what the school curriculum offers:

> I think I had too much faith in the system at the beginning that the system would educate my child. I feel ideally my role is to make sure they get the right education. It's really very important. In addition to that, because I know ideally what I would like, I have to fill in the gaps.

Linsey employed a tutor two evenings a week as well as working with her daughter on a regular basis on three other evenings.

Although only Anita, Jalil and Christine at Milner and Clare and Manju in Oak Park used the term 'compensate' to describe their relationship to schooling, a majority of middle-class mothers compensated through the use of paid tuition; they had the 'economic capital' to do so. Similarly, six of the seven black mothers in Milner compensated for a perceived lack of basic skills work and the absence of a black perspective in the curriculum by sending their children to Black Saturday school. For example, Manju at Oak Park employed a tutor for Negar and sent her to an Islamic Saturday school. She saw her own role as pivotal in her daughter's education:

> Education starts at home, starts from her time after school actually. She's in her fifth year and I feel she has to do some serious work at home because she hasn't actually covered a lot of the stuff at school. I find I'm having to compensate despite the fact that according to the school she is doing quite well.

Four times over the course of an interview she used the term 'compensate' to explain her rationale for the educational work she is carrying out in the home. Similarly, Clare claimed that Sophie's educational attainment was the result of the educational support she provided, both personally and through the employment of tutors, rather than anything emanating from the school: 'I have manufactured Sophie's educational success. Ask the school. Before I was made redundant Sophie was seen as an average ability pupil. Since I've been at home she has improved by leaps and bounds. That's down to me not the school.'

In contrast, the majority of mothers in Milner positioned themselves as supporters in relation to their child's schooling. Naseema told me, 'I try and do what Sharoff's teacher asks', while Betty said, 'They expect you to hear your child read so we'll do that two or three times a week'. Beverley said: 'They don't bring a lot of work home. There's the spellings and times tables you need to go over with them'. However, a focus simply on what mothers are doing does not tell the whole story. Conscientiously responding to school demands to support the curriculum meant very different things in the two schools. The demands Milner made of parents added up to far less of mothers' time and energy than corresponding demands made of parents at Oak Park. Complementing in Oak Park was of a totally different scale to supporting the curriculum in Milner. There was regular homework three or four times a week, in addition to spelling and dictionary work children were expected to undertake at home. Even so, few of the Oak Park mothers were content with simply complementing the school curriculum, preferring to draw on a mixture of all three strategies.

Relationships to Children's Schooling: The Influence of Cultural Capital

We can see how cultural capital played a crucial role in the extent to which mothers could weave in and out of strategies of complementing, compensating and modifying, and provide their children with what middle-class Lelia describes as 'the trimmings': 'School is there to take the main responsibility for her learning and we provide the trimmings' (Lelia, Milner).

Lelia was the only mother at Milner, who, in spite of her self designation as 'a complementor' of the educational system, was able to draw on cultural capital to weave, seemingly effortlessly, between complementing, compensating for, and modifying her child's school site provision. Her daughter, Naomi had a Maths tutor for over two years. Lelia's intervention on the school site resulted in Naomi's inclusion in a gifted writer's group, while Lelia read with Naomi every evening, and actively supported the school's curriculum offer in other ways. Other Milner mothers found assuming a range of strategies in relation to their children's schooling a much more conflictual process. Juile, whose interview displayed her intense involvement in her children's education, attempted all three strategies, but with varying degrees of success. In particular, she found compensating a very difficult course of action: firstly, because of her lack of material resources; secondly, because she found her compensatory role at odds with her understandings of what 'people like us should be doing' (Bourdieu, 1980a/1990a, p. 56):

> I shouldn't have to teach them, it's not my job. I did have a tutor but it was too expensive. It was taking up all my spare money. It got to the stage where it was either new shoes for George or the tutor so we had to stop.

Much of Julie's account expresses the tension between feeling a compensatory role was needed and not having the resources to provide it. Cultural capital was implicated in these mothers' ability to draw on a range of strategies in support of their children's schooling. Financial resources, confidence in relation to the educational system, educational knowledge and information about schooling all had a bearing on the extent to which mothers felt empowered to intervene in their child's educational trajectory and the confidence with which they embarked on such action. For Maria, whose account stressed, over and over again, the importance of education, her personal feelings of incompetence and lack of confidence mitigated against her embarking on any action with a sense of efficacy:

> I have tried, I really have. I knew I should be playing a role in getting Leigh to read but I wasn't qualified. Therefore it put extra pressure on me because I was no good at reading myself, it was too important for me to handle and I'd get very upset and angry at Leigh.

Attempting to modify the school's offer also had unpredictable and upsetting consequences:

> I always found if I went to the class teacher, she'd take it very personal and think I was attacking her. I wasn't. I was just bringing it to her attention in case she didn't know, you know, that in my opinion he's not progressing. But when I did go to the class teachers I think they took it too personal and felt I was attacking them when really it was that it is so important I couldn't let it go.

There are clearly articulated tensions in the accounts of mothers like Maria and Julie. They both felt inadequate to the task of compensating for what they perceived to be gaps in their children's educational provision. Maria, who attempted a different strategy of trying to get the staff to modify her child's curriculum offer, was only partially successful because the teachers view her as 'aggressive and overemotional'. In contrast, the relative affluence of Oak Park mothers meant they had choices which were not available to Maria and Julie; choices which were productive of cultural capital. Most of the Oak Park mothers, like Lelia in Milner, could range between all three strategies. They compensated through the employment of tutors, at the same time successfully modifying the provision the school made for their child, while continuing to confidently complement the school offer through their mothering work in the home.

Conclusion

Habitus as method enables a focus on the powerful influence of personal history on mothers' activities in support of children's schooling. Middle class women are predominantly engaging in a process of replicating habitus while their working class counterparts are attempting a much harder task; that of transforming habitus. Habitus provides a means of responding to the troublesome dichotomy between macro and micro levels of society. As I have attempted to establish in my analysis of the choices available to women within the sphere of involvement in schooling and the theme of generational continuity and discontinuity in maternal practices, habitus allows structure to be viewed as occurring within small scale interactions and activity within large scale settings. As such it is a powerful analytical tool for revealing the power dynamics of everyday interaction.

Generating cultural capital is no straightforward, seamless process. It involves a complex amalgam of time, effort and both material and psychological resources. Middle-class mothers were engaged in an extensive, systematic programme of generating cultural capital for their children whether it was straightforwardly educational capital through tuition, cultural capital through art, dance, drama and music classes, or social capital through orchestrating regular slots for their children to develop their own social networks and practice their social skills (Bourdieu, 1984a). In doing so they were, in part, responding to a range of external pressures; familial, neighbourhood and the pupil peer group. Dance, drama and music lessons were 'what people like us do' (Bourdieu, 1990a, pp. 64–5). The components of cultural capital that I identified at the beginning of my research study (available time, material resources, educational knowledge, information about the educational system and social confidence) all powerfully influence home–school relationships. Working-class mothers at Milner may have seen the school as a familiar site, but familiarity did not make a difference. Cultural capital did. It was middle-class women's confidence, their self-presentation as entitled, the certain conviction that their point of view was the correct one and their clearly articulated knowledge of the system and how it worked that counted.

I am not asserting, however, the existence of a unitary middle-class. Bourdieu's different 'fragments' of the middle-class are clearly represented in this study (cf. Bourdieu, 1979/1984a). Oak Park mothers do not constitute an homogeneous class grouping. Ruth has to go in and fight for extra school resources for her son. Other middle class mothers, like Judith and Pamela, used far more subtle strategies. They insisted politely and charmingly that they knew better than the teacher and so succeeded in getting what they wanted without the physical and emotional costs of Ruth's techniques.

An investigation of social processes embedded in home–school relations, such as the one that I have undertaken, provides the possibility of developing Bourdieu's concepts of habitus and cultural capital to include the influences of gender and ethnicity alongside those of social class. It also provides a vehicle for exploring mothers' activities in support of their children's schooling and how these relate to cultural reproduction. Cultural capital and habitus can be used to shade in the details of cultural reproduction through a focus on how social class advantage is maintained through everyday practices. As I have attempted to illustrate habitus and cultural capital as method are capable of highlighting the complex social and psychological processes underpinning maternal involvement. They also illuminate how the inequitable distribution of resources; educational, economic and cultural, contribute to a social class pattern in which working-class women's actions are undermined and those of middle-class women sustained.

The research raises important issues for policy and practice within the sphere of home–school relationships. All too often, partnership between parents and teachers appears to exist in name only in the two study schools. I would suggest there are implications for teacher education. A Bourdieuian analysis reveals the intricate dynamics of power which infuse all aspects of parental involvement. In a contemporary political climate where the focus in teacher education is increasingly on 'back to basics', awareness of, and knowledge about, the complexities embedded in teacher–parent relationships is increasingly seen as extraneous. In contrast, I would argue that Bourdieu helps us to keep key issues of social justice in the frame. Despite the current pervasiveness of homogeneous notions of 'parent' in both governmental and academic discourses, gender, 'race' and class continue to make differences that demand recognition and require reflexive consideration.

Chapter 5

Language and the Classroom

Michael Grenfell

Introduction

This chapter offers a discussion of language in the classroom in relation to Bourdieu's work.[1] The position and status of language generally in his writing is slightly ambiguous. On the one hand, it is central to his project. In his very earliest fieldwork in Algeria and south-west France, the study of language use was one of his major concerns (cf. Bourdieu and Grenfell, 1995). He has also published various academic papers and articles on language; some of which are grouped in two principal books: *Ce Que Parler Veut Dire* (1982b) and *Language and Symbolic Power* (1991a) (the latter is not simply an English translation of the former but includes some different papers, more extensive bibliography and a useful introductory chapter by the book's editor J.B. Thompson). There is in fact constant referral to issues of language across all his major works. Yet, Bourdieu's treatment of language is probably the least 'empirical' of all his topics of study. There are no linguistic analyses in the conventional sense of the term. And, his writing on the workings of the 'academic field' (1965/1994: with Passeron and de Saint Martin) do not include details of pedagogic discourse as such. In lieu of this apparent absence, the present chapter offers examples of language in classroom contexts. It does so to explore the concepts of habitus, field, capital, legitimacy and symbolic violence in terms of the language of teaching and learning. Examples from three separate sites have been selected in order to discuss these issues. Two are from primary schools; one of these being a mathematics lesson. The third is also from a mathematics lesson, but this time from a secondary school. Firstly, however, and in order to set a theoretical context to the discussion, I want to begin by addressing Bourdieu's main perspectives on language.

Language as Praxis

Bourdieu opens both his main books on language with full-frontal attacks on the contemporary founding fathers of linguistics: Ferdinand de Saussure and Naom Chomsky. He quotes Chomsky, disapprovingly, who, he argues, constructs linguistic theory in socially neutral terms:

Linguistic theory is concerned primarily with an *ideal speaker-listener, in a completely homogeneous speech-community, who knows its language perfectly* and is unaffected by such *grammatically irrelevant* conditions as memory limitations, distractions, shifts of attention or interest, and errors (random or characteristic) in applying his knowledge of the language in actual performance. This seems to me to have been the position of the founders of modern general linguistics, and no cogent reason for modifying it has been offered. (Chomsky, 1965, p. 3, quoted in Bourdieu, 1991, p. 44 — italics Bourdieu's own)

Chomsky's approach follows on from Saussure who posited the distinction between *langue*, an idealized linguistic universal, and *parole*, individual acts of communication. A similar distinction is made by Chomsky when he differentiates respectively between *competence* and *performance*. Both Saussure and Chomsky argue that the business of linguistics is to study *langue* or *competence*. Bourdieu does not agree:

As soon as one treats language as an autonomous object, accepting the radical separation which Saussure made between internal and external linguistics, between the science of language and the science of the social uses of language, one is condemned to looking within words, for the power of words, that is, looking for it where it cannot be found. (Bourdieu, 1991a, p. 107)

For Bourdieu, words are never just words, language is never just a vehicle to express ideas. Rather it comes as the product and process of social activity which is differentiating and differentiated; and thus, differentially valued within fields of social activity. Language is value-laden and culturally expressive according to standards of legitimacy and opposition to them. Bourdieu claims that such a sociological critique of language subjects the concepts of linguistics to a threefold displacement:

In place of *grammaticalness* it puts the notion of *acceptability*, or, to put is another way, in place of 'the' language (langue), the notion of the *legitimate* language. In place of *relations of communication* (or symbolic interaction) it puts *relations of symbolic power*, and so replaces the question of the *meaning* of speech with the question of the *value* and *power* of speech. Lastly, in place of specifically linguistic competence, it puts *symbolic capital*, which is inseparable from the speaker's position in the social structure. (1977b, p. 646)

Bourdieu argues that language should be examined in terms of the relationships from which it is generated. 'No one acquires a language', he states 'without acquiring a relation to language' (*ibid.*). These relationships are differential according to the principles generating social hierarchies because they are constituted by the same social processes and values attributed to their products:

. . . linguistic relations are always relations of symbolic power through which the relations of power between speakers and their respective groups come into being in a transfigured way. As a consequence, it is impossible to interpret an act of communication within the limits of a purely linguistic analysis. Even the most simple linguistic exchange brings into play a complex and rarefying network of historical power relations between the speaker, endowed with a socially specific authority and his audience who recognises his authority in varying degrees, as well as between the respective groups to which they belong. (Bourdieu and Wacquant, 1992a, p. 118)

It is possible to see a classroom as such a network of linguistic relations. However, it is helpful to begin by thinking of these relations in terms of Bourdieu's two basic analytic concepts: Habitus and Field.

Linguistic Habitus and Linguistic Field

Much of the discussion of Bourdieu's theory of practice in Chapter 2 fits his approach to language and linguistics like a hand in a glove. For habitus and field, we need only substitute linguistic habitus and linguistic field. Language is probably the exemplar of an objectifiable *structured* structure which is also *structuring* in practice. In other words, language arises out of interactions with language and between people, which are constructing and constructed according to intent, the limits of context, and degrees of shared meaning. There is a sense, moreover, in which language can be seen to be highly formal and objective, for example as in a dictionary or grammar book, or highly subjective and informal, as individuals' personal utterances.

To understand language in these terms, as an expression of field and habitus, is to see the latter as linguistic habitus: those features of language, and consequent thoughts, individuals are disposed to have and acquire in the course of their upbringing and trajectories through life, and which come into being in language used in a particular context or field. Linguistic field, in contrast, is a linguistically identifiable space that is structured in terms of positions and relations within it, which values and revalues features of language as an expression of the social differentiation which has generated it:

> On the one hand, there are the socially constructed dispositions of the linguistic habitus, which imply a certain propensity to speak and to say determinate things, which involve both the linguistic capacity to generate an infinite number of grammatically correct discourses and the social capacity to use this competence adequately in a determinate situation. On the other hand, there are the structures of the linguistic market which impose themselves as a system of specific sanctions and censorships. (1991a, p. 37)

The Linguistic Market

The market analogy is here used to refer to the ways linguistic 'products' have value in a particular field the way market products have value. Linguistic value is set by relations between different aspects of words and meanings and those of the established legitimate linguistic norm. This 'norm' is defined as the most prestigious language, possessing greatest *linguistic capital*, or the dominating style of language of those who speak from authority. It follows that a field will have its own linguistic norm to which everything defines and differentiates itself. Forms which are deviant in terms of one field can, of course, be the 'norm' in another field. It is in this sense, that the language of a field can then be understood as a 'linguistic market', as valuing is relative and 'open' to renegotiation. Much of Bourdieu's discussion follows on the basis of this understanding. For example, it is one thing to recognize the standards of the legitimate norm, it is another to have a practical operational knowledge of it: the distinction between *reconnaissance* and *connaissance* discussed in Chapter 2. Unsurprisingly, there is a difference between those who possess and generate knowledge norms themselves and the simple recognition of the norms in others. Bourdieu expresses this in mainly class terms: 'the dominated classes, and in particular the petit-bourgeois — are condemned to reconnaissance without connaissance' (Bourdieu and Boltanski, 1975, p. 8). Once this situation exists, those without the prestigious style constantly seek to appropriate it; even to the point of hypercorrection — a disposition to be 'over correct', to make over use of what are felt to be valued language markers. But this effort itself betrays the structural position of individuals within the linguistic field. Individuals with most linguistic capital may operate conversely: controlled 'hypocorrection', where those who are 'master' of the linguistic game demonstrate their total domination of language by 'descending' into the realms of the popular as a sign of 'confident relaxation and lofty ignorance of pedantic rules' (1991a, p. 63). Bourdieu concludes:

> Showing tension where the ordinary speaker succumbs to relaxation, facility where he betrays effort, and ease in tension which differs utterly from petit-bourgeois or popular tension and ease: these are the strategies of distinction (for the most part unconscious) giving rise to endless refinements, with constant reversals of value which tend to discourage the search for non-relational properties of linguistic styles. (*ibid.*)

It is by this dynamic that language develops, as do the social forces implicitly expressed in it. Linguistic capital is constantly being revalued in the course of such operating processes: language evolves.

Linguistic Examples

The study of language within a pedagogic context forms part of a vast academic field of linguistics and applied linguistics. Collins (1993, p. 128) identifies two principal approaches within these disciplines: quantitative linguistics, which he sees as representing the objectivist pole of socio-linguistics; and interactional linguistics, which represents the subjectivist pole. The first might be exemplified by the work of Labov (1972; 1977) which demonstrates language variation in social contexts; the second by Gumperz (1982), which focuses on the linguistic alterations made by individuals in conversation. To these we might add writers in social psychology who investigate the feelings, attitudes and motivations of speakers and their collective linguistic identities (cf. Giles and Powesland, 1975; Tajfel, 1982; Genesee and

Bourhis, 1982). Bourdieu's approach to a theory of linguistic practice is identical to his general theory of practice: it aims to go beyond such oppositions between subjectivism and objectivism. Nevertheless, it is possible to regard linguistic variation in use and individual attitudes to language in Bourdieu's basic terms. The sort of distinctions Bourdieu writes of are presumably identifiable at a range of levels in linguistic usage.

For example, at a *phonetic* level socio-linguists have identified variation attributable to individuals' positioning within the social hierarchy. In work on a linguistic corpus of French collected in Orléans, France, I was able to identify markers of standard and popular French to individuals in terms of their education and occupation (Grenfell, 1993). This distinction was *misrecognized* by those producing it, confirming Labov's finding (1972, p. 132) that speakers perceive their own phonetic intentions differently from the sound they produce. Moreover, the form of individuals' pronunciation differed remarkably when reading a full text rather than particular words: the latter being easier and therefore reducing 'linguistic insecurity'. Initially, it may be difficult to understand these types of strategies (hypocorrection, hypercorrection) as being central to the processes of pedagogic discourse. Nevertheless, school might be considered as the site in which phonetic differences in speech are reaffirmed; valued markers confirmed, deviant forms frowned upon. At this deepest level, social distinction is established. Such distinction will also apply at a *phonological* level. In linguistic analyses of the Orléans corpus, markers were identified between 'carriers' of 'langue légitime' (legitimate linguistic norms) and 'langue populaire' (popular language); for example, in the number of elisions and liaisons displayed, or pronoun dislocation in topic/anti-topic sentences, such as in 'moi, j'adore'. Of course, such tendencies are never fully determined on the basis of social class, but, by combining elements of habitus, education and occupation, it was possible to explain variations in linguistic activity. For example, a secretary registered as relatively modest in terms of education and occupational status (economic and cultural capital), but displayed a high level of linguistic capital by dint of her use of language as a tool of her trade. Other examples followed a similar pattern.

A socio-linguistic questionnaire was conducted during the Orléans collection in order to ascertain general subjective dispositions and attitudes, not only to language but other language issues of the day; for example, the use of the fountain as opposed to the ball-point pen, the type of writing paper to be used, and the slow adoption of English terms for modern, technological phenomena. Analysis of answers from those in the corpus group showed how there existed marked differences across social groupings with regard to these issues. Upper social groups showed dispositions:

- to be against reforms of spelling;
- to deny class differences in language usage;
- to do crosswords;
- not to use lined or squared paper;
- to feel standards of French were deteriorating.

Lower social groups showed dispositions:

- to be for reform of spelling;
- to be aware of social class differences;
- not to do crosswords;
- to use lined paper;
- to feel standards of French were improving.

These sorts of opposition are significant but it must be stressed that, for any one individual, they were never expressed in a complete form. Rather individuals showed themselves to be partly aware, partly unconscious of the value of specific aspects of language; such as the use of dictionaries, using fountain pens, the way others' speech affects them, their own habits and practices. There were individual configurations in terms of the degree to which linguistic norms were 'known', 'recognized' and 'misrecognized'. It seems reasonable to suggest that a specific configuration of attitudes and habits — linguistic capital — arises within an individual habitus, and is the product of family social milieu, educational experience, the interaction of these two, and subsequent personal and professional experience. Nothing is ever clear cut, nothing is pre-determined. These are dispositions which are based on the differentiating principles constitutive of Bourdieu's theory of practice.

Language and Education

More specifically related to classroom knowledge and talk, Edwards and Mercer (1987) have listed three principal approaches: linguistic, social and anthropological, and psychological. By linguistic they mean the analysis of classroom discourse by such researchers as Sinclair and Coultard (1975), Stubbs (1976), Barnes (1976) and Barnes and Todd (1977). These writers demonstrated how classroom knowledge was structured and built through identifiable patterns. For example, the I-R-F exchange structure, where *initiation* of talk by the teacher leads to *response* from a pupil, to which the teacher provides a *feedback*. Quantitatively, researchers in this tradition established the famous 'law of two-thirds': that, in the average classroom, two-thirds of time is spent on talk; two-thirds of this is by the teacher; two-thirds of which is based on lecturing or questioning. However, little account of the individual pupil was taken in this research, nor the message of the linguistic medium: who constituted it and its impact in specific contexts.

The opposite might be said about the sociological and the anthropological approach to classroom talk and knowledge. Here, broad ethnographic studies (Willis, 1977; Heath, 1983) have been used to account for the ways pupils' social class background contributes to their level of academic achievement. However, in these cases, a predominant message, that of class reproduction, appears to be more important than the medium. As Bernstein has put it: 'it is as if the specialised discourse of education is a voice through which others speak (class, gender, religion, race, region)' (1986, p. 206).

Edwards and Mercer's work can be located in the 'new' psychology of education; essentially, a socio-cognitive approach to the construction of classroom knowledge through discourse, and heavily influenced by the work of the Russian psychologist Lev Vygotsky (1962; 1978). From a Vygotskyan perspective, thought and language are very close, and are immanent in social interactions. For Vygotsky, whatever appears within any one individual's psychology, appears first at an 'inter-psychological' level; that is on the social plane of human development. Knowledge and learning are discursive and social, and occur in what Vygotsky called the *Zone of Proximal Development*, or 'the distance between the actual developmental level as determined by independent problem solving and the level of potential development as determined through problem solving under adult guidance or in collaboration with capable peers' (1978, p. 86).

Language and Pedagogic Discourse

Language, for Bourdieu cuts across and partially integrates these approaches. It is 'constructivist' in an almost Vygotskyan way; but also 'structural' in that it rests on the belief that generating structures, and the principles on which they are based, are identifiable.

We have seen that language for Bourdieu is essentially representative of social structural differentiation. It always relates to something. The relation is characterized by meanings that are valued according to differential values — the sense of words. What is in a word? For Bourdieu, a word is a socio-cultural time capsule packed with socially derived meaning — the use of the word. It derives its meaning from relations with other words:

> The all-purpose word in the dictionary, a product of the neutralization of the practical relations within which it functions, has no social existence: in practice, it is always immersed in situations, to such an extent that the core meaning which remains relatively invariant through the diversity of markets may pass unnoticed . . . The different meanings of a word are defined in relation between the invariant core and the specific logic of different markets, themselves objectively situated with respect to the market in which the most common meaning is defined. (1991a, p. 39)

The game of 'Scrabble' could not be played without the use of 'all-purpose' words. In such games recourse to a dictionary often functions to legitimate word-choice: a word either exists or does not exist, is either correctly or incorrectly spelt. In practice however, words get their meaning from their relation to other words. Meanings are determined by particular fields, in relation to 'core' or orthodox meanings. These words are 'things to think with' and express ideas. For Bourdieu, the basis of much of this meaning is the differential structuring of society:

> All agents of a particular social formation have in common a set of fundamental schemes of perception which receive an initial objectification in opposing adjectival pairs commonly employed to classify and qualify people and objects in the most

different sites of practice . . . the network of opposition between high (or sublime, elevated, pure) and low (or vulgar, flat, modest), spiritual and material, fine (or refined, elegant) and gross (or fat, rough, brutal, coarse), light (or subtle, alive, deft) and heavy (or slow, thick, obtuse, laborious, gauche), free and forced, wide and narrow, or, in another dimension, between unique (or rare, different, distinguished, exclusive, exceptional, singular, incredible) and common (or ordinary, banal, current, trivial, anything), brilliant (or intelligent) and dull (or obscure, faded, mediocre), has as principle the elite of the dominating and the mass of the dominated. (1979, p. 546, Own translation)

Words never exist on their own but in discourse, in relation to each other:

the form and the content of a discourse depend on the relation between a habitus (which is itself the product of sanctions on a market with a given level of tension) and a market (*field*) defined by a level of tension which is more of less heightened, hence by the severity of the sanctions it inflicts on those who pay insufficient attention to 'correctness' and to 'the imposition of form' which formal usage presupposes. (1991a, p. 79)

Words form part of fields and can represent them. By entering a field, a word takes on meaning from that field through its position within the *network of relations* immanent in the semantic field. Bourdieu argues that this attribution of meaning is a kind of imposition: It 'is both a transformation and a transubstantiation: the substance signified *is* the signifying form which is realized' (1991a, p. 143). Prescribed meaning becomes legitimate interpretation. The notion of 'symbolic violence' is pertinent to this discussion. If words come imbued with authority and prescribed meaning, they impose legitimate definitions in a way that does not tolerate non-orthodox versions; one form dominates, the other is suppressed. In this way, one social groupings' definition of meaning is established at the expense of another's, even though the latter may be perfectly valid.

Pedagogic language can be seen in these terms; as the product of a particular field context. As such, it will be governed by what is valued in that field, what is legitimate, what is excluded. This is apparent, not only in the language of an interaction, but the whole site — the time and place such exchanges take place — and the way a particular field connects with other fields within education. There is an issue of what is the legitimate and who defines it? There is another issue of how this is represented in schools and classrooms through language. A third is the effect of individual habitus, for both teachers and pupils, in the field. A fourth is the extent to which such differences of language can be expressed in terms of social class and what other generating principles might be present in classroom discourse. I now want to explore these notions with specific reference to particular pedagogic contexts.

Classroom Discourse

Language, for Bourdieu, is primordial. He is mindful of the way in which social reality is constructed in and through language. He has noted, as have Austin and

Searle, the illocutionary force of language; the way it seemingly can cause effects over and above the basic words 'in themselves'. The way ships are named is a good example of this, or the knighting of someone by the Queen. Both of these are acts of 'magic', where power is conferred on someone by the group to act in their name in allotting social prestige and status to others, places or objects. He refers to the case of the *skeptron* in Homer, which has to be held by the orator in order for him to have the right to speak. Again, the power is not in the object itself, but the acknowledged symbolic power ascribed to it by the group or field.

In the academic field, language is used to confer scholastic credit on individuals; this is as true in formal qualifications as in micro contexts of classroom assessments. The teacher has authority, or at least authority is given to the teacher, to act in certain ways and according to certain principles. But schools are each very different and give rise to very different cultures. The following three examples show how aspects of the pedagogic discourse look in practice.

My first example is taken from a bilingual primary school classroom (Bourne, 1992). The teacher in this study is 'progressive' and seems to be adopting an approach which is in keeping with the 'common knowledge' of Edwards and Mercer (1987); that is that knowledge is constructed between pupils and between pupils and teachers. Yet, Bourne finds that the teachers' classification of pupils conforms to a series of binary adjectival pairs that include and exclude certain pupils in terms of care, attention, intelligence, behaviour, etc. On the basis of these, the teacher constructs an 'ideal pedagogic subject' to which she operates and wants pupils to conform:

> the pedagogic discourse of the teacher is tuned to the construction of a common knowledge, and strategically avoids interactions which disrupt the smooth construction and presentation of the class as sharing and participating successfully within that common knowledge. The use of question, answer and response forms in a class where a number of pupils are in the early stages of learning English would endanger and possibly disrupt that smooth flow, and make language opaque and problematic, rather than being the transparent medium through which conceptual development can be monitored. (Bourne, 1992, pp. 316–17)

In other words, what is legitimate for the teacher constructs a certain type of classroom discourse which locates individual pupils' needs and expectations in relation to it, which in turn has effects on how they act with respect to each other. Bourne goes on to discuss the consequences that the avoidance of a certain type of pupil–teacher exchange has for pupils. The pupils elicit responses differentially from the teacher according to the way they engage with her. She concludes that this engagement itself is determined by a series of cultural expectations inherent in particular pupils. If we reinterpret Bourne's discussion in Bourdieu's terms, it would be necessary to detail the content of teacher/pupil discourse in terms of habitus specific expectation; in this case, pedagogic (teacher) and socio-cultural (pupil) as expressed through language and the range of activities mediated by it. Moreover, these discursive products and processes would have to be seen in terms of the organizational principles of the specific field site. It would then be possible to demonstrate, as Bourne does, how certain pupils are excluded from the discourse, or exclude themselves — not explicitly and with intent — but by the way they behave, respond to the teacher's demands, and connect with fellow pupils. For example, one pupil persists in initiating topics with the teacher, and, as this runs counter to the teacher's 'legitimate ideal', challenges her. The response the pupil receives quite literally 'puts her in her place' as a pupil. Her questions are often met with direct commands for her to go and fetch something, with no acknowledgment of her message. Other times, her initiations are ignored:

Lukon	Miss, it that one, that one?
Teacher	Tuk, read the next sentence.

This sort of distancing, between what is a legitimate or illegitimate way to proceed, is a strategy on the part of the teacher to self-regulate, to gain control over another, to maintain core principles of her own pedagogic habitus. Unable to be the pupil she wants to be, or the pupil the teacher wants her to be, the pupil is marginalized within classroom discourse and activity.

This marginalization will tend to re-emphasize the power of the original socio-cultural habitus (of the pupil) at the expense of the legitimate pedagogic culture (of the teacher). However, in a bilingual classroom at least, culture is never a uniform reference point of the whole class, or even recognizable group within it. Cross ethnic groupings are fraught with conflicts and misunderstandings as individuals express themselves according to the discourse fields they have encountered:

Nhan	Who believe in Jesus.
Child	God?
Nhan	You? Do you be'eve in Jesus? I don'. I don' be'eve in Jesus.
Najma	We say god is Jesus.
Nhan	Yes. Bu' you, do you be'eve in?
Najma	(*angrily*) You say if G — if I believe. I say . . .
Nhan	Wha' is tha'? Whad' I say?
	I'm no' like you.
Najma	You bad, man! You dare say tha'!
Nhan	I don' be'eve in Jesus.
Najma	You know when (. . .) Easter.
Nhan	Wha' Easter? (*pause*) Who I mean.
Najma	(*scornfully*) Yeah, *who*!
Nhan	I ask you wha' Easter
. . .	
Najma	I get you one (. . .) I show you 'e 's a god.
Nhan	We don'. We can' bring no thing to school.
(*ibid.*, pp. 446–7)	

Clearly, the children are speaking from two culturally derived positions on Jesus. These beliefs impinge directly on the children and establish their group relations over an issue, where the legitimacy of an ideal is being contested. Bourne points out how Nhan eventually appeals to the teacher's authority in the rule that 'things should not be brought in from home': a strategy used by the teacher to avoid confrontation and disruption of the 'commonality' of the classroom. The teacher indicates what to value, which is defined rather nebulously in terms of tolerance and equality rather than content or the relationship to knowledge. Yet, Bourne shows how, besides enlisting support from teacher's and parent's discourse (which we should see as being habitus specific), individual pupils draw on the discourse of older children, sometimes explicitly sexual, with which, one assumes, they could have very little literal understanding, as a way of exerting their own power by accessing more adult ways of doing and being (pp. 450–1). In other words, when the teacher seeks to deny differences and, indeed, establishes a class-room commonality in order to do this, the consequent effect is for the pupils to use their own means of re-establishing these differences. In the terms used in this chapter, the teacher's pedagogic habitus and its coming into being within the field context of work denies pupils' own habitus and thus excludes them from the ped-agogic discourse. Excluded, pupils have only their own habitus and field culture to fall back on. In this case, Bourdieu's approach would suggest that, within and across groups, unorthodox ways of thinking and acting actually operate as if they were legitimate for one group whilst being in opposition to other groups which are considered unorthodox by the first group, but are in fact legitimate in global terms.

This phenomenon is most explicit in relation to objective, observable dif-ferences of class and culture, which constitute the habitus of the pupils in this particular classroom. Such differences would occur in other classrooms, similarly misrecognized, where other elements of habitus might dominate. The next two examples explore these differential responses between pupils and teachers, between what is and is not legitimate, in terms of methodological approach.

In the Vygotskyan perspective taken by such researchers as Edwards and Mercer, educational knowledge is 'handed over' to pupils or made common as part of classroom interactions. The teacher constructs knowledge in classroom discourse and thus provides the 'scaffolding' for pupils to build their own understanding. Scaffolding is a metaphoric term coined by Bruner to designate the way the teacher makes it 'possible for the child, in Vygotsky's words, to internalise external know-ledge and convert it into a tool for conscious control' (Bruner, 1985, p. 25). It is a version of Vygotsky's 'Zone of Proximal Development'. Here is an example of a teacher in this supportive mode:

1	Teacher	OK right Paul, I'm going to give you a sum, right, and I
2		want you to just tell me how you are doing it. OK this is the sum.
3		You (*to Gary*) can do it as well and then I'll give you
4		you a different one — um — try and think of a nice . . .
5	Paul	(*interrupting*) hard one.
6	Teacher	Hard one, OK.
7	Paul	Oh no, oh no.
8	Teacher	OK that's it (*writing*) and it's a subtraction.

$$\begin{array}{r} 1\,3\,3 \\ \underline{6\,9} \\ \hline \end{array}$$

9	**Paul**	Oh no.
10	**Teacher**	Now tell me what you actually do to start with. What do you
11		say to yourself?
12	**Paul**	Well, 3 minus 9 you can't do.
13	**Teacher**	Yes.
14	**Paul**	Cross that out and make that 2?
15	**Teacher**	Yes.
16	**Paul**	So now you've got 13.
17	**Teacher**	Correct.
18	**Paul**	So that's 4.
19	**Teacher**	Yes, correct.
20	**Paul**	So that's 2 minus 6 you can't do so that's 1 take that's — down to zero.
21	**Teacher**	Yes.
22	**Paul**	And you get 120. Is that — is it 4 and 4?
23	**Teacher**	Say that again, 120, what do you mean 120?
24	**Paul**	Well (*Loud noise occurs in background*).
25	**Teacher**	That Mrs Hemington, she's so helpful, isn't she, with her
26		stapler. Go on, say it again, just . . .
27	**Paul**	Well, you've crossed that out (*indicating the '1' in the*
28		*hundreds column*).
29	**Teacher**	Yes. What are you going to do with it, now you've crossed
30		it out?
31	**Paul**	Move it on to here (*indicating 'tens' column*).
32	**Teacher**	Go on then. You haven't done yet. I can't see it in there. It's
33		vanished.
34	**Paul**	So that's three.
35	**Teacher**	Well, is it though?
36	**Gary**	Hang on, put a one in there Paul.
37	**Paul**	Right, OK.
38	**Teacher**	What did you say Gary?
39	**Gary**	Put a one.
40	**Teacher**	What is that one? Where have you got that from?
41	**Paul**	From the hundreds.
42	**Teacher**	Right. So what number is that there now? (*indicating the*
43		*'tens' column*).
44	**Gary**	That is now 13.
45	**Paul**	Um, what's that, oh, 12 (*makes choking noises*) sixty-four.
46	**Teacher**	Is he right?
47	**Gary**	Yes.

(Mercer, 1995, pp. 75–6)

This is a teacher carefully supporting a pupil whilst he grapples with a particular mathematical algorithm. In the first section, the pupil negotiates a 'hard' sum. In the second, the pupil starts off correctly and receives affirmative responses from the teacher. This continues in the third section, and then the pupil surprises the teacher with his conclusion of 120 in line 22. The pupil and the teacher do not agree at this point, and the teacher talks through the given method in order to bring Paul back into line with it. Another pupil is brought in to help this situation, and Paul eventually obtains a 'correct' answer. Mercer concludes that he is happy to call what the teacher is doing 'scaffolding', that this can be considered 'assisted performance', and states that Paul went on to do subtractions without any assistance.

All this may be true. However, what it does not account for is the different worldview between teacher and pupil; indeed, the distinct cognitive practices they each may be utilizing. This is most noticeable in line 22 where Paul comes up with the unexpected 120. At this point, the teacher does not investigate what thinking results in this utterance, rather she talks the pupil through (according to) her own (legitimate) method. Her intention to teach is more powerful than her intention to understand the pupil. By contrast, Rowland (1987) discusses what happens when the teacher does pursue the pupil's 'method', and how this leads to an enhanced interpretative understanding.

A methodological approach derived from Bourdieu would entail reconceptualizing this case site in terms of field and habitus. The field structure might be the hierarchy of methods within the mathematical discourse, the legitimate procedures and language used to represent them. Habitus would be present in participants, their present and past experience, and the schemes of thought — hard/nice, legitimate method, etc. — used in interaction with the constituted pedagogical discourse. The teacher has a clear method, procedure, sequence, to solve the problem. What happens when the pupil produces a procedure according to his own habitus (cognitive schemes to generate thinking), is that he is brought back 'on line'. What is left uninvestigated is his own habitus response, and how this might be productive in the pedagogic act. This is not to say that the pupil's 'wrong' answer should be accepted, or that he should be left alone to find the correct solution according to his own method. It is rather that it is a naive realist's view to accept what went on in utilitarian terms as 'scaffolding'. It is, as Bourdieu might say, 'too real to be true, since it grasps at once a mental category and a social category, socially produced only by superseding or obliterating all kinds of differences and contradictions' (Bourdieu, 1989c, p. 38*ff*). As an alternative, it is possible to 'deconstruct' the word 'scaffolding' in epistemological terms in order to analyse the full reality of the process, with all its tensions and contradictions.

In the above example, it is not a question of making a value judgment as to whether this is or is not a good teacher — her intent is to operationalize the algorithm. More pertinent questions would be: is this good practice?; is what she is doing effective? At the point she rejects the pupil's response, she is being effective in what she has chosen to do. The broader question is: is this good pedagogy? One might say that what she is doing is good 'scaffolding' without saying whether this is a good thing or not, for it puts the teacher in the superordinate position and gives legitimacy to her method and knowledge without accounting for the pupil's.

My third example of pedagogic discourse takes a different tack. What follows is an extract from secondary school a maths lesson with a class of 13-year-olds. So far in the lesson, the pupils have constructed boxes from squared paper:

```
 1   T    What I want to know . . . and what
 2        you're going to calculate . . . while I'm
 3        bringing the sellotape round is . . .
 4        how big your box is.

     [Pause]

 5   Ps   Area . . . It's the area.
 6   T    How big (Emphasizing) (Writes on board).
 7   P1   It's the area (tentatively).
 8   T    Not the area.
 9   P2   It's the perimeter.
10   T    Not the perimeter.
11        The volume.
12   P3   How much it contains.
13   T    How much it contains, exactly that,
14        the volume.

          . . .

15   T    Right. What I want to know is how
16        many small cubes you could put
17        in here . . . right . . . so the answer
18        to how big is . . . is how many
19        small cubes . . . can you get in here?
20        If you want the proper name for
21        them, they are called cubic
22        centimetres, aren't they?
```
(Edwards, 1994)

This is clearly not an example of exploratory talk; nor closed questions; nor handing over knowledge. Curiously, it seems that it is the pupils who are the first to present the 'legitimate language', the authorized vocabulary of the field — area (lines 5 and 7), perimeter (line 9) — whilst the teacher employs the 'non-legitimate' 'big' (line 4). It is not then an induction into the technical language of the subject. Later, in interview after the lesson, the teacher claimed that this was because she was 'training them': she was new in the department and the techniques she used were less traditional than those of her colleagues: 'I was trying to produce a practical activity and to avoid triggering formulaic solutions using volume = length × breadth × height'. She was doing this according to her own *pedagogic habitus*, her understanding of maths and how it should be taught. Because this ran counter to the departmental approach, in which pupils had been trained, it first appears that the teacher and pupils are speaking at cross-purposes, and the teacher is denying pupils access to technical language that will facilitate them in their action. Meaning is negotiated: first pupils show what they understand by 'how big' (lines 5, 7 and 9) and check out what they already know against 'how big'; second, the teacher introduces a technical word — volume — that a pupil defines (lines 11 and 12); thirdly, the teacher reintroduces the non-technical question 'how big' (line 18), connects it with a non-technical 'how many small cubes' (lines 18–19) and finishes the sequence with a technical definition, 'cubic centimetres' (lines 21–22).

In this sequence, the authority of the teacher is never in doubt; she has total command of the language and associated concepts. Indeed, she introduces technical language at two critical points: firstly, to bring pupils back into the discourse (line 14); secondly, to supply the target concept (line 21). However, she is showing to pupils that she does not value these as such — a kind of 'strategy of euphemism' to deny that which is most important and thus demonstrating one's command over it (cf. Bourdieu, 1991a, p. 80). In other words, there is a play here between orthodoxy and heterodoxy. The former is not being named but goes misrecognized. As such, it is for the pupils to guess what the teacher values. This valuing is symbolic and reproduces symbolic power 'capable of producing real effects without any apparent expenditure of energy' (Bourdieu, 1991a, p. 170). The teacher is operating this in a particular field site, by strategically subverting the pupils' normal pedagogic discourse. She does this in terms of her own pedagogic habitus realized in practice in the field context in which she finds herself, the present valued products of which she wishes to transgress in order to fulfil her own pedagogic aims. Pupils respond differentially to this: those in command of the legitimate terms are denied the teacher's confirmation. What they 'know' is devalued. They are reduced to work with the rest on the teacher's terms.

Earlier I referred to 'scaffolding' as a metaphor that tried to capture the dialogic nature of the social and the psychological. In some previous approaches to classroom discourse, the teacher is seen in a supporting role, subordinate to the pupil. Introducing the concepts of field and pedagogic habitus uncovers, at a practical and theoretical level, the underlying processes of pupil/teacher interactions with all the tensions and contradictions inherent in these. Knowledge is not so much mutually constructed or imposed but reproduced in specific subject contexts. In this reproduction, teachers are active agents, because, as in this example, they establish a value system within which pupils must work.

This value system is a product of the teacher's own pedagogic habitus within the field and generates knowledge that is valuable and valuing. Such a value system implies specific relations to knowledge and is inherently structured. The teacher asserts that structure, and, in so doing, reproduces subject knowledge and how it should be valued. Activities are the means to explore and develop knowledge, but simple scaffolding is not enough to express the dynamic involved. Indeed, the word scaffolding is a good example of the way a particular language can mislead by being so evidently 'true' that important facets such as processes, tensions and conflicts can be overlooked. Learning mastery of facts is never enough, induction into technical terms (as in strict didactic pedagogic approaches) is insufficient. If this is all that happens, pupils do not discover the irregularities of the system, do not have practical competence in it. To know and to learn is more than acquiring form. Yet, it would be similarly misleading to suppose that learning can be encapsulated as an activity of personal exploration. In order to go beyond these images of teaching, it is necessary to introduce field and pedagogic habitus, so as to highlight the relationship between teacher and pupil, located in time and space, together with the ways these are expressed in and through language. It is necessary to see these relations as governed by principles immanent in the structuring and structured structures identifiable in human discourse and praxis. Teaching knowledge is not the transference of known things to unknowing subjects (pupils), but the transformation from unknown to known things in relationships with a pedagogic other. The extent this can happen depends on pupils' and teachers' habitus and their interplay with a field context. Pupils learn when they interpret and take control of knowledge, but this arises in relationships which are imbued with field and habitus specific generating structures.

In legitimate mathematical discourse, volume and length are linked but this is often reduced to a numerical activity in which world relations, objects, are excluded. In the third example above, the teacher tries to reintroduce these relations by setting up some spatial experience. She does this by avoiding legitimate language *per se* in a covert way and not dealing with area/perimeter theoretical relationships overtly. The volume algorithm is itself valued but only when connected with space and experience before the explicit algorithm is taught. This is part of this teacher's pedagogic habitus, her tacit teaching competence.

Researchers such as Edwards and Mercer freely admit to underplaying tension and conflict in pedagogic discourse and to stressing the constructive and co-operative (Mercer, 1995, p. 121). It is not my intention to replace this view with a conflict model of classroom discourse. Rather, it is to connect features of individuals and context by employing concepts of field and habitus; to open up a space where the processes available in teacher–pupil exchanges are brought to the fore. Edwards and Mercer rarely look at teachers' implicit dilemmas, let alone habitus. They are too preoccupied with an application of the 'scaffolding' metaphor and the Vygotskyan perspective to the data they have collected in a way that matches theory with practice. Clearly, teachers have idiosyncrasies. The question is how these are related to legitimate ideologies and practices which might also be present but in a less clearly visible manner. Moreover, what are the processes and products of their interaction?

It is impossible to refer to teachers' thinking, teachers' intentions, in isolation. They must be connected to the hierarchy of valued practices and knowledge within the pedagogic discourse — the field. Habitus brings with it field and field the notion of habitus. The two are mutually constituted for particular, practical purposes. Habitus replaces intentions with past histories, contexts, and ideational structures in relation to the field. It is possible to unpick some of these as part of research practice. Field and Habitus demand that such research connects the context of individual dispositions with ideational, ideological structures immanent in the site. 'Scaffolding', on the other hand, often closes down such possibilities by focusing on the immediate interaction between teachers and pupils in a utilitarian way, and valuing what occurs, rather than seeing these as constituted by the pedagogic discourse which forms them and which they continually form. As such Habitus and Field offer a more dynamic framework for looking at the process of pedagogic action.

Conclusion

In this chapter we have looked at aspects of classroom discourse in terms of Bourdieu's theory of practice. What has become clear is that not only is the role of language in pedagogic discourse prone to misunderstanding but the language we use to talk about it is also problematic. The 'legitimate' is a helpful concept in highlighting the orthodox ways of conducting teaching and learning, and the consequent effects it can have on different pupils according to their cognitive approach, culture and learning style. Moreover, it is clear that these effects often go misrecognized by the teachers themselves, preoccupied as they are with their own routines which are based on their own developing pedagogic habitus. Yet, understanding classrooms in terms of individuals' habitus and the site field they find themselves in, shows how the structure of pedagogic discourse is constructed at the intersection between those taking part in it. The structural principles and generating processes in pupil–teacher exchanges at least offer the possibility of individual teachers becoming aware of the meaning and consequences of their action. This understanding must have a constitutive effect on future methods of teaching and their outcomes. Without this continual 'reflection' on the deep structure of classrooms, teachers risk perpetuating the inequalities and disjunctions for which they are, admittedly rarely consciously, responsible. Bourdieu states it:

> It is impossible to imagine a teacher able to maintain with his own discourse, his pupils' discourse and his pupils' relation to his own discourse, a relation stripped of all indulgences and freed from all the traditional complicities, without at the same time crediting him with the capacity to subordinate his whole pedagogic practice to the imperatives of a perfectly explicit pedagogy which could actually implement the principles logically implied in affirmation of the autonomy of the specifically scholastic mode of acquisition. There is indeed every difference in the world between a teaching orientated by express intention of minimising code mistakes by continuously and methodically stating the code, and the forms of teaching which are able to dispense with expressly teaching the transmission code because they speak by tacit agreement to a public prepared by insensible familiarization to understand their tacit meanings. (Bourdieu, 1972/1977a, p. 126)

Note

1   I should like to extend my thanks to Jill Bourne of the Open University and Cheryl Edwards, formerly of Southampton University, for allowing me to use their transcripts for my own purposes. More than this, it was their original work that inspired me to rethink in the terms of this chapter.

Chapter 6

Career Decision Making and the Transition from School to Work

Philip Hodkinson

Introduction: The Context of the Study

A key area of educational research is the transition from school to work. There has been considerable change to policy and practice in this area in England and Wales, over the past few years. For example, the school curriculum prior to the transition has been transformed by the introduction of the General Certificate of Secondary Education (GCSE) and the National Curriculum. The post-16 alternatives to work at 16+ now focus on the new General National Vocational Qualifications (GNVQs) alongside the long-established A levels. There have also been dramatic changes in the patterns of progression between the ages of 16 and 19. Far more young people now stay on in full-time education. It is as common now to leave education at 17+ as at 16+. Very few teenagers move straight from school to a job. The numbers on youth training schemes have steadily diminished. Indeed, the nature of youth training has itself changed. The Youth Training Scheme (YTS) has become Youth Training (YT). Training or Youth Credits (see below) and the Modern Apprenticeship have been introduced. There has also been a transformation in the management of post-16 education and training, with an emphasis on measurement of outcomes, contract compliance and inspection, in a context of deliberately created 'quasi-markets' supposedly driven by 'customer choice' (cf. Hodkinson and Sparkes, 1995). To many people working in the area, there seems to be no end to these continual changes.

This chapter looks briefly at a study which set out to examine one part of this complex situation: the transition from school to youth training of a small number of young people who were involved with one of the first Training Credits pilot schemes. Training Credits were piloted in 11 areas in England and Scotland from 1991 and in a further 9 areas in a second pilot phase from 1993. In the summer of 1995, they became national in scope. By this time, the name had been changed to Youth Credits. I retain the original name here, because that was the one used when most of the data was collected. The Training Credits scheme is based on the principle of issuing each school leaver with a voucher, or Credit. In theory, the young person with the Credit is a customer, using it to purchase training.

The use of such vouchers illustrates two key characteristics which underpin education and training policy in the UK in the 1990s — a focus on individualism and a belief in rational choice. When I, Andrew Sparkes and Heather Hodkinson examined the literature around the transition to work we discovered two interesting paradoxes. Firstly, most of the recent policy literature took an unquestioning advocacy position in relation to individual rational decision making as the driver of education and training activity. Yet, on the other hand, a significant body of sociological and educational research seemed to deny the very possibility of meaningful individual choice. Secondly, whilst there had been an almost complete transformation of policy, curriculum patterns and management structures in recent years (see above), many deep-seated problems seemed to persist. To put it another way, the two different literatures polarized, with much policy discussion giving a strongly optimistic and uncritical picture of the current developments and the immediate future, whilst most academic studies appeared pessimistic, predicting either no improvement or that things were getting worse. It was in trying to identify a credible position, which made sense of the data we had collected and did justice to elements of both arguments whilst allowing them to be compared and evaluated, that we turned to the work of Pierre Bourdieu. Before engaging with our actual study and the significance of his work to us, I need to illustrate these contradictions in relation to career progression, career choice and career decision making.

Career Progression, Career Choice and Career Decision Making

One influential statement about the centrality of individual choice came from the Confederation of British Industry (CBI). It argued that pride of place should be given to the individual and his/her responsibility for self development in a market environment. This should be done through, amongst other things:

- An individual focus through personal profiles incorporating records of achievement and individual action plans, in education and training.
- High class professional and independent careers advice and guidance.
- Incentives for all young people through financial credits, to empower and motivate them and arm them with real influence and buying power in a new education and training market. (CBI, 1993, p. 13)

The assumption was that if each young person took responsibility for their own education and training and were given a Credit, to buy education or training of their choice, their individual purchases would drive a market in training provision. This would ensure the efficient use of training resources and force training providers to raise quality in order to attract customers. Because young people who are making choices about education or training are surrounded by others with vested interests, such as teachers who may want them to stay on in school to make courses viable, neutral careers guidance was seen as essential.

Central to this view is the belief that 'as they approach 16 and beyond, young adults need: — high quality careers education and independent guidance to help them make the *right* choices' (British Government, 1994, p. 35, emphasis added).

These one-off 'right' choices will set young people on track for their future educational and employment careers. Such careers are seen rather like ladders. The right choice places the person on the right ladder. He or she then progresses upwards, in a relatively straightforward and predictable manner. Further change will only happen if, for example, a staging post is reached where a choice of further ladders exists, or if a young person 'falls off' a ladder, because an 'incorrect' decision was made.

The actual choice process is seldom discussed in this literature. Rather, there are assumptions that it is, or should be, completely rational, as young people consider dispassionately all the relevant information about the options available to them, and then make a reasoned decision about which option to select. For example, Bennett *et al.* claim:

> We assume that, knowing their capacities and other personal characteristics, individuals form an estimate of expected earnings resulting from each education, training and labour market option, and, taking into account their taste for each, choose the stream which offers the greatest net utility. (1992, p. 13)

In the Training Credits scheme investigated, such rational decision making was built in via a Careers Guidance Action Plan. This Action Plan was divided into four sequential parts. Part 1 explored the young person's existing achievements, focused on 'the skills I have gained'. Part 2 specified career aims, the skills required for these aims, and 'how I can work towards my aims'. Part 3 described the planned learning programme. Part 4, to be undertaken after training was completed, was a review of the learning programme. When we interviewed, Part 1 was left to the schools; the Careers Service worked with pupils to complete Parts 2 and 3; and Part 4 was to be done by the Careers Service after training had been finished.

Often unarticulated in such policy-oriented writings lie two assumed theoretical positions in relation to career decision making. The first is trait theory, which sees career decision making as matching person to placement, by identifying traits of personality, skill and interest that are needed in certain jobs, and finding out to what extent individual young people possess those qualities, ending with what Kidd (1984) calls 'a process involving a matching of self and occupation' (p. 25). Both she and Law (1981) criticize this model as at best oversimplified. The second position is that of rational choice analysis. As Hindess (1988) says, 'models of maximising behaviour are widely used in economics, and rational choice analysis can be understood as extending that economic approach to other areas of human behaviour' (p. 1). For example, Elster (1978, 1986) claims that analysing personal actions on the assumption that choices are rational normally provides the best explanation of patterns of human activity.

In contrast to all this, much research literature points to significant differences between the career paths of young people from different backgrounds. Twenty years ago, Ashton and Field (1976) identified three broadly different types of work in Britain. These they called 'long term career jobs', which were dominated by the middle classes; 'working-class career jobs', which included technical, clerical and skilled manual occupations; and 'low-skill' jobs including unskilled manual and shop work. Since they wrote, there have been many major changes to the British educational system and to the labour market. Yet despite these changes, recent research still confirms the general validity of the Ashton and Field hierarchy (Furlong, 1992; Roberts, 1993; Kerckhoff, 1993), though the actual nature of careers has changed in all three levels, with casualized labour, part-time working and rising unemployment. In effect, the picture is now more complicated, with this largely class-based hierarchy overlain by Hutton's (1995) 40–30–30 society, where 'Only around 40 per cent of the workforce enjoy tenured full-time employment or secure self-employment, . . . another 30 per cent are insecurely self-employed, involuntarily part-time, or casual workers; while the bottom 30 percent, the marginalised, are idle or working for poverty wages' (p. 14).

Contributors in Bates and Riseborough (1993) describe considerable differences between experiences, attitudes and background of young people across a range of post-16 education and training provision in Britain. Such studies confirm deep seated inequalities in the British labour market and that entry into the different career trajectories was largely dependent on levels of qualification gained at 16+. This, in turn, was strongly influenced by social class, which was itself a major independent factor in explaining career route. Gender marked out strongly the type of occupational area likely to be entered (Griffin, 1985) and ethnic origin further restricted opportunities for some groups (Blackman, 1987; Cross and Wrench, 1991). Finally, Banks *et al.* (1992) show that geographical location was a significant factor, due to variations in unemployment and job opportunities.

Such analyses often imply a structurally determinist viewpoint that seems to understate the contested nature of social reproduction and the degree of choice that faces many individuals. For example, although Furlong (1992) acknowledges the importance of what he calls the 'subjective realities' of young people in making career decisions, the nature of his work makes it difficult for these to be examined. His and other similar large scale survey studies provide valuable descriptive data, but do relatively little to help us understand how and why such patterns persist. Contributors in Bates and Riseborough (1993) provide snapshot insights into the widely differing experiences of different groups of young people and show how, once on a chosen route, they are socialized into a narrow, focused set of goals and ambitions, for some groups significantly different from those with which courses were begun (Bates, 1990; 1993). They do not, however, fully explore the processes by which the original choices were made.

In examining career decisions from within a similar sociological research position, Roberts (1968; 1975) argues that decisions are not determined by the individual but by 'opportunity structures' in the youth labour market, which are strongly influenced by the nature of industrial organization and employment, government regulation and social class.

Bourdieu and Choice

At first sight, Bourdieu's work seems to fit with this academic literature. Like some of the studies cited above, Bourdieu's fieldwork usually concentrates on patterns of relations, and he is deeply suspicious of an individual subject's own understanding of actions and reasons for them. For example, in *Homo Academicus* (1988) Bourdieu gets close to exploring issues of choice. He describes and analyses the complex inter-relationships between 'positions', 'dispositions' and 'practices' amongst French university academic staff in the 1960s. These seem to leave little space for individual choice; for example, of views about what counts as academic activity or even political belief. Rather like Furlong (*op. cit.*), Bourdieu can be read as demonstrating that subjective choices of individual academics are actually determined responses to the 'relations of force' within which they are locked.

Indeed, Bourdieu seldom talks explicitly of choice or decision making in *Homo Academicus*, and when he does, the use of inverted commas clearly indicates a spuriousness which he sees in the term. For example, he argues that 'the success of a university career depends on the "choice" of a powerful head' (1988, p. 93). By 'head', he means an academic leader and figurehead. But this choice is not a real choice, for it 'expresses that sort of sense of inextricably intellectual and social investment which leads the best qualified supplicants towards the most . . . prestigious position' (pp. 93–4). This picture mirrors very closely the ways in which research shows that middle class, white, male young people more easily fit in to the more prestigious courses and jobs (Roberts, 1993). As we analysed our data and thought deeply about the relationships between choice, decision-making and career progression, we felt that parts of Bourdieu's theorizing offered the best available way to explain what we had found. This was because one of Bourdieu's concerns was to distance himself from two polarized positions in French intellectual thought in the middle part of this century — the structuralism and implicit determinism of Levi-Strauss and his followers on the one hand, and the existentialism of Sartre on the other, with its assumptions that we are all really free agents, if only we have the will to change our lives. There are some parallels between these intellectual polarities, and those already described between sociological research literature and recent policy writings around the transition to work. Bourdieu was exploring the middle ground, and so were we.

The Training Credits in Action Project

When we began this research, Bourdieu's work was far from our minds. We did not plan the research as he would have done. Rather, we approached the enquiry from within an interpretative framework (cf. Smith, 1989). We were primarily concerned to understand the meanings the Training Credits scheme under investigation had for the participants engaged within it, and sought any means to do so. We adopted an 18 month longitudinal perspective to data collection, with four interview sweeps. After each sweep, data was analysed and used to focus questioning in subsequent sweeps. We studied the second cohort of Training Credits trainees, following 10 young people from their final term in school until they were 15 months or more into their training. Sampling was in two stages. We began by interviewing 115 school pupils, mainly in small single gender groups. Of these, 91 were in year 11 (age 16 approximately) and 26 in the 6th form (17–18-years-old), 59 were boys and

56 girls. They were attending six secondary schools, selected to give geographical spread. Pupils were selected, by their careers teachers, as being likely to at least consider using Training Credits. We also interviewed ten careers officers and eight careers teachers from those schools.

From the 115 pupils, we selected 14 to follow through, though this was rapidly reduced to 11 and eventually 10. They were selected as interesting cases who would be using Training Credits — with a gender mix, from different geographical locations and working in different occupational areas. We attempted to balance cases where unusual features were apparent with those that appeared to be more straightforward. For each trainee we also interviewed parents, employer(s), training providers, careers teacher and careers officer.

Interviews were semi-structured and tape-recorded. Each researcher took responsibility for whole networks, to maximize understanding of inter-relationships. Regular team meetings ensured consistency of approach and we used standardized but open-ended interview schedules, separately drawn up for each stakeholder group and each of four interview sweeps.

Analysis was at three levels which over-lapped chronologically. We began by examining each stakeholder perspective separately. Secondly, we took each trainee as the centre of a network and built up his/her career story through a mixture of stakeholder perceptions. Analysis was done through repeated listening to tapes, to tease out harmonies and dissonances within and between perceptions. Thirdly we focused on specific issues raised by both these types of story and by relevant literature, and synthesized these elements heuristically into a more comprehensive, theoretically rich picture of the Training Credits scheme and decision-making within it.

The Research Findings

This was a large research study. The findings are therefore far too complex and detailed to be adequately summarized here, but have been described more fully in Hodkinson *et al.* (1996). Here I shall concentrate on career choice and decision making, as these were the areas where Bourdieu's work was of most relevance.

We asked the 115 pupils why and how they had decided on a particular course of action for the next year and beyond. From those who had made decisions, some patterns emerged. Many said that they were influenced by relatives or neighbours who worked in the same fields. However, this 'influence' was more subtle than simply listening to advice. It was grounded in long term experiences:

> [I want to be a] light vehicle mechanic . . . most of my family have done it already — my dad, my brother, my grandad and people like that. [For work experience] I went to [garage name]. I like it all, just like fixing things and taking it out on test drives . . .

> . . . They [my parents] wish I'd go into secretarial work because they think it's not a girl's thing . . . But he [dad] says if it's what I want to do I should go for it. (year 11 girl)

I did want to be a mechanic but I don't want to do that now. Well, no-one employs girls really. They all want men. Well, I asked a few garages and they said they wouldn't take you 'cos it was a girl. I prefer hairdressing. It's warmer . . . Dad laughed, he thought I'd do something like that. I'm always doing stuff with my hair. (year 11 girl)

I intend to leave school at the end of the year going to college part time on the building trade. My dad does building so I'll be able to work with him. He's got contacts as well like if I want jobs. I'd rather work with someone else but . . . he'll take me on. (year 11 boy)

Previous work experience strongly influenced many pupils, some positively and some negatively. In some cases it helped them in getting a job:

I want to do hairdressing YT. I was looking for a Saturday job and my mate had had . . . two offers so I thought I'd go for it, hairdressing, and I ended up really liking doing it . . . Before I wanted to go into hotel work but I did my work experience and hated it. Fussy, it was too fussy, especially doing it at [named hotel]. (year 11 girl)

I'm getting on to engineering, a firm in [named town]. Well it's a training, a two year training placement, but they're taking me on at the end. Let me go on to do another two year course at the tec. [FE college] . . .

. . . It was my second choice, after computer programming. I'm getting a night school course to learn all that stuff . . .

. . . My stepdad works for [named firm] . . . and I started working there. Then when we joined the 6th form we had to do one day a week work experience, so I decided to do it there. And they choosed me out of four other people. (year 12 boy)

Some of the pupils have particular interests which they would like to incorporate into careers, and childhood ambitions sometimes survive in some form. Enjoyment of a job was often felt to be an important consideration.

Well I've wanted to do that [caring] since I was 7. I wanted to be at work. First I wanted to be a nurse, then my mum was in hospital two or three weeks ago and decided I didn't want to be a nurse just in case my family was in there. So I decided to carry on with the disabled . . . in a school . . . I've got a disabled family, disabled cousins and friends. (year 11 girl)

Some changed their minds, while others were still unclear and undecided:

I'm working with my dad painting and decorating . . . because I enjoy doing it. I work like after school and at the weekend, at the moment anyway, and I enjoy doing it. I changed my mind 'cos I was working with my mum . . . shop work. But I changed my mind about doing that one 'cos I thought it might not suit me. So I'm doing this one [painting] now. (year 11 boy)

A few described considered decision-making leading up to the choice of a job.

I started off doing geography and maths [A levels]. Geography didn't work out for me, and then, the maths course, they had a half way exam and unfortunately I didn't achieve the right result to carry on to the Upper Sixth. So I carried on with economics, and took up doing accountancy in my own time. I originally planned to go to University, but once I decided I wanted to be an accountant and with the geography and maths, I realized I wouldn't get in . . .

. . . The main aspect was a friend of mine who works. He's actually doing his accountancy technician training with a firm in [named town]. We were talking through, I like working with figures. I like to think I'm good at maths, so I thought that would be a nice job for me to do. It appeals to me after starting the accountancy course. It's sort of become more attractive and keeping it all laid out . . .

. . . I've talked through various careers. At first I wanted to go in the RAF but that went out the window when I failed the eyesight test . . . So then I looked at manual work. I like engineering, I've worked as a mechanic for a year as a Saturday job. That appealed to me, but after working there for a year it made me see what it was really like. So then I moved to look at what I was really good at, what I enjoyed doing, and accountancy was the main result, after talking it through with them [parents] and my friend as well and the careers people here. I sort of talked it through and looked at all the aspects of accountancy and the best one that I thought would be for me was a technician working with the figures and numbers. (year 13 boy)

This data could not be adequately explained from either of the two polarized positions described in the literature (see above) but, rather, appear to require a combination of the two. It seemed to us that these quotations demonstrated three key qualities. Firstly, the pupils describe making decisions. They have all been instrumental, to a greater or lesser extent, in determining what career they will eventually follow. Secondly, they appeared to have largely rational reasons for making their choices and for changing their minds. They are often choosing jobs they know a lot about and the source of information is often an insider who has no vested interest in 'selling' a vacancy and whose judgment they can trust because they know them personally. Alternatively, the information comes from actually doing some aspect of the job themselves.

Finally, these rational decisions were pragmatic. There are several dimensions to this pragmatism. The decisions were based on partial information which was localized, being based on the familiar and the known. The decision making was context-related, and cannot be separated from the family background, culture and life histories of the pupils. The decisions were opportunistic, being based on fortuitous contacts and experiences. The timing of the decisions was sporadic, in that decisions were made when the pupil felt able to do so and were reactions to opportunities as they were encountered. Decisions were often only partially rational, in the sense of being influenced by feelings and emotions. They were partly intuitive.

The career decisions of these young people can only be understood in terms of their own life histories, wherein what Bourdieu calls *habitus* had developed and evolved through interaction with significant others, and with the culture in which the individual has lived and is living. I am using 'culture' to describe the socially constructed and historically derived common base of knowledge, values and norms for action that people grow into and come to take as a natural way of life. As young people grow up, they absorb and reinterpret meanings drawn from the culture which they inhabit.

We used habitus to encapsulate the ways in which a person's dispositions are partly individually subjective but also influenced by the objective positions and cultural traditions in which that person lives. As discussed in Chapter 2, habitus involves more than perceptions. Bourdieu sees it as deriving from, and being part of, the whole person or body. This concept was particularly useful, because it can incorporate multiple and over-lapping identities; for example as tennis player, sister, mother and shop assistant.

Bourdieu says relatively little about the ways in which the habitus of certain individuals develop, or their personal cognitive strategies. He seems to have no need either of accounts of particular psychologies. What follows, therefore, may deviate from anything which he himself would accept. We argue that, from childhood, young people amass conceptual structures (schemata) which serve as tools for understanding aspects of their experiences (Rumelhart, 1980). A schema structures what a person knows of the world, by filtering out 'irrelevancies' and allowing sense to be made of partial information. In this way, two lights seen from a car in the dark can be turned into a cat or an approaching vehicle. A repertoire of schemata contributes to the dispositions that make up habitus. As new experiences are gained, schemata are modified and developed and as they change so does what is recognized in the surrounding world. In this interactive way, the life history of the individual shapes and is shaped by his/her common sense experience. In choosing any action an individual uses his/her own dispositions. We finally conclude that no-one can step outside such personal development and therefore decision-making can never be context free.

Young people make career decisions within what we refer to as *horizons for action*. The horizons are the perspectives on and possibilities for action given in any field or intersection of fields. Such action includes choice, as the latter has practical consequences. We can see how the dispositions of habitus and the positions of education and the labour market both influence horizons for action and are inter-related; for perceptions of what might be available and what might be appropriate affect decisions, and job or training opportunities are simultaneously subjective (perceived) and objective (out there).

Because 'schemata' filter information, horizons for action both limit and enable our view of the world and the choices we can make within it. Thus, the fact that there are jobs for girls in engineering is irrelevant if a young woman does not perceive engineering as an appropriate career. On the other hand, we have seen an example of a young woman who considered working in a garage, because her life history was such that this particular, stereo-typically male occupation was seen as both possible and plausible.

It is also possible to widen our analysis in order to incorporate the ideas of capital in the field.

The Training Credits Field

Within the Training Credits field, a wide range of stakeholders with different positions, dispositions and capital (economic, social and cultural) interacted. It was by thinking in Bourdieu's terms that we were able to do two vital things in interpreting the data. Firstly, it was possible to retain some sense of individual decision making and agency on the part of the young people. As players in the field they had capital, which they used to try to achieve the ends they desired, remembering, as has been already explained, that their actions in using their capital, and the availability of capital itself, were themselves both constrained and enabled by their habitus and their individual horizons for action. Secondly, the notion of field allowed us to simultaneously acknowledge that the actions and choices of the young people were inseparable from the actions and choices of the other players, also using their own capital, derived from their own habitus, and located in their own horizons for action. A couple of examples will illustrate this point.

Clive wanted to work selling cars. He decided on this career because he had always liked cars, and because he did well on work experience and in a part time job with a local garage. The job he eventually got was specifically created for him, in that same garage. As the employer put it:

> The people who work for me are hand picked, and we tend to take someone when someone suitable came along for what we want to do, rather than, if you like, being inundated with enquiries, or whatever. . . .

> As he [Clive] progressed along [working part-time, whilst at school], he became obviously higher than the average ability . . . and he seemed ideal to come and work with ourselves. So I then obviously discussed this with his parents, before broaching the subject with him, because Clive, being very keen on cars, would have said yes to that anyway. I'm not interested in having someone employed here just to have a dead end job. . . .

> He's a very very nice young man, exceptionally so. . . . His whole family are. Which is another basis for when we employed him. Having met the whole family, and done business with them, . . . giving ourselves an insight into them, they are very very pleasant, and you can see just why he's the way he is.

We might interpret this as Clive using his cultural capital in order to get this placement, and making a decision that he wanted to work with cars in this particular garage. However, his eventual placement also depended upon the way in which the cultural capital of his parents was used to his advantage. In this context, the employer had the most capital and the greatest access to power. From the dispositions that made up his habitus, positioned as a working class small employer in a local community, this employer decided that he needed another worker, and that Clive was the right person for the job. Of course, some of the capital which Clive used only had value because of the dispositions of this employer. Had he applied for another job, where the 'relations of force' between the positions and dispositions of himself, his parents and the employer had been very different, he might have had less cultural capital available. It is quite possible that the very attributes which helped him get this job would have handicapped him for some others.

Helen's story (see Hodkinson *et al.*, 1996) raises similar issues. She was also taken on, coincidentally in a garage, this time as a car body sprayer. Once more, she got the placement through complex inter-relationships between herself, her father and the garage owner. Just like Clive's employer, this man saw his new trainee as having the appropriate attributes to fit his needs, as located in the dispositions of his habitus from his position in the field. For example, he explicitly told us that all his workers came from 'good working class families'. Helen fitted that criterion, which gave her cultural capital that a middle class young person, or, probably, someone of ethnic minority, would not have had.

A very interesting aspect of Helen's case was the fact that she was given a placement to train in a stereotypically male job. By examining what her employer told us, and by using the concepts of habitus and horizons for action at an individual rather than a group level, this breach in the normal, stereotypical pattern can be understood. For this employer, the fact that Helen was from a good working class family, whose 'pedigree' he knew and valued, was more important than her gender. This, he told us, was because he had already employed another young woman as a car sprayer, and she had been highly successful. He took this other young woman on, because she came with a man whom he rated as one of the best car sprayers in the area. When he managed to attract this man to work for him, the woman was, in his terms, 'part of the deal'. Because she had been successful, he was now prepared to take Helen on. In other words, the dispositions which made up his habitus had changed slightly, in the light of his experiences and, in changing, had strengthened Helen's cultural capital.

Sometimes, relations of force within the field resulted in conflicts. Where this happened, it was often the young person who lost out, for they had less capital than most of the other players. Ironically, this happened to Helen, six months after she had begun her training. At this point in time her employer decided to end her placement. As a result, she eventually had to abandon car spraying as a career, and, in our last contact with her, was working as a shop assistant. The details of this case have been fully described elsewhere (Hodkinson *et al.*, 1996), but it remains unclear whether or not her gender had any bearing on the dismissal.

The final way in which Bourdieu's concepts helped interpret the data, was that it enabled us to see the field as more than either a set of structures or a set of rules. The practices of the different players in the field and their relations to each other and to the structures of the field contributed to the constitution of that field. This could be most clearly seen by comparing what the Training Credits scheme planners thought should happen, with what actually did. Again, a concrete example makes the point.

As has been explained, the scheme designers believed that the scheme would work as follows. Becky, let us say, would decide what she wanted to do. She would then use her voucher to allow her to choose the best training to meet her needs, in cooperation with her placement employer. The assumption was that she would find an employer first, and that together they would choose the training. But the field was not structured by the rules of the Training Credits scheme. Becky had wanted to become a nursery nurse, but decided she could not face the full-time course recommended to her for that career. She then went to a training provider, who, having talked to her, searched around for any training placements he could find. He approached a dentist he knew, and asked if he would take on another trainee. This dentist did not really need anyone, but allowed himself to be persuaded to say yes, partly because he trusted the training provider to send someone who would fit in. The provider asked Becky if she wanted to give it a go, and she said 'yes'. She told us that she was not sure if she wanted to be a dental surgery assistant, but that she was enjoying the placement.

Almost none of this should have happened if the field had been determined by the scheme rules. The training provider chose the employee, rather than the other way round. But the existing relationship between the two of them, with their associated practices, derived from their dispositions and horizons for action, were much stronger than the official rules. It was the relations and practices of these and other players which constituted the field.

Career Progression: Moving beyond Bourdieu

As I have demonstrated, Bourdieu's inter-related concepts of habitus, capital and field proved a powerful heuristic device in making sense of the career decision making revealed in our data, avoiding a polarized explanation focused either on social structures or individual free choice. We used these ideas to present an explanation for some of the practices found in the field, and, indeed its structure. However, we also found it necessary to extend the basic theory of practice for use in our own context; in particular, to explain the underlying processes of career progression.

Strauss (1962) suggests that we often describe careers according to either of two metaphors. The first is that of the career ladder. This metaphor has already been identified as implicit in much of the recent policy literature on post-compulsory education and training in England. The other metaphor for career development, according to Strauss, is that of cooking an egg. Whether we poach it, fry it, boil it or scramble it, it will always be recognizably an egg. This metaphor is seen in studies which emphasize the segmented nature of career progression due to factors such as class, gender or ethnicity. Working class males, let us say, can develop in a variety of ways, but their central 'working class maleness' will always allow the expert outsider to predict the range of opportunities and types of trajectory that they will follow. We have seen that career patterns in large populations are indeed strongly patterned by social class and other factors (Furlong, 1992; Banks *et al.*, 1992; Kerckhoff, 1993; Roberts, 1993). However, it is a fallacy to apply models based on the explanation of patterns in large populations to the interpretation of the actions of single individuals. There can be a logical circularity about such trajectory models. Because the patterns resulting from behaviours of many people can be measured, it is sometimes assumed that they are a sufficient explanation for the individual actions that they are made up of. Having made that assumption, individual behaviours, based on class, gender and ethnic identity, are then assumed to 'explain' the patterns with which we started. Some find this sort of determinism in Bourdieu (see criticisms in Part I).

For the individual, Strauss (1962) claims that neither the ladder nor the egg metaphor for career development is appropriate:

> Development, then, is commonly viewed either as attainment, or as sets of variations on basic themes. In either case, you as the observer of the developmental pattern are omniscient; you know the end against which persons are matched, or you know the basic themes on which variations are composed. Neither metaphor captures the open-ended, tentative, exploratory, hypothetical, problematical, devious, changeable, and only partly unified character of human courses of action. (p. 65)

He goes on to talk about career development as a series of 'turning points'. 'These points in development occur when an individual has to take stock, to re-evaluate, revise, resee, and rejudge' (p. 71). Strauss claims that turning points are found in all parts of our lives, including occupational career. In many careers there is a predetermined structure to these turning points, some of which involve formalized status-passage. However, even within organizations where official structures resemble ladder-like trajectories, many individuals fail to match the predetermined norms. He describes, for example, problems of pacing and timing, and of mismatch between personal motivations and official structures.

In many life course studies, similar notions of turning points are often used. Denzin (1989) calls them 'epiphanies'. Working in Finland, Antikainen *et al.* (1996) talk about life changing learning events, whilst Alheit (1994), writing about youth unemployment in Germany, talks of 'biographical discontinuity'. In all cases, the central idea is the same. At a turning point a person goes through a significant transformation of identity. Career development can be seen as an uneven pattern of routine experience interspersed with such turning points. Within each turning point, career decisions are pragmatically rational and embedded in the complex struggles and negotiations of the relevant field.

In our data it was possible to discern three different types of turning point. *Structural* turning points are determined by external structures of the institutions involved. One such structural change comes at the end of compulsory schooling, when young people have to choose whether to stay in full time education or leave. Other turning points are *self-initiated*, that is, the person concerned is instrumental in precipitating a transformation, in response to a range of factors in his/her personal life in the field. Finally, turning points are *forced* on some, by external events and/or the actions of others. This happened when Helen was made redundant by her garage owning employer.

As a person lives through a turning point the habitus of the person is changed. Sometimes this change resembles incremental development, as when one of our trainees changed from trainee farm worker into full-time student at agricultural college, but remained en route for his chosen career of farm manager. On other occasions, a turning point results in a much more dramatic transformation, as when Helen changed from car sprayer to shop assistant.

Most studies using the idea of turning points and epiphanies (Antikainen *et al.*, 1996; Denzin, 1989; Strauss, 1962) concentrate on the turning points rather than the interspersed periods of routine. Yet turning points are inseparable from the routines that follow and precede them, and those routines are of central importance to career transformation. There are several different types of routine, and we identified three in the Training Credits study.

Some routines are *confirmatory*. That is, they reinforce a career decision already made, so that the new identity develops broadly in the way in which the subject hoped and intended. Such confirmatory routines can also be understood as part of the development of habitus. The divide between routine and turning point is largely arbitrary. It is the combined effect of the two which is important.

Another type of routine is *contradictory*. This time, the person's experiences undermine the original decision, as he/she becomes dissatisfied and either begins to regret an original change or, alternatively, decides that the current experience is no longer adequate or appropriate. One of our subjects, Laura, went through two contradictory routines, in a shop and later in a nursery school. In both cases, after a very short confirmatory period, her experiences made her less and less satisfied with her lot and she resigned. The result of such contradictory routines is to undermine the identity assumed at the previous turning point. The result can be either a self-initiated further turning point, a change in job location whilst still continuing a career, or the development of coping strategies such as a focus on home or leisure interests to deflect attention away from dissatisfaction with work.

Other routines are *socializing*. That is, they confirm an identity that was not originally desired. As we have seen, Helen wanted to be a car body sprayer, but was made redundant. When she first took another placement in a record shop she saw it as a stop gap and still intended to recommence her car spraying career as soon as the opportunity arose. However, six months later she had become socialized into seeing herself as a shop assistant, intending to continue car spraying only as a hobby. It was the turning point combined with the socializing routine that followed it that brought about her transformation of identity. Bates (1990; 1993) describes a similar process as a group of young women were socialized into the role of caring for the elderly and their original ambitions to work with children were cooled out.

As we envisage them, routines and turning points can only be understood in combination with habitus, horizons for action, capital and field. The notion of a 'horizon' of action links Bourdieu's epistemology with the Husserlian phenomenology as referred to in Chapter 2; for example, through the work of Schutz (cf. 1962/1982). In turn, these ideas help explain how habitus can change as circumstances change. In so doing, it clarifies the point that habitus does not determine our actions or futures in a mechanistic way such as Jenkins (1992) suggests. Rather, there is a reflexive relationship between positions, dispositions, practices and relations (Bourdieu and Wacquant, 1992b). At any one moment in time, what people do, therefore, is contained by their horizons for action, which are partly, but only partly, derived from the habitus. However, as people act, as others around them also act, and as positions within which they are located change, so their habitus is modified. For most of us, for most of the time, modifications to habitus fall within the patterns of trajectory identified in studies of the transition from school to work, and, in different contexts, in Bourdieu's own writing. However, in relatively unusual but far from rare circumstances, significant transformations can and do occur.

Implications for Policy and Practice

There is space here for only the most brief discussion of the implications of this research (see Hodkinson and Sparkes, 1993; 1994; 1995; Hodkinson *et al.*, 1996 for a more comprehensive discussion). In this chapter, I will concentrate on two points.

Firstly, there is clearly an urgent need for policy and practice on the provision of careers education and guidance to recognize the complex nature of career decision making, and thus attain more realism. At the time of writing, English policies and practices are focused on individual action plans with careers officers, which are supposed to take place once a comprehensive careers education has prepared the ground. All is geared to making a correct decision. Guidance is officially valued as a means of achieving such correct decisions, which are seen as a means of increasing efficiency of resource use, as fewer young people will drop out of the courses they have chosen (Audit Commission, 1993). This approach cannot succeed, because, as our analysis demonstrates, there can be no such thing as a 'correct decision'. Choice is a pragmatically rational process. Further, people and their situations change, so that what was appropriate in June may not be so even by September. Yet, young people do make decisions and many value the careers guidance they are given. In the current policy climate, therefore, the guidance services face a double dilemma. They are expected to achieve types of decision which are unreal and unrealistic. Yet if they fail to demonstrate their effectiveness in applying such a policy, the value of guidance itself may be unfairly thrown into doubt.

Secondly, there is a futility about using notions of choice in Credits which drive an educational or training market. It is the complex relations in the field which determine the choices young people make, and, as our research shows, the ownership of a voucher does little to change these relations of force in that field. Attempts to improve the quality of education and training, or to improve the lot of disadvantaged young people, therefore, need to be based on different and more sophisticated strategies, developed with an understanding of the complex realities of the education, training and employment fields.

Chapter 7

Higher Education *Field*-work: The Interdependence of Teaching, Research and Student Experience[1]

David James

Introduction

Teaching and research are increasingly regarded as separate entities in higher education, to the extent that there is now a literature which explores the nature of the separation and the prospects for various forms of reintegration. However, as Rowland put it in a recent article, '. . . the category distinction between teaching and research may owe more to the demands for accountability than to logical or pedagogical differences between academic roles' (Rowland, 1996, p. 13).

The topics of research study can be seen to be similarly constructed; that is, more by the demands of a political field than the conceptual apparatus of practitioners. Indeed, such practitioners might have good grounds for regarding themselves as better informed observers of practice than those politically placed to research it. We might draw a parallel with student experience and views about teaching in higher education, which for all its potential richness and diversity is increasingly conceived in terms of the narrow measurement of various forms of customer satisfaction.

As Rowland also notes, Bourdieu sees notions like teaching and research as impediments to understanding because they obscure practices and underlying principles. This chapter attempts to show how a Bourdieuian approach to the study of practices in higher education can open up new ways of understanding research, teaching and student experience — not as separate entities, but as dimensions of a particular *field*. It begins with a brief indication of the nature of Bourdieu's work on higher education. It then turns to look at some contemporary treatments of the relationship of teaching and research and the way student experience is conventionally discussed. This is followed by some case study data from a UK university faculty: one major theme of this data is discussed within an approach in keeping with Bourdieu's methods and analysis. The result is an interpretation which highlights possible degrees and types of relatedness and interdependence of teaching, research and student experience.

Bourdieu's Work on Higher Education

Of all the areas of social life studied by Bourdieu, it could be argued that it is the study of higher education that demonstrates his integrity in terms of the willingness he shows to subject his own world to a form of 'participant objectification' in a way that many scholars, even sociologists of education, seem reluctant to countenance (see for example Burgess, 1984; Walford, 1992, p. 197). Higher education has certainly been something of an abiding concern in the work of Bourdieu and his collaborators over the last 30 years or so. For Robbins, as we saw in Chapter 3, Bourdieu has 'been prepared to turn his intellectual training against itself'. Robbins (1993a) has also suggested that this work on higher education can be divided into three emphases, which correspond roughly with the 1960s, 1970s and 1980s. However, despite this division, Robbins also stresses that there is a composite picture of Bourdieu on Higher Education, and the later work interacts with and incorporates the earlier work. The early work is characterized by Bourdieu's 'Algerian vision' in which, following the destructive influence of French colonialism, a social and cultural reconstruction is conceived as possible via educational means. Important elements of this vision were extended to France, where Bourdieu saw parallel structured inequalities which had become part of the established order. This approach was developed into a 'sociology of higher education', in which existing data on the underrepresentation and underachievement of working class students in French higher education was supplemented with new data and explained in terms of relative cultural proximity to the curriculum. The term 'cultural capital' was used here to denote variations in the amount and type of cultural endowments (Bourdieu and Passeron, 1964/1979).

As we saw in Part I, this work, like other sociological analyses, played its part in contesting predominant assumptions about how differences in educability could be attributed to 'natural' differences of intelligence. However, unlike some other accounts, it went on to suggest a solution to the problem along the lines of cutting free the culture of higher education from its class anchorage, instituting a 'rational pedagogy' which would deal in independent, autonomous discourses that would not advantage one group over another.

Robbins suggests that the 1970s saw a break with this 'Algerian vision'. *Reproduction* (Bourdieu and Passeron, 1970/1977) was based on a wider range of researches, included more prestigious parts of the French system, and presented a more pessimistic view. Here concepts such as 'pedagogic action' and 'symbolic violence' were presented as a series of logical propositions which appear to claim universal applicability. Regardless of the truth, validity or utility of any actual content, a pedagogic process is more or less efficient by virtue of how well it enables an interest group to reproduce itself. This principle, it was suggested, applied to all educational processes and provided the means to understand them. The shift in emphasis from the earlier work is considerable, in that Bourdieu moved from a discussion of rational pedagogy (an idea dependent on the possibilities of a kind of cultural 'free zone') to a discussion of the cultural being 'arbitrary'. Education systems are engaged in the reproduction of competing social interests and groups, and as Robbins puts it, 'the success of pedagogic work in every specific context could be measured in terms of the degree of identification established between individuals and institutions. Pedagogy was transformed from an instrument of instruction to one of socialisation' (Robbins, 1993a, p. 157).

This analysis connected to other work in the 1970s which began to tackle the relationship between competing fields, and especially the means by which fields distinguish themselves from each other. Of particular note is Bourdieu's attempt to grapple with the relationship between the fields of education and of employment, which continually try to appropriate and accommodate one another's interests:

> Just as in the conflict between the religious and the secular, that between education and employment takes the form of strategic and reciprocal appropriation: the field of employment seeks to appropriate the values of education whilst the field of education seeks to accommodate the field of employment. (Robbins, 1993a, p. 156)

Examples of these two processes might include the adoption of educational means (such as a curriculum and certification) in management training, or the incorporation of work-based learning — or employment competencies — into the curriculum.

The work on higher education of the 1980s takes up earlier fieldwork and analysis and reinterprets it with a focus on institutions and their relationships with individuals. Robbins mentions *Homo Academicus* and *La Noblesse d'Etat* in this context, before suggesting that each successive phase of work has accommodated what went before without invalidating it. The 'composite picture' includes the idea that through work like Bourdieu's, people might acquire sufficient knowledge of the institutional constraints in which they are enmeshed to enable them to change or modify those institutions.

Robbins' article gives us a useful overview of the development of Bourdieu's thinking in relation to higher education. Later in this chapter, I will make use of direct quotations from a work more recently available in English, namely *Academic Discourse*, with a secondary purpose of giving a little more detail of Bourdieu's approach. Subtitled 'Linguistic Misunderstanding and Professorial Power', this work is an English translation of an otherwise unaltered text from 1965 entitled *Rapport Pédagogique et Communication*. Like *Homo Academicus*, it is another example of what Bourdieu means by the term 'participant objectification'.

Some of the main themes of Bourdieu's work on higher education are reflected in the empirical concerns of this chapter. For example, it focuses on aspects of the academic world, indicating a willingness to subject this world to scrutiny. It illustrates how processes which appear to be simply educational in nature can be understood as a form of pedagogic work and socialization within a particular field. However, before turning to these issues I would like to give brief consideration to the ways that teaching, research and student experience are most often discussed.

Teaching and Research: Complementarity or Conflict?

In educational literature the relationship between teaching and research is often discussed at a fairly high level of abstraction, rather than in terms of the practices of tutors and students. Some writing has pointed to notions of complementarity, where the learning of tutors and students amounts to the same set of processes in a university setting. This idea is quite explicit in Newman's *The Idea of a University*, a collection of lectures written in 1852, which, as Scott reminds us, continues to have a great deal of rhetorical importance (Scott, 1993). The notion of complementarity also appeared in the work of Parsons and Platt (1968) for whom teaching and research were 'two aspects of a single task' (p. 517). It could be argued that both the way that the now-defunct UK Council for National Academic Awards (CNAA) regarded research, and the element of 'scholarly activity' in the contracts of many ex-polytechnic university staff in the UK both bear witness to a basic assumption about a relationship in which research necessarily *underpins* higher education teaching. This is the usual 'direction' for thinking about complementarity. It is also possible to find examples of a form of complementarity in the opposite direction, such as those argued as desirable by Garnett and Holmes (1995) in their discussion of the 'symbiotic' relationship between teaching and research. There were examples of this in my own study (see below) and in that carried out by Rowland (1996), where on some occasions teaching provided academics with opportunities for data collection or analysis or the development or refinement of research questions, depending on the field and the level in question.

Nevertheless, most recent work points to *conflict* between the activities associated with teaching and research. The American work of Fox (1992) investigates publication productivity in a large stratified sample of social scientists in four fields. She looked at declared interests, time commitments and 'orientations' of faculty members and measured the degree to which these variables were associated with publication productivity. She concludes, for example, that:

> ... the findings point to a strain between research and teaching ... Those whose publication productivity is high are not strongly invested in *both* research and teaching. Rather they appear to trade off one set of investments against another. (p. 301)

and

> ... with some variation by the degree-granting level of the faculty's departments, the data indicate that, in practice, good — or at least more productive — researchers have less classroom contact with students, spend fewer hours preparing for courses, and consider teaching much less important than research. Thus, the findings suggest that research and teaching ... activities do not represent aspects of a single dimension of interests, commitments, and orientations, but are different dimensions that are at odds with each other. (p. 301. Emphasis in original)

Another study has shown that tutors who 'could give evidence for actually using results from their own research explicitly in their teaching published less than those who could not' (Magennis and Woodward, 1992, cited in Elton, 1992, p. 257). Elton also mentions an Australian study by Ramsden which suggested that attitudes towards teaching were inversely related to attitudes to research amongst academic staff. Fox herself goes on to discuss some of the 'institutional dilemmas' which may underlie the strain or tension. At the heart of the discussion is the issue of the greater status or prestige of research activities and the fact that academics are often hired to do one thing and rewarded for doing something else. Elton suggests that the 'prestige gradient' across institutions might be made less steep by the separate funding of scholarship, which he argues has to underpin good research *and* good teaching (Elton, 1992).

What Is Student Experience?

The abundant discussion about teaching, research, and the relationship between them in Higher Education contrasts with a much less-developed discussion of student experience, at least in the UK. The editor of a recent book entitled *The Student Experience* noted in her introduction that the experiences of students in higher education had long been a concern amongst American researchers, but that in the UK we tended to see students primarily as *learners*, so little work had been seen as necessary (Haselgrove, 1994). In a climate of customer charters and marketization, vague notions of the quality of the student experience have become a prime justification for measuring the quality of teaching, and have therefore become subsumed within teaching as a topic of concern.

A distinction is often drawn between the experiences of those going on to Higher Education after compulsory schooling, and 'mature' students. In a review of a wide range of literature on mature students I carried out recently, I found that the predominant representations drew on a range of sociological and psychological ideas, but were concerned to isolate mature student experience as distinctive from other student experience on the grounds that mature students were intrinsically different. These 'species' conceptions (as I called them) did not allow for situated and contextualized accounts of student experience (James, 1995). In fact, student experience appears to have only recently come to be problematized, and this is usually on the grounds that a particular group of students (mature, black, female, part-time, overseas, disabled etc.) are likely to have a different experience in some sense. But different to whom?

It seems to me that there are two principal groups of conceptions of student experience in circulation in UK higher education. The first of these I would call *marketing* conceptions, which have as their main focus such things as the 'brand' of higher education represented by different institutions and the demonstration of 'customer satisfaction'. Promoted by governments bent on increasing their control by reducing academic autonomy in the name of quality (cf. Alderman, 1996), the idea that students are customers lies behind the UK government's *Charter for Higher Education*. This was launched as part of a wider 'charter initiative' in the early 1990s which sought to make all kinds of public service more accountable. The idea that students can be considered as customers has been roundly criticized for its poverty in relation to the purposes of higher education (e.g., Barrett, 1996). However, marketing conceptions sit well with the vast bureaucratic apparatus that links institutions to funding bodies and quality agencies.

The second type of conception is one I will call a *learning* notion of student experience. Here the stress is on the effective utilization of students' previous experiences in the curriculum and in teaching methods, sometimes through arguments about the validity of affective (as well as cognitive) dimensions and sometimes through the application of various models of the learning process derived from humanistic psychology. Closely related is the issue of the recognition of students' previous experience-as-learning through the use of accreditation processes.

These two conceptions can of course overlap. For example, it can be argued that quality of teaching would be improved by making more use of students' prior experience, and that this would enhance the student experience itself and become quantified via evaluation questionnaire responses. In any case, the two conceptions do not exhaust the ways in which student experience is discussed. Occasionally, there is public debate on matters as practical as poverty amongst students. Other conceptions are quite abstract, treating student experience at the level of the 'nourishment of persons' in social, political, moral, practical and intellectual dimensions (Goodlad, 1995). But whichever concepts are adopted, surely student experience has to be understood in relation to practices of teaching and research, as part of a larger picture?

Teaching, Research and Student Experience at Robbins University (RU)

I want to approach this problem via the presentation and discussion of some empirical data, before moving to illustrate what I consider to be theoretical ideas which help us to see the interconnections — indeed, the interdependence — of the triad: teaching, research and student experience.

Between April 1991 and November 1994 and as part of a PhD study (James, 1996), I conducted a series of interviews with a group of 21 mature undergraduate students (all of whom were over 25 years old on entry) and 9 tutors in the social science faculty of 'RU', an institution which came into being as one of the new technological universities after the Robbins report of 1963 had proposed a particular form of higher education expansion. Nowadays, it would be called an 'older' university in the UK context. The interviews were spread over almost four years, so followed some of the students through the whole of their degree courses and a little beyond. A case study approach was adopted after a considerable amount of epistemological deliberation. Put briefly, the approach reflected an interest in the subjective meanings held by actors in a carefully chosen case, with a view to achieving high validity in interpretation and some generalization at the level of social relations (as opposed to the 'morphological level' in the words of Bertaux, 1981). Practically, this meant that I did not want to seek out 'representative' individuals to build up a sample consisting of the 'right' numbers of men, women, black people, local people and so on. Instead, I took the mature students on a particular cluster of courses as my case study, and contacted all those over 25 years of age within social science degree courses in one institution. They constituted a third of a particular year's intake, which was a very high proportion for the subject disciplines, the institution and indeed the sector. What was perhaps less surprising was that 15 were female, 6 were male, and all were white. Later, and partially through a developing familiarity with some of Bourdieu's work, I came to the view that I wanted to achieve a situated understanding of mature student experiences that would not become trapped in individual subjectivities, nor lost in researcher-defined categories. Examples of both these tendencies in research were explored and rejected for their apparent construction of mature students as a 'species', as mentioned earlier. The interviews were augmented with some observation, some use of documentary sources, a research diary and a large number of conversations. Interviews with students had three areas as their main foci: successful and unsuccessful learning experiences; the perceptions of mature students held by various significant others; and perceptions of the self. The interviews with tutors, reflecting by then a degree of analysis of student interview data, had as their main foci a comparison between teaching first and second year courses, the nature of good teaching, and the relationship between teaching and research.

There is only the space here to give a brief indication of the sort of data generated and the themes which were constructed within it. For the purposes of illustration, I will begin with an issue which was of almost universal concern amongst students. The earliest interviews with students produced an astonishing level of dissatisfaction with teaching during the first year of the courses, in both of the formal categories (i.e., lectures and seminars). Students all had recent experience of being taught in other formal learning situations (which included a wide variety of courses leading to advanced level academic; advanced level vocational; professional; and access to higher education qualifications). Three of the students were themselves qualified teachers of adults, whilst the prospectus suggested that none of their teachers were so qualified. The following two extracts from student interviews are typical in terms of the impressions they convey. Both come from experienced and successful learners: Cathy is herself a qualified teacher of adults with a management qualification and some years of FE teaching experience; Maurice has a series of professional qualifications as well as the A levels he took to gain entry to the university course:

David   ... have you seen any good teaching?

Cathy   There hasn't been any great teaching ... they don't teach as such. [Elsewhere] I've seen great lecturing which was very stimulating indeed, and made difficult things seem very easy ... [here] most of the teaching is terrible, not engaging the room at all, mumbly, teaching things so they don't sound interesting but which turn out to be interesting once you've found out all about it yourself ... [amongst the lecturers, I can think of] two boring, one cynical and one who really doesn't want questions or interruptions. In lectures you want someone who is quick, interesting, in control and who orchestrates the room and the material. (first interview)

And similarly, in another early interview:

Maurice   A lot of the teaching is bad. In fact a lot of it isn't teaching at all. Mostly they don't teach us at all. They should, you know. I think it's just vanity to think that you can just throw material at the students. Most of the lectures are totally boring. Next year I will go to fewer and fewer lectures. I'm better off spending the time reading. Good teaching involves enthusiasm for the subject; enjoyment; and is dependent on appreciating the levels of the student and the teacher . . . Some of them talk non-stop for two hours. (first interview)

In nearly every one of the 21 initial interviews with students there were negative evaluations of the quality of teaching in first year lectures. By far the most commonly expressed wish was for a greater degree of structure in lectures, though there was also sufficient agreement among the students for me to construct an 'ideal lecture' which included such features as lecturer enthusiasm, student participation, clear signposting and the clear display of key terms. These interviews produced almost as negative a view of seminars, which seemed only rarely to conform to a shared ideal of participatory discussion. Departures from the ideal included what I termed a 'casualization', reported by Myra, Maurice and Mike, where seminars would sometimes 'break down into general chatting'; or conversely a 'formalization' reported by Melanie, Bruce, Helen and others, where the seminar amounted to a lecture given by a student reading a paper or turned into an impromptu 'mini-lecture' given by a tutor:

David   What are they [seminars] like, are you satisfied with the way they are run?
Bruce   No.
David   Why not?
Bruce   . . . well we all take turns in presenting the seminars, and there are some people who try to turn them into mini lectures. I mean I would expect a seminar to be someone talking for five or ten minutes, and then a discussion. It often works out that they're talking for . . . you know, it'll be an hour long, they'll be talking for maybe 40 minutes, then you'll get a very brief discussion at the end of it.
David   . . . so you don't get much of an opportunity . . .
Bruce   We don't. I mean if I was doing one, presenting a seminar paper in this room, I'd make sure I put the chairs in a circle first. There doesn't seem to be any effort to get the dynamics right. It's quite often one will sit in front of a row of desks so you're looking at the back of people's heads. They [seminars] are not as lively as I'd like them to be. (first interview)

There were interesting comparisons with what the tutors told me about their efforts to run successful seminars. What intrigued me most, however, was that these strongly held views about teaching began to change after the end of the first academic year. The change to a more positive assessment of the quality of teaching was sometimes attributed by students to a relative personal naivety during the first year, and sometimes to changes in the way in which teaching was organized or carried out. Doreen, along with several other students, was concerned that I should revise her earlier assessments of the quality of teaching:

Doreen   . . . the thing is I've learnt a bit more now, the tutors here are really under a lot of pressure to do research stuff, which is a government-pushed thing, isn't it . . .

David   Absolutely.

Doreen   . . . I heard there was some question . . . that lecturers' pay will be based on students' views of them . . . it's a big contradiction, isn't it, saying well you've got to do loads of research, but that means that you can't give time to the students, and then the students are going to . . . I mean most of them [tutors] would have a bill at the end of the day, wouldn't they? You owe us! . . . I think you just come to terms with it in the second year. (second interview)

This exchange reflects an increasing appreciation amongst the students of the circumstances under which tutors work as well as the identification of some contradictory pressures. Bruce recalled a colourful mnemonic which helped to explain the situation:

Bruce   I was told that it was fourth priority, teaching.

David   What here?

Bruce   Yes.

David   Who told you that?

Bruce   (Tutor X), he says it works out P,R,A,T, remember PRAT, it's publish, which is first priority, research, admin work, and teaching is four.

David   . . . PRAT! That's interesting. Do you think that's a view shared by most of the staff here? Or is it at least a set of priorities they would hold?

Bruce   I would imagine so, yes.

David   OK. Do you feel that that gives you a suitable environment in which to do a degree?

Bruce   I find . . . well I used to do the Open University before I came here, so I was used to working on my own. I don't find it a problem, though I would certainly have found it a problem if I had been a younger student straight from school . . . I think I'm probably in a minority. (second interview)

Bruce sees his recent experience as an independent learner helping him to survive in an environment in which teaching is 'fourth priority', and other comments of his suggest that an initial surprise soon gave way to acceptance of this state of affairs.

As the course progressed, students felt they were less of an undifferentiated mass in the eyes of tutors, and felt that their tutors were more interested in them. Some also felt more challenged (e.g., Melanie) and that there was much more thematic connection between their courses (e.g., Maurice) which seemed more integrated (e.g., Rachel). Theresa pointed to a great improvement in the second year, particularly in a course taught by the very same person she had considered to be the 'worst lecturer' during her first year. Myra spoke for many of her contemporaries when she said 'the whole feeling of the second year is different'. Such shifts in the perceptions of students between year one and year two (particularly with regard to sympathy with the plight of tutors and recognition of the demands on their time in addition to teaching) prompted me to ask tutors about the relationship between teaching and research-related activities. I had expected to find areas of comple-mentarity and conflict between these two, and also some evidence for assessing the degree to which they enjoy differential status. Even so, I was surprised by the size and nature of the gap that became apparent. Trevor Turner, who had for several years been responsible for the overall management of the cluster of degree routes, was the first to alert me to this:

David   I'd be very interested to know how you think of the relationship between teaching and research. I know that it has been in the news a fair bit in recent years, but more really your perception, particularly for yourself, of the relationship between teaching and research.

Trevor   Yes. Well I think in an ideal world, the good teacher is also the good researcher, and the up-to-date researcher, and I can think of certain people in . . . [this Faculty], either here now or, you know, relatively recently with us who are like that. I fear though that the other problem is the researcher who doesn't really want to teach very much and certainly not undergraduates, and certainly not poxy spotty first years . . . I'm ser-ious, you know that really is the attitude. And I even know of colleagues who tell students well if you've got any problems don't bother to see me, you know, go and see someone else. And they're supposed to be tutors (. . .) first year teaching in particular is seen as you know a sort of a flock as opposed to later years where your own research interests can come into their own and be drawn upon. As far as I'm concerned I really don't like that at all.

Later in the interview we turned to the topic of various tensions between teaching and research:

Trevor   I don't think there ought to be [tensions between teaching and research] . . . I think there are enthusiastic and very well advanced re-searchers here, recognized in their field nationally if not internationally. They're also very good teachers. But unfortunately I think a good re-search record is no guarantee that you can teach. This University now runs a sort of introductory series of sessions for new lecturers that's obligat-ory for all new lecturers . . . but it is very much part time, and you know, the come-back, if you don't make the grade on teaching, seems to be, so far at any rate [gesture indicating insignificance] because presumably some of them don't make the grade. On the research side I mean we have someone on the way out now who's not made the grade on the research side, but there's never been any query about that person's teaching ability.

David   Yes.

Trevor   What I'm trying to say is that it has been possible, more often than not I think to get away with being a good researcher and an indifferent teacher. It's been quite possible. Now whether we are into the sea-change now where that's not going to be the case in the future I'm honestly not sure . . . So people who are strung out on the lecturing and director of studies and what have you will be on a slow track to big promotions. Erm, you know the fast trackers, are still on the research side quite frankly.

One of Trevor's 'fast tracker' colleagues made this same point quite independently, citing Trevor himself as someone who would be unlikely to gain promotion by virtue of the fact that his teaching and course management functions were systematically undervalued. In Rowland's study, heads of department all saw research as more influential than teaching when it came to promotions, and Rowland makes some interesting links between this point and male and female stereotypes (Rowland, 1996, p. 9). However, further reflection on the interviews with staff alerted me to a more revealing point. I found that the most senior and established academic staff seemed much less capable of discussing (or were much more reluctant to discuss) issues of pedagogy than were those lower in the academic hierarchy. Taken together with a range of other data, this left me with a strong impression that 'pedagogy' was on the whole considered unproblematic, or that what notions of pedagogy there were in circulation tended to be subordinate to conceptions of an academic discipline.

Practices in a Field: The Academic Discipline

The academic discipline can be taken to refer to both the forms of knowledge and the knowledge communities in question. As Becher has shown, these are empirically much the same thing, though they may be separated for analytical purposes (Becher, 1989, p. 20 and p. 53). Following Bourdieu, the academic discipline may be regarded as a field within which there are relative positions of dominance, subordination and equality with regard to the holding of different stakes, or forms of capital. The academic faculty or department itself occupies such a position in relation to other similar faculties or departments, nationally and internationally. A particular faculty will also have a 'standing' in relation to other component parts of the institution. Within the department or faculty individuals and groups will also have relationships which may be objectified to some extent by describing their holdings of various forms of *capital.*

One of the most important forms of capital here is revealed in the differential holdings of prestige and honour associated with different types of activity (teaching and research, for example) and with different types of publication and research contracts. Symbolic capital like this is sometimes codified (as in the results of the UK quadrennial Research Assessment Exercise, which awards groups of researchers an ordinal score between 1 and 5; or in the number of prestigious Research Council grants held), but is essentially beyond most measuring instruments. As Becher reminds us, it is not political power or wealth which are primarily at stake, but *reputation* in the academic community that is the most highly prized commodity (Becher, 1989, p. 52). Reputation is a form of symbolic capital. It is related, sometimes converted, to other forms of capital, such as cultural capital (e.g., differential holdings of valued knowledge) and economic capital (the resources — and jobs — which flow from success in research competitions). I do not want to suggest that the academic discipline is a kind of grand causal variable in all this. Rather, it seems to me to be a key to getting some purchase on a whole series of overlapping social spaces (or fields) within which power relations are played out. I am concerned to 'break in' to the complex interlocking circles which go to make up the social reality of studentship.

The systems of power relations *within* the faculty can be similarly conceived. The operation of a field both rests upon and regenerates belief in the value of the capital(s) at stake in the field. I have drawn attention to the negative evaluations of teaching in the first year of the cluster of courses, and to the shifts in perception amongst students after they had spent some time in their second year. The unfavourable comments on the quality of teaching in the first year are produced with reference to other educational settings. This is what one would expect from the nature of my questions and, perhaps, from mature students with so much recent experience of other educational activities which had led them to new opportunities and the prospect of major life changes. Yet it is important to recognize that my approach as a researcher invited the invention of models of teaching which were divorced from their social, cognitive, disciplinary and physical contexts. Interviewees were, in effect, being asked to devise an ideal-typical picture of a lecture or seminar and to measure their new university experiences against the ideal. For all their willingness to do this, the exercise could only produce a technicized picture which rested on factors assumed to be trans-situational, mostly qualities within the individual (teacher or student). However, there is another way in which data on differences between first and second year perceptions may be accounted for.

It could be argued that the early part of the first year of the degree programme is too soon in the students' academic socialization processes at RU for them to make fully contextualized judgments, in the sense of being fully acquainted with the stakes in the particular field. By 'socialization' I also mean the gaining of a sense of the game, or sense of (a particular) reality, such that the habitus becomes attuned to the stakes of the relevant fields sufficiently to operate strategically. As individual students come to value locally conventional constructions of the subject discipline and its values, they will also increasingly value the processes by which it is constructed, that is the pedagogy in operation. The comments of tutors suggested that this pedagogy is one that is quite fully subordinated to progression through the subject matter of the academic discipline. This point is illustrated particularly well by Mick Taylor, who described part of his approach to teaching by comparing what happened with groups of students within the academic discipline to what happened with those from outside:

> **Mick** . . . I should make an observation which I'm still, I haven't sorted out after many years, is the teaching that I do to first year students on a Business Studies course, and the teaching that I give to Sociology students, on what is virtually the same course, though it's continuing to diverge, it had its origins in the same course. The business students are a different animal as it were, and . . . I feel I've got to do more missionary work with them, I've got to keep arousing their interest and keep them interested, and I've got into the habit with them in probably 50 per cent of the lectures we start with a question, which I write on the board, and they

either respond spontaneously, with immediate replies, or jot a few things down on paper, and we get into debate. So for example, recently in one of those lectures I put on the board the question 'In what ways might management control be restricted by social factors external to the workplace for example family and so on . . . make some comments' and we had a debate which went on . . . and then we had another one on — which is always a good one for discussion and getting them involved and interested — was on gender, erm, 'is it in the interests of business to have more equal opportunities . . .'. Doing that with those students they get very interested, and they get used, some of them are participative types by nature, and doing it that way tends to maintain their interest better. The sacrifice you have to make is you don't transmit as much knowledge because you spend part of the time debating these questions. Now why I mention that is because, by contrast, I do relatively little of that with the sociology students, A) because I think I've got to transmit more basic knowledge, and B) because in the past, I've never been as successful in stimulating this dialogue . . .

David   That's interesting. Are they assessed at the same sort of level in the same sort of way at the end of the course?

Mick   They're both assessed by course work and exam, yes, although the level is probably lower . . .

David   The level is intentionally different, is it?

Mick   It's slightly lower for the business students, so [facial gesture suggesting this was of concern]. And as I say, I haven't quite worked out exactly if I'm on the right lines with this, if I should be using the same approach with both groups, and I've continued to work on those principles, it seems to work with both groups.

A common interpretation of this sort of situation might be that Mick is simply responding differently to different student needs, or learning styles, or preferences (see for example Honey and Mumford, 1992): the students are, as Mick put it, 'a different animal' in each group. However, such explanations only tell half the story. In Mick's articulation of the comparison he seems at one and the same time aware and unaware of the way in which his practices might reproduce the primacy of the relatively pure strain of the subject discipline. There is a 'sacrifice' with the Business Studies students, but both he and his Sociology students would seem to see any such sacrifice as inappropriate for their needs. I would suggest that it is more than coincidental that, as a newer and more eclectic discipline, Business Studies would be valued somewhat lower than Sociology in a traditional academic hierarchy. This is not to say that in some other fields it cannot be, or is not, valued more highly.

The pedagogy embedded in the academic discipline would appear to be one which places a high premium on independent endeavour and achievement. Rather as joint publications are judged in some circles to offer a less valid indicator of academic worth than sole authorship, so the means by which academic progress of students in higher education is assessed is predominantly (exclusively in the case study setting) by reference to individual assignments and individual examinations.

As Pamela and other students suggested during interviews, seminars are not able to provide the discursive element that some tutors and students claim to expect of them. Perhaps this is because they function as opportunities for practising and demonstrating the acquisition of the individualized skills associated with the presentation and re-presentation of the discipline. If this is correct, they are, predominantly, opportunities to show that one can do what tutors do in lectures. This suggests that there is very little scope for individuals — tutors or students — to make much difference, even if they rearrange the furniture in the way that Bruce implied would be useful (see above). As Bourdieu *et al.* suggested in a work first published in 1965, with reference to the links between professorial power and language in French higher education,

> The chair from which a lecture emanates takes over the tone, the diction, the delivery and the oratorical action of whoever occupies it, whatever his personal wishes. Thus the student who delivers a paper in place of his professor inherits the rhetorical manners that go with the chair. So rigorously does the physical situation govern the behaviour of both students and lecturers that attempts to establish dialogue between them quickly degenerate into fiction or farce. Questions to the audience are often mere rhetorical gestures, belonging to the exposition, rather than interrupting it . . . The lecturer can call on students to get involved or voice objections, but there is really no risk of this ever happening. (Bourdieu *et al.*, 1994, p. 11)

Our present cultural and temporal distance from this picture should not blind us to its continued relevance. Interestingly, Bourdieu and Passeron go on to say how, whilst they may from time to time question this situation and request change to it, students are

> . . . in many of their most deeply held attitudes . . . firmly wedded to the traditional teaching situation. For this also protects them, and it is one of the few models of scholastic behaviour open to them . . . most students remain faithful to the traditional space of communication, even in their imagination. (*ibid.*)

A little later, it is suggested that 'the space of the teaching relationship imposes its law of distance so strongly . . . because it captures and expresses so much of what the university, as an institution, stands for' (p. 12). The evidence and argument underpinning these comments is about physical spaces and the practices of individuals within them. Such physical spaces are a manifestation of social relations which set the context for activities, which then contribute to the furtherance of those social relations. The crucial point for my own data here is that interviewees' accounts of teaching and learning cannot be taken as face-value evidence of the quality of a 'service'. These accounts are even problematic as indicators of customer satisfaction or dissatisfaction with a service. Students are never mere recipients, even where the dominant pedagogy constructs them as such (cf. Barrett, 1996).

Where teaching and learning operate as the individualized inculcation of the academic discipline, there is less to them than meets the eye. Becher's interviews produced a similar picture to mine. Amongst the academics he talked to,

> the large majority preferred to focus on their activities as seekers after knowledge rather than as communicators of it. The reason for this, it might be inferred, is that membership of the academic profession — at least in elite departments — is defined in terms of excellence in scholarship and originality in research, and not to any significant degree in terms of teaching capability. Had the programme of interviews included non-elite institutions, the pattern of responses might have been different. However, if it is indeed the leaders in the field who set the norms, those norms do not for the most part appear to include pedagogic considerations. (Becher, 1989, p. 3)

Bourdieu and Passeron talk of attempts to rationalize pedagogy in higher education as clashing with an existing view of teaching amongst academics 'whose disdain for the "elementary" nature of a reflexive pedagogy reflects the superior level of the education system which they occupy' (*op. cit.*, p. 6). Roger Fender, one of the most senior of my interviewees was often cited by students as being a giver of particularly clear lectures. Nevertheless, he was reluctant to exchange 'cliches' with me about teaching method, and complained of the need to think up 'silly examples' to make social scientific content more accessible, all the while being aware that I came from an Education faculty. Perhaps the relative ease with which I was able to arrange interviews with tutors was also related to a sense of security engendered by established reputations within the subject discipline. After all, what would an eminent academic in a University have to fear from a registered student from a (then) Polytechnic, least of all an *Education* faculty in a Polytechnic?

A pedagogy which amounts to little more than a rationalization for a structure designed to inculcate an academic discipline is also unlikely to problematize notions like student ability or capability with any degree of sophistication. Something akin to the 'ideal pupil' conception developed by Becker, and subsequently employed by other educational researchers, seemed to help me to understand the way that student capability was seen. Ideal pupils are those whose actions support teachers' interests, but of greater significance is the idea that teachers might categorize other pupils with reference to their departure from an ideal. A similar notion — that of the 'fictive student' — featured in Bourdieu and Passeron's account of the relationships between professors and students in French higher education as one part of a 'fiction of linguistic understanding which the academic world needs in order to function':

> ... academics display two complementary and contradictory attitudes. They address themselves to fictive subjects, avoiding the risk of putting their teaching practice on trial. It is up to the student to cover the whole of the ground, and if he does not live up to the being which he ought to be — his 'being-for-the-teacher' — the mistakes are always wholly attributable to him, whether out of error or out of spite. Addressing the student as he ought to be, teachers unfailingly discourage him from

asserting his right to be only what he is. Moreover, they are able to justify their disdain for the real student, since only the fictive student deserves their respect, and a handful of 'gifted students' — objects of all their care — prove that the fiction exists. (Bourdieu *et al.*, 1994, pp. 16–17)

My interview with Paul Cooper, the most 'junior' member of academic staff (i.e., the least established in terms of conditions of employment), provided a very interesting parallel here. He spoke of the way in which many of his colleagues categorized students:

> [they] make all sorts of assumptions. For example, at . . . [admissions] interviews you get people saying, on the basis of a few minutes' interview and some comments on the form, 'Oh, obviously a two-one type of person'. How can anyone base that kind of judgement on just . . . it's appalling.

Another tutor described the first year as an opportunity for 'weeding out' students who feel below a particular threshold of ability or whose motivation was less than adequate. This tutor made no reference to the extensive admissions procedures which, for all their rigour, still seemed to him to produce a significant number of 'mistakes' each year. By the beginning of the second year, students had 'either left if they haven't got it, or they've learnt what it is'. But it is in relation to the final years of the degree programme that tutors made the most revealing comments as regards perceptions of student ability. For example, Bob Waverley told me about a colleague with whom he had shared several courses, and whose stance on teaching was quite clear-cut:

> [my colleague] is quite clear that he's only interested in the small number of exceedingly bright students, and he knows that and he says it without any degree of shame or upset. That's what he's interested in, and his system is great for people like that . . . he was one of the tutors I had working with me when I was doing the first year methods course, and he . . . came to see me at least once a year, usually twice, and said look, you're going to have to take this person . . . she can't learn anything from me.

This statement refers to one of the most senior members of staff in the faculty, whose *habitus* seems best understood in relation to the economic, cultural and symbolic *capital* of a *field* in which research activity almost eclipses teaching activity. The pedagogic elements of his practices are entirely subordinated in this field. The popular psychological notion of 'orientation to teaching' (see for example Samuelowicz and Bain, 1992; Gow and Kember, 1993) completely sidesteps this issue, giving the impression that a little re-education, though difficult to bring about, could change a teacher's approach. The data here suggests that we should not forget that it is the practices of Bob Waverley and the students which perpetuate the subordinated pedagogy as much as anything that the colleague in question wishes on his own. His *habitus* describes a sense of limits which is a practical, situational and structural product, and which cannot be reduced to a psychological construct like 'orientation to teaching'.

Conclusion

The foregoing discussion demonstrates that a Bourdieuian approach facilitates the interpretation of qualitative data on student experience in useful ways. Areas of study which on their own can become quite impoverished — such as measuring the satisfaction students express with regard to particular teachers or teaching methods — can be seen as part of a wider picture which connects structure and agency without losing sight of either. Once considered, this wider picture reveals that the discussion of teaching, research or student experience on their own involves too much reification and isolation to provide much insight. Using such concepts as *field*, *capital* and *habitus* helps us to see the integrated and interdependent nature of teaching, research and student experience. The approach taken suggests that students' daily experiences are intimately connected to such structural features as the processes of quality measurement of research. It also suggests that the pedagogy in operation is only understandable in relation to the academic discipline and the nature of the academic community in which it is located. It is of particular interest that a strong early reaction against this pedagogy by students gives way to an acceptance of its terms, as students become socialized, and their *habitus* reconfigures within the new *field*. The interests and priorities of students come to be intricately locked together with those of tutors, whose general level of investment in teaching reflects the generally low stakes attached to pedagogy in the particular academic setting. Although it is possible for higher education institutions or their critics to take refuge in disconnected and decontextualized notions of 'high quality teaching' or 'good practice' (even to the extent of producing league tables), these notions are rather limited if we wish to understand student experience. A dynamic and relational approach to the social practices of students and tutors helps us to see a degree of interdependence which conventional conceptions obscure.

Note

1   I would like to thank Frank Coffield, Harold Berlak and the participants in a session at the 1996 European Conference on Educational Research for comments on an earlier version of this chapter. I would also like to thank the students and staff at RU for their time and trouble during the period of fieldwork.

Part III

The Practice of Theory

In Parts I and II in this book we have been concerned to give an account of Bourdieu's theory of practice and show how it might be used in particular research contexts. In effect, we have offered both theory and practice. However, the main underlying theme of this book is that these two are not separate but joint activities as they both involve the same epistemological issues. The present chapter acts as a link between the practical applications in Part II, and the discussion of basic guiding principles for conducting research from a Bourdieuian perspective to be found in Chapter 9.

Chapter 8

The Practice of Theory

Introduction

This chapter is entitled 'The Practice of Theory'. It is concerned with what it is to use Bourdieu's theory in practical research. However, its main preoccupation is not methodological technique but the theme of 'reflexivity'. Bourdieu writes very often of the fundamental role of reflexivity in his work. The subtitles of the English versions of two of his books (1990a; 1992 with Wacquant) refer to 'Reflexive Sociology'. The arguments he sets out for this again implicate the whole way we construct research, the role of theory in it, and how conclusions can be formulated. In brief, he is drawing attention to how we develop an understanding of a topic of research, and what the nature of the understanding might be. However, it is clear that what he has in mind is a very different concept of reflexivity than is conventional in western social sciences. Nowhere in his work will the reader find a chapter entitled 'how to be a reflexive researcher'. Similarly, despite claiming a pivotal role for reflexivity in research, what he calls 'objectification of the objectifying subject', he rarely involves himself in the kind of personal researcher introspection which may be expected from such a phrase. Nevertheless, Chapter 3 discussed how, in a book such as *Homo Academicus*, Bourdieu does analyse his own professional milieu and his part in it. This is an example of objectifying the research field and the researcher. Derek Robbins also commented on the way Bourdieu's own history shaped his practical and theoretical concerns. This chapter extends these issues to the researchers whose contributions make up Part II of this book.

What follows is something of an epistemological experiment, an 'essai' in what might be possible. What is at issue here is the researcher and their research 'eye'. The chapter steps back to consider the researchers themselves before going on to the practice of research itself. Following the drafting of the chapters in Part II, the four authors were invited to contribute material to this present chapter in the form of four 'reflexive accounts'. We wanted to examine how it was possible to objectify important aspects of the relationship between researchers and their various objects of study. In so doing, we are aware that the accounts sometimes cover biographic information and introspection in ways which are more personal than Bourdieu's own 'reflexivity'; although he does talk quite openly in places in terms of his personal social and academic trajectory and its effect on his research and writing (see for example Bourdieu and Grenfell, 1995; Bourdieu and Wacquant, 1992b, pp. 209–15). In order to guide the authors' reflection, we listed some possible dimensions of reflexivity, which we were able to discern from Bourdieu's discussion of it. Later we will argue that what is important in these accounts is the relationships they display, which, although necessarily present in the research, usually remain at an implicit level. This chapter tries to show how these dimensions might be individually expressed.

We start the chapter by giving a brief consideration to the nature of reflection and reflexivity in social research in order to better locate a Bourdieuian meaning. Our authors' 'reflexive accounts' are then presented thematically, using the device of a different typeface to distinguish between these and the main 'voice' of the chapter.

Reflection and Reflexivity in Educational Research

In modern western societies, there are few professions untouched by the notion of the 'reflective practitioner', which in its simplest formulation denotes a shift away from the idea of once-and-for-always certification of bodies of professional knowledge towards the idea of continual learning supporting professional problem-solving, requiring reflection-in-action and reflection-on-action. There is no reason to expect educational research (which is after all a profession for some people) to be any different.

However, the idea of 'reflection' in social scientific (including educational) research goes much deeper than this, touching on important and widespread shifts in the perception of what counts as valid knowledge and the means of attaining it. This is not to say that social scientists all mean the same thing by the terms 'reflexivity' or 'reflection'. Within one recent collection, reflexivity is presented as a criterion for judging the quality of research in times where the traditional touch-stone of objectivity has been abandoned (Henwood and Pidgeon, 1993); as the way to develop a critical stance on previous research paradigms (Jupp and Norris, 1993); and as a way of empowering researched people by assisting them to see the significance of their own actions (Papadakis, 1993). So how are we to make sense of the variety of meanings here?

Woolgar proposes that we think of a continuum, 'ranging from radical constitutive reflexivity to benign introspection' (1988, p. 21). At one end of this continuum, the relationship between the scientific product and the social world is seen as one of mutual interdependence and similarity, where, in Garfinkel's words, 'Members' accounts . . . are constituent features of the settings they make observable'. At the other end of the continuum, where the scientific product and the object of study are conceived as distinct entities, reflexivity is a 'concession' consisting of 'loose injunctions to "think about what we are doing"' (p. 22). Better termed 'reflection' than reflexivity, this activity has, as its goal, the task of increasing confidence in scientific conclusions by helping to confirm that the scientific product is indeed an accurate representation of (but nevertheless quite distinct from) the reality it portrays. Social sciences, says Woolgar, 'espouse distinction and admit similarity' (p. 22), leading to tension, not least in terms of reflexivity.

Arguing principally from a consideration of anthropology, Woolgar himself advocates a 'radical constitutive reflexivity'. This is achievable through the minimization of notions of the exotic in research; through making it a constant intention to look for the similarities between our actions and the actions of those studied; and by trying to 'recover and sustain the uncertainty which exists in the early stages of ethnographic enquiry' (p. 28). Furthermore,

> It is insufficient to reveal the actual circumstances behind the production of ethnographic texts, as if this revelation was itself a neutral, passive process. In short, we need continually to interrogate and find strange the process of representation as we engage in it. (pp. 28–9)

This argument is similar to one put forward by Hammersley and Atkinson for a 'reflexive ethnography' (Hammersley and Atkinson, 1983). Arguing against what they call 'naturalism' in qualitative research, Hammersley and Atkinson point to a paradoxical tendency on the part of naturalists to distance themselves from theory (not wishing to 'distort' reality) whilst seeking to uncover the theorizations of actors in social situations. In doing this, such researchers deny themselves the very tools they study in others. Ironically, this is linked to an epistemological project remarkably similar to that of the early physical scientists, attempting to observe the world 'as it really is'. A reproduction model of research follows which, like the correspondence idea of truth, relies on the ontological assumption that the social world is simply 'out there', waiting to be discovered.

Reflexive ethnography seeks to dispense with the 'joint obsession' of positivism and naturalism to maintain 'the distinction between science and commonsense, between the activities of the researcher and those of the researched' (*ibid.*, p. 14). It proposes a recognition that we are part of the world we study, and that reactivity, as a fact of investigatory life, is to be exploited rather than resisted. Scientific methods are merely refinements of techniques used in everyday life to understand, predict or control events, and scientific theories are a kind of 'advance guard' of common-sense thinking. These methodological implications of reflexivity are paralleled by implications for the practice of some research, where, it is claimed, there is a need for an 'experimentalist mentality' (*ibid.*, p. 18) to enable the constant comparison of data and explanations, much as encouraged within Glaser and Strauss's notion of grounded theory (Glaser and Strauss, 1967). Hammersley and Atkinson argue that both grounded theorizing and analytic induction go some way to overcoming the problems they have identified with naturalism, though they remain of the view that the first of these is substantially an 'over-reaction to positivism' in that it concentrates on the generation of theory whilst neglecting theory-testing.

Reflexive ethnography represents one influential set of ideas about the nature of reflexivity. However, this is by no means the only way in which the issue is discussed in educational research. For example, feminist researchers adopt epistemologies within which there are very strong notions of reflexivity. One example of this is where the researcher's own experience is a significant or sole source of data, making reflection indistinguishable from data-gathering. According to Reinharz, 'The impulse

... does not stem from opportunism or exhibitionism but rather from the desire to eradicate the distinction between the researcher and researched' (1992, p. 234). Reflexivity is also fundamental in models of action research and practitioner research. This is particularly true of one strand of action research which advocates the examination of practices by teachers in the light of their values (cf. Whitehead, 1993). Whatever the range of goals or objectives, action research usually elevates the improvement of practice to pole position. Commonly, it is the researcher's own practice that forms the focus, though occasionally a project will also realize something of the democratic flavour of Lewin's original thinking. Whilst there is not the space here to do more than mention such examples, it is clear that several notions of reflexivity are in evidence within educational research. This is not surprising given the wide range of other disciplines which educational researchers draw upon. In the context of this book, the next question must be whether or not an approach derived from Bourdieu offers us a notion of reflexivity which is distinctive or which promises to help us do anything beyond those we have seen so far.

Reflexivity for Bourdieu

... strictly speaking, knowledge of the conditions of production of the product is one of the conditions of rational communication of the findings of social science ... [however] ... The finished product, the *opus operatum*, conceals the *modus operandi* ... You are never taken into the back-rooms, the kitchens of science. (Bourdieu, 1993a, p. 158)

What does it mean to be taken into these back-rooms and kitchens? By way of example, let us take a translation of a contribution Bourdieu made to a Paris conference in 1975 on colonialism. Having raised the question as to why a group of social scientists should come together to discuss such issues, Bourdieu says:

If we've met here to talk about it, that's because we think it is interesting. But to say we are interested in a problem is a euphemistic way of naming the fundamental fact that we have vital stakes in our scientific productions. Those interests are not directly economic or political; we experience them as disinterested. The distinguishing feature of intellectuals is that they have disinterested interests, that they have an interest in disinterestedness. We have an interest in the problems that seem to us to be interesting ... All that is just a preamble to say that one should make it a rule never to embark on sociology, and especially the sociology of sociology, without first, or simultaneously, undertaking a self socio-analysis (in so far as that is ever completely possible) ... The subject of scientific discourse needs to be asked the same questions that are put to the object of that discourse. (Bourdieu, 1993a, p. 49)

In arguing that researchers must ask of themselves similar questions to those they ask of prior research, Bourdieu advocates the gaining of a situated understanding of previous scientific discourses and products, via the notion of field. This includes an understanding of how the scientific field in question also connects with other fields, in this instance the field of colonial power and the wider intellectual field at certain periods. Bourdieu also considers the sorts of difficulty we face when the very essence of what we want to know may reside in silences or absences, especially in documents. Orthodoxy and heterodoxy may be readily apparent, but what of doxa, what of 'everything that goes without saying'?

Bourdieu ended his short presentation to the conference on colonialism with a concise recommendation for a specific form of reflexivity:

> The important thing is to be able to objectify one's relation to the object so that discourse on the object is not the simple projection of an unconscious relation to the object. Among the techniques that make this objectification possible, there is, of course, all the equipment of science; so long as it is understood that this equipment must itself be subjected to historical critique . . . (Bourdieu, 1993a, p. 53)

This illustrates the centrality of the idea of a 'second break' with objectivism, something we saw introduced in Part I of this book. It shows that in a Bourdieuian approach, reflexivity has a distinctive meaning. It is not limited to the 'benign introspection' Woolgar identified, yet nor is it a sign of the wholesale pursuit of the re-unification of researchers and their objects of study via subjective meanings, such as is implied in his 'radical constitutive reflexivity' with its ethnography of the text. It is both of these and more. It amounts to an argument that the researcher's social relationship to the object of study is itself a necessary object of study. This act of *reflexion* involves a positioning of oneself in relation to fields (and therefore capital of various kinds) so as to reveal as much as possible of the nature of the sources and maintenance of one's *interest*. The elements of a reflexive social science for Bourdieu are well summarized by Postone, LiPuma and Calhoun, as follows:

> . . . in attempting to transcend the opposition between science and its object, Bourdieu treats science and scientists as part and product of their social universe. The scientific field can lay claim to no special privilege as against other fields; it too is structured by forces in terms of which agents struggle to improve their positions. Science seeks to analyze the contribution of agents' conceptions to the construction of social reality, while recognizing that those conceptions frequently misrecognize that social reality. By the same token, scientists' constructions of their own reality — the scientific field and the motivations for scientific behaviour — often misrecognize that reality. Consequently, it is essential to advance and endorse a reflexive science of society. (Calhoun *et al.*, 1993, p. 3)

The following accounts move towards this type of epistemological examination of the processes of the products of research.

Acts of Reflexivity

The authors of the four chapters in Part II were asked to comment reflexively on their own experiences of using Bourdieu's work in their particular research fields. These reflexions necessarily involved aspects of the authors' habitus and the academic space they occupied, both in carrying out the research and presenting it to their peers and other audiences. As a presentational device, we have grouped individual comments under a series of foci, which allude to particular dimensions of reflexivity. The thematic headings take us through the material in the following sequence:

1 Self socio-analysis: objectifying relationships between self, Bourdieu's work and the research object;
2 Objectifying relationships with the researched;
3 Points of theoretical departure;
4 Theoretical development;
5 Critical engagements; and
6 Reception in the field.

Given the nature of the issues discussed, there are inevitably many overlaps between the material presented here under each heading. Moreover, we have preserved the individual voice of each account as much as possible, rather than create a smooth narrative. The accounts are offered for illustrative rather than comparative purposes, and to throw up a range of particular issues.

Self Socio-analysis: Objectifying Relationships between Self, Bourdieu's Work and the Research Object

One of the main themes of the reflexive accounts is to do with the identification of facets of the researcher's own social trajectory and location, within various fields. This we may call 'self socio-analysis', to borrow a term Bourdieu has used himself. It reveals a little of the formation of individual *habitus*. The following extracts illustrate some of the possibilities that lie in this direction.

Diane Reay   Despite some major reservations I have increasingly used Bourdieu to understand and deconstruct my own position in both the research and the academic field. To a growing extent my research has become a process of self analysis in which I have needed to grasp at a conscious level my own dispositions in order to make sense of those of the women that I have interviewed. I, like the women, am deeply embedded in the research field I have been investigating. My own children attended Milner (one of two principal research sites), I worked as a teacher in the school for 20 years and still live in the catchment area. I also, like seven of the mothers that I interviewed, am dealing with the disjuncture resulting from contradictory class positionings. I grew up as a working-class girl on a sprawling council estate housing coal miners' families. Bourdieu's theory, in particular his concepts of habitus, field and cultural capital have been very useful in making sense of both the social space I have crossed and the contradictory position I occupy in the research field as a result. I have also started to write reflexively about my position as a female contract researcher in the academic field (Reay, 1997a) and the ways in which it parallels my earlier position within the wider social field.

David James   There was always some sense in which doing a study about mature student experiences was a quest to understand my own history, holding out the possibility that I would be enabled to answer fundamental questions about the way that educational processes had marked a number of significant turning points in my own life. Selection processes at the age of 11 gave me a real sense of educational failure against which to measure considerable success later on as a mature student in a degree course in one of England's most prestigious universities. Or again, a movement from under-confident child (to whom teachers seemed culturally far removed) to an adult whose professional work has often included helping established teachers to develop their confidence! I now feel that such a history cannot fail to engender some sort of fascination with the part that educational processes play in legitimation, or in the shaping of identities, or in cultural location and dislocation. Like Bourdieu, Derek Robbins has suggested that he may be described as an 'oblate', such that a lower middle class disposition finds expression in rigorous intellectual pursuit (and the accumulation of cultural rather than economic capital) (Robbins, 1991, p. 7). My own background in a 'respectable working class' family has some parallels to such a trajectory, yet the overriding impression is rather one of having travelled a great cultural distance, of a changed orbit, with various costs and benefits but no prospect of retracing one's steps. The main point here is that a particular personal and professional history has provided both the conditions for an interest in Bourdieu's ideas and an object of study for those ideas.

Michael Grenfell   I first came across Bourdieu as part of a sociology course during my undergraduate degree. This degree was in French Social and Economic Studies, so we studied Anglo-American sociology, history, economics etc. before specializing in the French equivalents. This was in the late 1970s, and Bourdieu had already made an impact in the Sociology of Education through the publication of *Reproduction* and his contribution to *Knowledge and Control*. Our first encounter with him, as students, was not really as a French sociologist at all, but simply as a contributor to debates in the sociology of education. In my final year, and after spending a year in France, I came to Bourdieu as part of a French Sociology course. As such I was able to situate him in terms of a whole French tradition: Montesquieu, Tocqueville, Comte, Marx (on France) Durkheim, Mauss, and later figures such as Crozier, Tourraine and Boudon. *La Distinction* was just published, and I read it in French. I still find it easier to understand Bourdieu in French than in English. I accept his language is often difficult — I have struggled with an odd page or two for many days in some cases. Generally, however, I find his language enjoyable as pieces of prose. At the time, I did not realize that my own education itself positioned me in a particular way with regard to Bourdieu, his work, and the academic fields to which it related. I was a sociologist (although not purely so, compared to other undergraduate courses), but coming from a French rather than an Anglo-American tradition. I read French and interpreted his works in their own cultural terms rather than through a translator's language.

At the time, it seemed to me that Bourdieu was addressing traditional debates in sociology in a much more subtle and sophisticated way than other sociologists. The connection with my earlier undergraduate studies was through *The Social Construction of Reality* (Berger and Luckmann, 1967), and Bourdieu seems to borrow their phrase: 'the internalisation of externality and the externalisation of internality'. In particular, I was impressed by the ways Bourdieu's approach seemed to go beyond the traditional concepts and notions in which many sociologists had got themselves bogged down: definitions of class, status and power, control/direction, rules, roles, subjectivity/objectivity, etc. Once one adopted a Bourdieu position, many of these debates became obsolete.

After graduating, I went straight on to teacher training. As one of my option courses, I took a Sociology of Education course. I was immediately struck, again, by how many of the 'hot' debates became rather 'non-issues' when viewed from Bourdieu's theory of practice; in other words, the problems discussed arose through a lack of theoretical and practical sophistication. I decided to write my major assignment on Bourdieu and Education. This turned into something of a magnum opus, and gave me the opportunity to read a lot more Bourdieu; not only the books but a whole range of articles in French and English, as well as various commentaries. I had great respect for my lecturer, who was an associate of Bernstein. Bourdieu was known as the 'cultural capital man'. Still, even after a long and careful discussion, I was amazed to find Bourdieu (or at least my account of him) being charged with determinism, schematicism, resistance to change, etc.; all the things I felt the work sought to avoid. Paul Willis' Learning to Labour was in vogue and I read it through a Bourdieuian eye, and could not understand why Willis had not himself made the many possible connections.

After working as a language teacher for two years I took an MA in Applied Linguistics. During the course, I was amazed how researchers in this area were still adopting relative positions of Objectivity (sociolinguistics) and Subjectivity (social psychology) without reflecting on the limitations of such, and indeed, seemingly oblivious to Bourdieu's efforts to propose a method which went beyond them. I completed a dissertation on a corpus of French, but I was too French, not a sociologist, not a sociolinguist, too philosophical. I understood such reactions in terms of Bourdieu's 'struggle of classifiers', as an attempt to position me (ultimately a form of symbolic violence) in terms of existing academic (legitimate) fields. I met Bourdieu on different occasions at this time: he sympathised and encouraged!

The first two of the above accounts focused on social location in a wide sense, whilst the third set out to position the researcher via a brief history in relation to formative events in the academic field. The next section takes the relationship between the researcher and their research a little further.

Objectifying Relationships with the Researched

For analytical purposes it is possible to separate the general issue of the positioning of the researcher in relation to the object of study from the changes and developments that occur as the research proceeds. Some of these are addressed in the following account:

David James   What of the relationships between the researcher and the researched in my study? Firstly I think we have to recognize that there are a number of ways in which mature student experience can be constructed and expressed as an object of study. These would include a focus on particular examples of interaction in learning situations through to a collective if rather abstractly defined 'higher education' experience. Taking for a moment the categories 'staff' and 'student', it is possible to make some observations about the way in which relationships developed.

In the first instance I had to negotiate access to a case-study setting. This involved the making of approaches in accordance with internal practices and structures, so there was an exchange of correspondence with a senior figure before any staff and students were approached directly. Like other researchers, I engaged in quite a lot of 'positioning' work, particularly when making arrangements for early interviews. By 'positioning' I mean seeking to maximize the success of attempts to establish contact by emphasizing the ways in which I could be said to be similarly located to the people I wanted to interview. With students I stressed that I was myself a mature student, and that I was (at the time) actually registered as one. I underplayed my employment as a lecturer working in higher education, though I did use letter-headed notepaper to add authority to an initial request for participation. By contrast, letters to staff emphasized what I had in common with them. They avoided any implication that staff interviews had been partially motivated by students' expressions of dissatisfaction with the quality of teaching. At the time there was mounting public criticism of higher education teaching, albeit often simplistic and unjustified: I knew that this, in tandem with funding cuts (known as 'efficiency gains') was taking its toll in terms of staff morale.

Similar points can be made about the interviewing itself. Research interviewing is sometimes discussed as if it began and ended with the skilful management of interpersonal relations. I would argue that all relationships with interviewees were characterized by a professionalism and a degree of mutual respect and were in keeping with the usual ethical guidelines. Yet in my interviews with both staff and students I became increasingly aware that habitus was also at issue. In any given interview, two histories, trajectories and current positionings were, to some extent, under scrutiny — mine and the interviewee's.

I believe that this goes some way to explaining why it was that some staff were more forthcoming than others when it came to detail about teaching, learning and assessment. In general, those with least capital in the local academic field (fewer publications, least involvement in externally funded research work) had much more to say about students, about their colleagues and about teaching, learning and assessment practices than those further up in the particular hierarchy. Some approaches would put this down to 'orientations' or 'investments' on the part of the academics interviewed, as if it was all a matter of individual choice. However, I would argue that the tendency is as much to do with my relative position in the academic field. As a holder of negligible symbolic capital in the particular field, some data would be more accessible to me than others. The rapport I enjoyed with staff in the lower positions in the field was a social product.

There are some parallels with the relationships I established with students. Sometimes they seemed to want me to be a kind of conduit for their many concerns about (for example) the way they were taught or assessed. Again, there were differences between them, and I did find myself being more 'strategic' when it came to interviewing students from completely different backgrounds to my own. This notwithstanding, I noticed how important areas of real commonality became in the achievement of a rapport in interviews. There were many examples of this, including the discovery by some interviewees that I had failed the 'Eleven-plus' and attended a non-selective secondary school, or when others found out that like them I had given up a secure and well-paid job during my 20s in order to become a full-time student. Perhaps the most dramatic example was when I cancelled an interview so that I would be present at the birth of my second daughter. When rearranged, the interview began with a long, lively and detailed chat about childbirth during which a cultural affinity (attendance at pre-natal classes, knowledge of pain relief choices etc.) found expression. It also went on — predictably in my view — to produce some particularly rich and interesting material which was very close to my fundamental research questions.

Defining the object of study actually proved to be a complex matter. I started out wanting to understand mature student experience, having assumed that other studies were right to simply claim this was a discrete object of study in its own right. Before long, however, I saw mature students first and foremost as students, but as students who were particularly good informants (in relation to me) about the practices of students and tutors in a university department. At one level this is because they tend to be learners with a range of experiences of educational situations which can be used for comparative purposes. Though important, this on its own does not explain just how productive the interviews were. My feeling is that this is mostly to do with the proximity — much of it authentic, some of it undoubtedly manufactured — between the habitus of the researcher and that of many of the researched.

Finally, my relationship with the researched and the research site must be understood in terms of a contrast with the groups of people and the institutions to be found in most educational research. Several writers have commented on the seeming reluctance of educational researchers to study their own situation or situations close to it, at least in the UK. Various reasons can be suggested for this tendency. At a purely technical level, it is much more difficult to maintain anonymity of a site when it is one of only a few possibilities and is located in a field in which there is a high degree of shared knowledge. However, there are other facets to this. Studying higher education is a risky business, and not just because a site is difficult to keep anonymous. Issues of power and interest are also involved. In the case of a university-based researcher studying a primary school, the power differential between the researcher and the researched is probably large, and it is the former's ethical responsibility to use this differential wisely so that the interests of the researched — and of course the research community (conceived collectively for this purpose) — are not damaged. Where the researcher studies an academic unit of organization in their own or a similar setting, the power differential may be absent or even reversed. What this contrast illustrates is that the preservation of anonymity of a research site is only partially to do with the care and ethical competence of the researcher. It is also a political function of the resources and motivation, or interest, of the researched, in relation to the particular researcher.

I would suggest that my own educational trajectory has produced a habitus which is sufficiently 'unbelonging' to make the taking of such risks possible. Bourdieu's theoretical tools have played a crucial role in both the substantive direction of the research and in encouraging a consideration of the positioning of the researcher.

To use Bourdieu's own terms, we might say that the general relation to the object of study, therefore, is the product of the researcher's habitus, whilst the negotiations and decisions he or she makes within the possibilities presented are examples of *strategy*. The scope for strategic actions is virtually limitless in one sense, but we are never in a position to do our research just as we please.

Points of Theoretical Departure

A third major cluster of material in the reflexive accounts is concerned with the way in which researchers started out with theoretical tools which came to be seen as inadequate for the task in hand, or which required augmentation to overcome some fundamental limitation. The following extracts give some indication of the possibilities for this kind of reflection:

Phil Hodkinson   As is explained in Chapter 6, we did not approach career decision making and the transition to work from the perspective of Bourdieu's work. Indeed, we did not originally intend to research career decision making at all. Rather, we started with the intention of exploring the meanings different stakeholders held of a Training Credits pilot scheme, their inter-relationships and inter-subjectivities, and the ways in which their practices and meanings were reflexively inter-related. However, working as we were within an interpretative framework (Smith, 1989), we did begin with two apparently, but not necessarily, contradictory assumptions: that there was no such thing as an external truth to be discovered, for the researcher is inevitably reflexively related to the topic and people investigated; but that what we know and understand through research is partly determined by the subject that is investigated, and that 'truth' is not merely a subjective construct of the researcher.

Reflecting on the research now, nearly five years since it first commenced, I am inevitably drawn to the question 'where did our theorizing come from?'. Indeed, I have written more extensively on this subject elsewhere (Hodkinson, 1996). In this section, that question can be reformulated into a more restricted form: 'what was the place of Bourdieu's thinking in the construction and evolution of our theorizing?' At a practical level, the relationship between his work, our data and our eventual theorizing is described in the chapter. Here I am more centrally concerned with the question of reflexivity.

One commonly held view of qualitative research is that thinking and theorizing should arise predominantly from the data (Glaser and Strauss, 1967; Strauss, 1987). Superficially, there is some evidence that this may have happened here. For example, the idea of pragmatic rationality came to us when we compared what pupils were telling us about the ways in which they made career decisions, contrasted with the ways they were supposed to make them in the scheme (Hodkinson and Sparkes, 1993). Similarly, we turned to Bourdieu's writing, together with that of Anthony Giddens, when it became apparent that we needed some new ideas to make sense of what our data showed.

But such a 'grounded theory' interpretation of what we did is grossly over-simplified. Though we did not begin the research with a clear focus on career decision making, or with a predetermined Bourdieu-centred theoretical frame, we did not approach the data with open, or blank minds. Indeed, we would argue that it is impossible to do so. Our choice of research topic, choice of research techniques and choice of which questions to ask in the interviews, were inevitably coloured by our prior understandings. With the benefit of hindsight, I would argue that we approached the research from within our horizons for action, which were simultaneously influenced by our own habitus, and by the positions we occupied in relation to our academic careers and the Training Credits scheme, and also by the characteristics of that scheme and of the people working within it. In Bourdieu's terms, we were players in the field of this research investigation. We had capital, but the characteristics of the Training Credits research field was determined by the relations of force around the project.

David James   . . . there is another way in which the relevance of Bourdieu's ideas came to the surface. During my time as a mature student on a full-time social science degree course in the late 1970s I came across the epistemological problem of reconciling structure and agency. With hindsight, I think that 'reconciliation' is the wrong term for what was on offer in sociological theory, at least as presented to me at that time. On the one hand, a highly structural Marxian theory and a number of its derivatives were doing battle with American functionalism and middle-range theory. On the other hand, interactionists, ethnomethodologists and ethnographers, sometimes allied to a politics of liberal individualism, developed a micro sociology which championed subjective meanings and their negotiation by actors, often drawing on the sociology of Max Weber. Although there were always exceptions, most new sociological texts could be read as belonging to one or another of these 'two sociologies'. I completed my course without taking the problem any further, putting it down to some sort of inescapable philosophical dichotomy. In any case, like most of those who study in higher education, I soon became, once more, *extra mural*, stepping back outside the walls of the university and developing other concerns. Nor did my new work as a teacher in further education cause me to revisit this particular dichotomy, since the vast majority of social science at pre-higher education level was constructed to exclude so fundamental a problem.

This perception laid rather dormant until some 13 years later, when I began the fieldwork connected with the PhD study. By this time I had read a number of studies of schooling, many of them ethnographic and many informed by an interpretivist sociology. My interests in methodology were stimulated by what increasing numbers of educational researchers were claiming about the relationship between empirical data and theory. Two prominent strands here were interpretive sociology and grounded theorizing, both of which, it was often claimed, could incorporate emancipatory goals (for example, 'giving voice' to individuals and groups whose oppression meant that a particular perspective was normally excluded or denied). By the time my study was under way, I had conceived my method and approach as a mixture of 'reflexive ethnography' and grounded theorizing.

But some problems are inescapable! There were controversies about the nature of theory in ethnographic work which were, at very least, mildly disturbing. I began to have concerns about whether anything of the diversity and change represented in my large volume of data could be adequately expressed within what had become an established qualitative tradition. Layder's critique of grounded theory resonated with these concerns. Whilst he acknowledges some strengths in the approach, Layder's account points to four serious limitations. Firstly, grounded theorizing highlights the immediately apparent and observable, deflecting attention from the interweaving of structural features. Secondly, and connected to the first point, concepts of power are usually rather narrow. Thirdly, grounded theory usually operates on the principle that data should limit theory, whereas there are good reasons for wanting it to guide theory instead. Finally, there is often an insistence that theory produced should be recognizable to the people studied, encapsulated in the notions of 'fit' and 'relevance' (Layder, 1993). This, I agreed with Layder, places unhelpful constraints on the researcher.

Layder's solution is a 'realist' approach to researching the social world. This is expressed as a methodological formulation, combining four levels of social organization (self, situated activity, setting, context) on a 'resource map' which has two main purposes. First, it reminds the researcher that whatever their primary emphasis, the other three levels of social life are always present; second, it enables the making of various connections with general social theory, allowing different kinds of theory testing.

I found a striking correspondence between Layder's proposals for a 'realist' social research and my first impressions of Bourdieu's broadest aims. Layder argues for the use of research strategies which integrate theoretical and empirical concerns, but also structures and practices, suggesting that 'setting and context are more profitably thought of as rather different but complementary aspects of social life' (Layder, 1993, p. 89). Macro and micro aspects of social activity are 'deeply embedded in each other, even when we are dealing with specific substantive details' (*ibid.*, p. 106). Concepts like habitus, disposition, embodiment and field must — if they do anything distinctive — facilitate thinking across these levels. As is well known, for Bourdieu 'The socialized body (what is called the individual or the person) is not opposed to society: it is one of its forms of existence' (Bourdieu, 1993a, p. 15).

Michael Grenfell   When I first came to educational research, I did not know about ethnography as an approach. I was, and still am, unhappy with it. It seemed rather woolly and theoretically and conceptually weak, despite interesting but ultimately inconclusive discussions by the likes of Hammersley. Again, Grounded Theory, Symbolic Interactionism, etc. seemed to be rooted in issues that were obsolete when viewed from a Bourdieuian perspective. I could see the implications of his work for educational research; in other words, Bourdieu outside of sociology. However, the direction of my own work did not take a pure Bourdieu line.

Four years after completing my MA, I got a job in a University as a language teacher trainer. My main empirical work for education using Bourdieu was carried out for my PhD: a study of teacher education based on a group of teacher trainees. In terms of this work, the originating source was phenomenology. I read authors like Van Manen, Vandenberg, Husserl and Merleau-Ponty in the light of my own earlier encounters with French philosophy. I wanted, above all, to give an account of the 'lived experience' of training. I therefore engaged in a whole lot of phenomenological writings, which now, I realize, somewhat mirrored Bourdieu's own early phenomenological studies of the affective life. I wished to avoid cutting up the data I had collected in a way which was/ is common in ethnography. I wanted the students to 'speak for themselves'. All the time, therefore, my own position not only with regard to the students (I was also their trainer!), but the data itself was an issue for me. Eventually, I ended up with five case 'stories' (I employed this word somewhat ironically and under the influence of post-modernism as well to acknowledge their constructed nature) amounting to some 250,000 words! They were personal, subjective accounts, by me and the students, but lacked any categorization, or indeed explicit analysis. I was unsure how phenomenology delivered the essential, or grounded, structures it promised. Certainly, many texts I read seemed conceptually sophisticated but empirically naive; even bordering on self-indulgence and solipsism.

It was after a lot of consideration in the light of my own 'encounter' with the data — a kind of reliving of the events — that I felt Bourdieu offered the best way of proceeding by re-thinking the students' experiences in relational terms. I could then see the training field as a structural map; as a set of interlocking sites and consequent influences. It was also clear that the students came with their own dispositions. I felt that habitus was the most dynamic way to describe these. I therefore worked on the notion of developing professional competence as the interaction between particular site/field contexts and students' individual habitus. I renamed habitus as 'pedagogic habitus' to take account of those aspects of student dispositions which were especially pertinent (came alive!) in particular aspects; for example, linguistic competence/background for language teachers, or previous professional experiences. A sense of time and place seemed all in understanding what they did and thought.

Again, I felt that the approach derived from Bourdieu was helpful in showing up the processes of teacher professionalization in a way which others were not. A good deal of teacher education seemed to be constructed around oppositions — theory/practice, school/training institution — which were debated in ideological and political rather than epistemological terms. Similarly, many approaches to teacher education got bogged down in particular academic disciplines. What they have to say about training was therefore symptomatic of the limitations of the disciplines themselves; for example, Colin Lacey's classic Socialisation of Teachers, or the radical critiques of Ginsburg and Popkewitz. Other approaches, for example, teacher 'craft knowledge' and the 'reflective practitioner', seemed to be based on romantic metaphors, rather than the reality of personal engagement that the habitus/field approach gave.

I was aware that the approach itself was highly problematic. In particular, I was departing from Bourdieu's own 'sociological' preoccupations by applying the same epistemological perspective to the development of pedagogic knowledge or competence, which is not primarily an issue of class, or status or power. But I could find no other way to show the dynamic interaction between individuals and the surroundings in which they find themselves. Most phenomenology was too subjective; sociology, too class preoccupied; structuralism, too static. Ethnography was based on the construction of commonalities, which did not place the students in time and space in terms of particular context and individual dispositions — and, most importantly — the interactions between them and eventual outcome.

The first of the above extracts might be termed 'reflexion on the role of reflexivity in theorizing'. Its argument with grounded theorizing was picked up in the second account, which referred to a detailed critique of the approach and how this led to a need for a relational stance. The third pointed to limitations perceived in ethnography and allied approaches and drew attention to a phenomenological element present in a Bourdieuian approach.

Theoretical Development

As we saw above, Bourdieu's theoretical tools have provided a number of 'springboards' that might be termed points of theoretical departure. However, it is also clear that in all four of the chapters in Part II, further theoretical developments are suggested via interaction with concepts from outside the core ones that Bourdieu supplies, or by extending these in new ways. In the extract which follows, we see an example of this in relation to cultural capital and habitus. Habitus, it is proposed, provides a way in which one might theorize gender in a sophisticated manner without marginalizing social class and without resorting to the 'essentialism' of some feminist writing.

Diane Reay Cultural reproduction is a problematic concept. With its connotations of passivity and lack of change it fits uneasily into 1990's academic poststructural orthodoxies. Social class is another misfit. Social class is increasingly viewed as an outmoded concept which fails to capture the complexities of 1990s Britain (Clark *et al.*, 1993; Pahl, 1989). The starting point for my research was a desire to develop a different version of cultural reproduction and social class from that represented in conventional accounts (Goldthorpe, 1980; 1983; Goldthorpe and Marshall, 1992). As a feminist I felt that social class categories ignore the multiplicity of women's social positionings within contemporary social life (Barrett, 1991; 1992; Mahony and Zmroczek, 1997).

The relationship between gender and class remains a difficult one to theorize as long as conceptualizations are rooted in paid employment status (Roberts, 1993). In particular, position in the labour market tells us very little about how social class processes are played out in social relationships. Cultural capital seemed to offer a solution. Initially, I read Lamont and Lareau's excellent article on using cultural capital as a research tool. They define cultural capital as 'widely shared legitimate culture made up of high status cultural signals (attitudes, preferences, behaviours and goods)' (Lamont and Lareau, 1988, p. 164), and argue that a productive way of operationalizing cultural capital in empirical research is as a basis for social and cultural exclusion. I decided at that point that cultural capital offered possibilities for understanding class practices, whilst also allowing for analyses which recognized the complexity of class. As such it provided a much richer alternative to socio-economic categorization which I increasingly felt led to gross simplifications of how social class is experienced by women in contemporary Britain.

However, when I came to analyse women's accounts I began to feel that the notion of cultural capital with which I had started out did not sufficiently capture the complexities of their lives. Half way through the process of analysing the data I started again using Bourdieu's less well-known concept of habitus as a way of understanding women's attitudes and activities (Bourdieu, 1985). Habitus with its incorporation of both structure and agency seemed to provide a way of understanding women's activities in support of children's education as gendered, classed and racialized processes. Habitus produces action but because it confines possibilities to those possible for social groups an individual belongs to, much of the time those actions tend to be reproductive rather than transformative. Although the concept of habitus is primarily linked to social class in Bourdieu's own work, I have attempted to develop understanding of habitus as both gendered and racialized (Reay, 1995a; 1995b).

Habitus is primarily a method for analysing the dominance of dominant groups in society and the domination of subordinate groups. Bourdieu describes habitus as a 'system of dispositions common to all products of the same conditionings' (Bourdieu, 1990a, p. 59). As such it can just as readily be understood in terms of 'gender (or racial and ethnic) disadvantage' as well as social class (McClelland, 1990, p. 105). Habitus can be used to focus on the ways in which the socially advantaged and disadvantaged play out attitudes of cultural superiority and inferiority ingrained in their habitus in daily interactions. As McClelland highlights, such dispositions are powerfully influenced by both gender and 'race'. I have tried to develop conceptualizations of racialized habitus in earlier work (Reay, 1995b). However, I am still attempting to develop understandings of gendered habitus that work satisfactorily for me.

As a feminist I have tried to interweave Bourdieu's research tools with the insights of a range of different feminisms, in particular that of the Canadian sociologist, Dorothy Smith. Bourdieu's conceptual framework is often compared to Giddens's theory of structuration (Giddens, 1987). However, I found stronger parallels with Smith's theory of institutional ethnography. Both work with notions of the taken-for-granted and relations of ruling, both conceptualize structures as constituted through the activities of individuals. I would argue strongly that Bourdieu's work offers itself to feminist adaptation. Although I disagree with some of Bourdieu's perspectives on male domination (Bourdieu, 1990a), he is a rarity among eminent male sociologists. Few male sociologists, eminent or otherwise, have recognized male domination in their work let alone extensively researched its repercussions for both females and males in the way that Bourdieu has (Bourdieu, 1990c; 1993a).

There are potentially productive convergences between feminist writing on embodiment and Bourdieu's concept of habitus. Both contemporary feminist writing and Bourdieu's work discuss and theorize gender as embodied in ways which avoid essentialism. However, it is Bourdieu who has been at the forefront of work which analyses how social class is embodied. I found his work in this area a really useful stimulus for my own thinking on how class and race are played out, not only in individuals' actions and attitudes, but in a whole range of bodily gestures (Reay, 1995a; 1995b; 1997b).

A key reason, therefore, that I have used Bourdieu is because he offers an effective foil to mainstream feminisms which marginalize social class in their analyses. As Beverley Skeggs points out very little feminist theory has explanatory value in relation to working-class women (Skeggs, 1997). As a result drawing on feminist theory exclusively makes it difficult to avoid viewing working class lives in terms of deficit and deviation from middle class norms. In contrast, Bourdieu provides another way of seeing; one that constantly keeps in play the exigencies of working-class lives alongside a focus on agency.

It is difficult to untangle and separate out the influence of Bourdieu from that of feminist theory and methodology on my research endeavours. He is much more helpful in illuminating the ways on which gender and class intersect, complicate and contradict each other. On the other hand feminism also has a long history of urging reflexivity in research and I am as much steeped in that literature as in Bourdieu's writing. In some ways I feel more at ease with feminist writing on methodology (for example Maynard and Purvis, 1994) than Bourdieu's somewhat daunting accounts which appear to advocate a 'properly scientific' way of undertaking research.

As a full-time researcher I am constantly aware of the imperfections of the research process. When I have tried to write reflexively about problems that I have encountered in the field (Reay, 1996a; 1996b), other feminist accounts have been more facilitating than Bourdieu's perhaps because he appears to be so confident in his approach to research and does not express his doubts in the same ways that I, and many other feminist researchers, have. Feminist accounts which also include the mistakes, oversights, cul de sacs and anxieties which permeate the research field are paradoxically both more reassuring and enlightening.

Class still remains very confusing for me and I am aware that I am using cultural capital but more particularly habitus in order to clarify some of that confusion. Habitus is a useful tool for challenging sociology's dominant conceptual categories, particularly socio-economic categorization. It also helps to reveal the taken for granted assumptions of the researcher as well as the researched. As I have argued in an earlier article the concept of habitus helps, not just in providing answers, but primarily in revealing better questions to ask:

Habitus is a way of looking at data which renders the 'taken-for-granted' problematic. It suggests a whole range

of questions not necessarily addressed in empirical research; How well adapted is the individual to the context
they find themselves in? How does personal history shape
their responses to the contemporary setting? What subjective vocations do they bring to the present and how are
they manifested? Are structural effects visible within small
scale interactions? What is the meaning of non-verbal
behaviour as well as individuals' use of language? These
questions clearly raise issues of gender and 'race' alongside those of social class. (Reay, 1995a, p. 369)

Whilst the most obvious reading of gendered habitus in Bourdieu's
own work depicts women as complicit in viewing gender divisions
as natural and universal (McCall, 1992), I have attempted a feminist
reading which sees gendered habitus as more fluid and shifting
across time and space. Bourdieu describes habitus as 'a power of
adaptation. It constantly performs an adaptation to the outside world'
(Bourdieu, 1993a, p. 88), thus enabling us to understand women as
a complex amalgam that is always in the process of completion.
There is no finality or finished identity.

As well as incorporating challenges and subversions to the
prevailing gender order, the concept of gendered habitus holds
powerful structural influences within its frame. Gendered habitus
includes a set of complex, diverse predispositions. It invokes understandings of identity premised on familial legacy and early childhood socialization. As such it is primarily a dynamic concept, a rich
interfacing of past and present, interiorized and permeating both
body and psyche.

The above account is lengthy. However, we include it in its entirety as the
articulation of the interplay between feminist methodologies and Bourdieu's, which
resulted in the notion of 'gendered habitus'.

Two further extracts follow under the 'theoretical development' theme. The
first shows how researchers found a particular area of Bourdieu's thinking very
productive and how this was combined with concepts from elsewhere to provide a
new framework:

Phil Hodkinson As our research progressed, our thinking, both discursively and
intuitively, changed as we inter-acted with others. The data did
indeed change us and the ways we thought about the issues.
However, as Moustakas (1990) suggests, the changes in us were
partly intuitive, and did not arise only from systematic analysis.
More importantly in the context of this section, our thinking
was also changed by the reading we did, including some
Bourdieu.

As we read about capital, habitus and field, we began to
view the data we had collected differently. The language and
ideas we were beginning to use changed our thinking and some
of our practices. We began to read our interview transcripts

differently, and to analyse them differently. I would now argue that, for us, the research process was an evolutionary routine. That is, though there were no transformations at key turning points, the ways in which we worked and thought evolved. Further, though aspects of this evolution could have been predicted because of the dispositions within our (starting) habitus, others could not, because we changed as the research progressed. For example, given our interpretative, symbolic-interactionist beginning, we expected, and others might have predicted, that it would be thinkers like Denzin or Giddens that we would find most useful and, as I have explained, one article by Strauss was highly influential. At first sight, Bourdieu's rejection of the value of people's perceptions as adequate research data to explain their practices, and his consistent focus on group patterns rather than individual experiences, suggests that his work was less likely to be acceptable to us. Yet, as I have explained in Chapter 6, it was his thinking which, in the end, proved to be the major single influence on our work.

However, the relationship between our research and his ideas was not one way. Although his ideas changed us and the way in which we interpreted our data, we, in turn, interpreted Bourdieu's work in the light of that data, and from our own, moving standpoint, within our own horizons for action. Thus, we have focused on aspects of Bourdieu's thinking that we interpreted as relevant to our work (habitus, capital and field), and largely ignored other aspects that did not resonate with our thinking about our data in the same way (his work on language, practice and reflexivity, for example). I am not claiming that these ideas are not relevant — indeed, others may feel that they are, and that our thinking and understanding would have been greatly improved had we utilized them. The point is that we used his work in a partial way. Furthermore, the meaning of his thinking has inevitably been changed in our use of it. We may not be using habitus, for example, in the same way that he does.

In making sense of this last point, Gadamer's (1979) thinking is useful. He argues that truth is and can only be interpretation from a standpoint. Thus, for example, Bourdieu's texts only have meaning when a reader interprets them, by merging the horizons of the writer with those of the reader. That meaning is, therefore, an inevitable amalgam of the original text and the perceptions of the reader. In a sense that lies close to our interpretation of the spirit of Bourdieu's own work, the meaning is neither objective nor subjective, but simultaneously both. Our research, and the notion of research reflexivity, can also be understood in that way. Thus, we interpreted our data, which only had meaning in that interpretation. As I have described, we did this from an evolving standpoint, strongly influenced, towards the end, by Bourdieu's work. Similarly, we interpreted and gave meaning to Bourdieu's work from that same evolving standpoint. In this way, the data, our habitus, Bourdieu's and other writings which we used, and the relations of force in the field within which the research took place, were all reflexively related, and can only be artificially untwined in attempting to make sense of the origins of the eventual reports and writings we have constructed from that research.

The final extract under this theme is a general discussion covering several examples of the sort of theoretical development which a Bourdieuian approach provides.

Michael Grenfell I have continued to rethink particular educational phenomena in Bourdieu's terms, in order, in a way, to get to the processes behind the academic metaphors used to describe them. Language seemed a good example of this. Over the past two or three decades, there has been a move from very teacher-centred to learner-centred classrooms. As the latter became more of a problematic concept, academics have moved to describe classroom discourse in terms of 'constructed knowledge', which is 'scaffolded' by the teacher. I have wanted to get beyond the idealism of such metaphors. In the examples I quote, I think there are questions of 'legitimate' cognitive processes at stake, as well as individual pupil thinking (my marking of 'legitimate' here is used in a similar way to the phenomenological technique of bracketing in order to render visible the non-common sensual understanding of a particular term). It is not a conflict or 'contested knowedge' model, but one, I believe where questions of individual pupil thinking — based on culture, class, gender, etc. — are less frequently lost.

In this sense, I want to avoid being captured by the language used by researchers and to investigate the individual particularities of site contexts. This is why I think the Bourdieu approach has such practical relevance: ultimately, we are talking about education and learning. If we can see these in terms of orthodox ways of thinking, teachers' and pupils' cognitive dispositions (habitus) and site contexts, we may better understand the way some knowledge is constructed and some knowledge is excluded in learning situations. I do not think one can work to eliminate differences between individuals, but I do feel we can see how they might be used to our advantage and disadvantage, and to avoid the worst extremes of pedagogic imposition.

That being said, I am aware how difficult it is to represent such analyses. My chapter in this book does cut up dialogues in a way I would wish to avoid, and I earlier described the mountain of text I ended up with when I tried, modestly at the time I felt, to present a comprehensive picture of five teachers in training. In order to construct these, I used interview, questionnaire, and observation techniques, along with diary accounts (mine and the students') and other materials analyses. In many of these, I was constantly aware of my own position in the research. Trainees were looking to please me, to pass the course. They did not, therefore, tell me everything they were thinking. The question is whether, out of all these separate data sources, the essential generating principles emerge.

In the project described in this book, I only recorded one of the examples of classroom language. The others are second-hand: taken from other researchers' transcriptions. Still, I wanted to show what a Bourdieu approach brings to them. I see these as illustrative discussions, rather than empirically grounded as in the case of my teacher education research. Both have their place, I think.

'Reflexive objectivity' is always relative, and I often wonder if even Bourdieu himself fully recognizes his own misrecognitions as much as he thinks he does. I think, however, it is probably sufficient to engage in an effort to work in this manner: there is always more to objectify than any one individual act of objectification.

The extracts above give some indication of the diversity of theoretical development possible in particular research practices. The next section takes reflexivity still further.

Critical Engagements

Reflexivity is, by definition, endless. Given the will and the resources, it should be possible to continue to refine an analysis of one's relation to the object of study time and again. Similarly, the interaction between the main conceptual tools utilized and others which seem closely related can be re-examined. Under this theme of 'Critical Engagements', the first extract draws on correspondence which formed part of the preparation for this book. It deals with the extent to which 'rationality' has a role in a Bourdieuian approach. It also explores the way habitus may be augmented with various other compatible concepts. It demonstrates a process of reflexion on reflexion:

Phil Hodkinson After reading an earlier draft of this reflexive account, together with a draft for my chapter, the editors for this book raised further points with me. They asked that I consider the possibility that 'the [career] decisions you studied were *rationalized* rather than *rational*' (their emphasis). To illustrate what they meant, David James kindly provided me with a quote from Bourdieu that I had not come across:

> Action guided by a 'feel for the game' has all the appearances of the rational action that an impartial observer, endowed with all the necessary information and capable of mastering it rationally, would deduce.

And yet it is not based on reason. You need only think of the impulsive decision made by the tennis player who runs up to the net, to understand that it has nothing in common with the learned construction that the coach, after analysis, draws up in order to explain it and deduce communicable lessons from it. The conditions of rational calculation are practically never given in practice. (Bourdieu, 1990b, p. 11)

My reaction to these comments, which I found very helpful, was two-fold. Firstly, I accept totally that all interview accounts involve a degree of rationalization. Indeed, there is now a growing literature, for example in the life history field, which suggests that we understand our lives only through such created stories. Elsewhere (Hodkinson, 1995) I have argued, following Haugaard (1992), that one escape from the determinism which some (e.g., Jenkins, 1992) see as implicit in Bourdieu's notion of habitus is that we are not trapped by our past, partly because that past changes as we re-story it from the present. This account of our research process is precisely such a reconstruction.

Secondly, my interpretation of the Bourdieu quote given above, is that, with one exception, it coincides exactly with our own position, and our attempted usage of his ideas. It is a powerful, concise and effective attack on rational action theory, which I believe is paralleled by the one I presented in my chapter. However, as the editors also recognized, I would argue that Bourdieu goes too far. At least in the field we investigated, our evidence strongly suggests that many of the 'actions guided by the feel of the game' were partly or, more precisely, pragmatically rational. In this context, Bourdieu's use of the tennis analogy is misleading. The tacit knowledge used by the player had almost certainly been partly consciously learned, as the player and the coach made conscious, rational decisions to change the way in which a stroke is played. Furthermore, some of the actions taken during the game were almost certainly the result of pragmatically rational decisions. For example, the player may have consciously decided to concentrate more on the opponent's forehand, feeling that he or she has detected a weakness there.

I think that one key difference between Bourdieu's position and mine reflects our differing foci. Despite his use here of an individual example, his prime concern is to explain patterns. However, we cannot use analytical tools designed to explain patterns in order to interpret individual actions. In this quotation at least, Bourdieu appears to make the same logical mistake as the rational action theorists he attacks. What we claim our research shows is young people who were being pragmatically rational, and we find that consistent with an analysis of the field predominantly based on Bourdieu's ideas.

This extract illustrates individuals engaging productively with Bourdieu's ideas within sight of a practical research project. The value of such an encounter may well be more to do with insights highlighted in the engagement than they are with any one particular outcome. The second extract, given below, alludes to one researcher's rejection of some aspects of Bourdieu's work whilst larger ideas from it were being developed.

Diane Reay   My utilization of Bourdieu's theory is not an uncritical one. I have experienced problems both with the condescending ways in which he has conceptualized working-class people (however, see Bourdieu 1993a for a notable exception) and the ways in which he seems to suggest that female gendered habitus is intrinsically complicit with male power (Bourdieu, 1990a). Neither made coherent sense in terms of my own experience nor that of the mothers in the research study. I have tried to move beyond Bourdieu's parameters to develop more sympathetic conceptualizations of both working-class and female habitus.

Both these extracts show reflexion as part of a continuous engagement with both the researched and the work of Bourdieu.

Reception in the Field

Finally, a number of reflexions focus on how work which has been inspired by Bourdieu's thinking has been received. Just two examples are given here. The first mixes experiences and some educated guesswork to suggest how different audiences react to an analysis:

Phil Hodkinson   With hindsight, I wish we had collected data about the way our work has been received — though that is very difficult to do, given the reluctance of some people to be completely honest with an author about his/her work. However, we did not do that, so all I can do here is hypothesize some of many plausible responses.

Firstly, those readers with a commitment to views of career decision making different from ours are unlikely to accept our findings and analysis uncritically. They will have interpreted our data from within their own horizons, their own habitus and from their own standpoints. Some may have merged their understandings with those of our writings, to create new meanings, which, for example, retain a belief in rational decision making, branding ours as untypical and undesirable. One correspondent, for example, claimed that what we described would only be true for people 'with low cultural capital'. He did not use the term, but that was what I think he meant.

Others, we know, have received our thinking with enthusiasm. This was no doubt because we had argued the case convincingly, but also because, from their standpoints, within their habitus and horizons, the views we expressed were acceptable. Such people will have created new meanings out of our writing, some of which would be very close to our own. Incidentally, our own meanings change and evolve over time, so it makes no sense to see them as either fixed or completely 'real'.

The second extract mentions a need to guard against coming to be regarded as some sort of disciple for Bourdieu, before moving on to note the difficulties that seem to arise in positioning work which often falls outside the usual academic categories.

Michael Grenfell   I have written about being captured by language, and in some ways, I think my own work on Bourdieu could be viewed in this way; that I have been captured by an epistemological position and its conceptual metaphors — habitus, field, capital, etc. Certainly, talking to Bourdieu on different occasions since our first encounter, I have been aware of, and guarded against, becoming an acolyte or disciple: carrying out the 'master's' work, as it were. In many ways, however, I think my work extends Bourdieu's own in the field of education, and it is not certain whether or not he would approve of these adaptions and applications. In order to understand any social activity, I always tend to think of it in terms of the individual habitus dispositions of those involved; the structure of the field and its relation to other fields; the dominant valued products of the field and how they are defined. I am certainly aware of this in my own positioning in higher education and my place in the academic field. As I said above: I am a teacher educator, and therefore involved in practical tasks themselves and in theorizing about them. I talk about sociology, but I am not really a sociologist. I work in linguistics but do not consider myself an applied linguist. I believe that what I say has value. For academic credibility, one has to publish. However, getting published involves a whole series of strategies. Sometimes the work can seem not to be practical enough to go into a professional journal; not philosophical enough for a philosophy journal; not strict sociology; and perhaps too continental for some education journals. I see this as a problem of positioning.

To an extent, I sometimes feel that Bourdieu's approach is more an attitude of mind than a methodology. Ultimately, I ask myself if my own understanding of educational phenomena and the processes of researching them is more complete by working through Bourdieu. And to this question I must answer in the affirmative. I feel my own 'academic habitus' has been changed by encounters with Bourdieu and his work. It is this which I bring into the research field, and which I constantly draw upon in objectifying what I am doing, why, and the status of the outcome. I do not see such objectification as necessarily negative, self critical, or a simple acknowledgment of the limitations of research. Rather I see the construction of a research topic/project, designing techniques to undertake it, analysis of data, and presentation of results as part of the same epistemological stance.

All four authors have commented on the problematic issues of writing in areas which are not yet clearly located within any one orthodox academic field. Nonetheless, all writers have chosen to engage critically with the work of Bourdieu as a methodological basis for their research projects.

Conclusion

This chapter has sought to explore and exemplify what seems to us to be the meanings of 'reflexivity' in a Bourdieuian approach to educational or social-scientific research. This was done through a brief consideration of other uses of the terms reflection and reflexivity, and then a glance at some attempts at definition from Bourdieu and commentators. What is distinctive about reflexivity for Bourdieu is a sense of social location in terms of the relationship between the researcher and the object of study. Accordingly, this theme (and the closely related one of relationships with the researched) was highlighted in the reflexive accounts which followed. Beyond this, several other related themes have been identified and illustrated, ending with 'reception in the field'. Examples of all these themes have been 'objectified', at least in the sense of being rendered visible.

We have presented the material in this way because reflexivity runs right through Bourdieu's work as a constant thematic presence. The most recent of his writing emphasizes its importance in 'dispossessing the knowing subject of the privilege they take for themselves from the ordinary' (1997, p. 21, own translation). Bourdieu is sensitive to the special relationship the researcher sets up in taking something from the social world as an object of study. He argues that this is only possible because the researcher is not of the 'world' they study, and therefore, can separate out theory from practice: their own theory and the practice of the researched. This is inevitable, yet problems begin when the researcher takes their own constructions as a representation of reality. The only way to avoid this is also to raise for analysis the presuppositions which the researcher includes in the research. Bourdieu states that these presuppositions are of three distinct orders:

> there are first of all those associated with the occupation of a position in the social space, and the particular trajectory which has led to it, as well as belonging to a particular gender . . . There are next those which are constitutive of the particular *doxa* of different fields (religious, artistic, philosophical, sociological, etc.), and, most precisely, those which each individual thinker owes to their position in the field. There are finally those presuppositions which are constitutive of the *doxa*

generically associated to the *skholè*, to the leisure, which is the condition of existence of all the fields of 'knowing'. (*ibid.* own translation)

As long as these are kept in mind and objectified for each researcher and each
research endeavour, the researcher can avoid the symbolic violence of imposing an
interpretation on reality. The only question then is how much this objectification
needs to be explicitly stated in the research itself.

We know that this chapter goes some way beyond anything that Bourdieu
himself does or is likely to advocate as a textual product. Yet the three orders of
presuppositions stated in the last quotation from Bourdieu are everywhere apparent
in the researchers' accounts given in the chapter. We have chosen not to explicitly
name them in these terms. Instead we invite the reader to compare these elements
for 'objectification of the objectifying subject' with the reflexive accounts in the
chapter and with the research discussions in Part II. Bourdieu is certainly not
arguing that such objectification negates the findings of research. Neither is he
dismissing research as ultimately relativist. However, he is claiming that without
the presence of this type of reflexivity at every stage in undertaking research, we
run the risk that the outcome will be more about the researcher than the researched.
The extent to which the 'reflexive objectivity', to which he urges us to aspire is
possible, is an issue which the reader may want to reflect on themselves in the light
of the above, and then, perhaps, turn back on themselves in their own research
encounters. This mutual undertaking and understanding can then provide a backdrop to Chapter 9, in which we take forward our discussion of the realization of
'theory as method' in a Bourdieuian approach.

Part IV

Theory as Method

So far in this book we have outlined Bourdieu's basic theory of practice and discussed its emerging profile in an educational context. We have also offered examples of educational researchers using his theoretical terms and approach in various practical situations; including issues of reflexivity for the researchers involved. In this chapter we go on to explore what constitutes an educational research endeavour from a Bourdieuian perspective. We want to avoid a 'how to do it' prescription. It is clear from Part II that there are various ways of using Bourdieu within the scope of the theory he offers. At the same time, the strength of his work and its applicability to educational research can only ultimately be evaluated once it is used in real-life contexts.

In this chapter, we offer some description of the possible stages, techniques and methods for conceptualizing and conducting a research project. Some of these involve issues of principle; others include implications for practice. Out of this discussion, it is intended that a picture will emerge of how to go about carrying out research within a Bourdieu-based framework, and the character and ways of presenting knowledge produced as a result of such an undertaking. The core of this section systematically considers procedures and techniques. Throughout the chapter, we employ Bourdieu's own voice as a commentary on the issues raised.

We begin by turning our attention to the main theme of the chapter expressed in its title: theory as method.

Chapter 9

Theory as Method

In Chapter 2, we raised the issue of paradigms as a way of highlighting philosophical positions on knowledge and knowledge production necessarily present when anyone undertakes a research project. Stating them in an explicit manner allows us to see the various implications of each. Questions of epistemology are at stake; namely, different ways of knowing and understanding, and the means of expressing them. We saw that it is often the case that either/or scenarios are constructed between each of the paradigmatic approaches — positivist, hermeneutic, critical, action-based — and this may lead to an overly rigid research perspective. Nevertheless, it is useful to list the issues at stake between the researcher and the researched in terms of subjectivity, objectivity, theory, and practice, etc. as a way of positioning the work being carried out. Theory is obviously a problematic word, which might refer to anything from any one individual's subjective, personally based rationale, or intuitive feeling, to highly formalized general statements with a strong predictive power. Both extremes, as well as various forms in between them, are of relevance and use in education and in the research activities engaged in to understand its processes.

Faced with this variety and choice, it may be felt that Bourdieu offers a highly formal, even inflexible, theory. There is an insistence on a dialectical relation between subjectivity and objectivity, which is never easy to grasp in reality. At the same time, it is a theory which appears to give rise to a number of schematic metaphors, which might equally be seen as reifying the very educational processes, whose dynamic it seeks to be able to capture. To this extent, Bourdieu might be considered highly theoretical. But, let us follow through in some detail his own response in interview when questioned on these issues of theory and practice:

> Let me say outright and very forcefully that I never 'theorize', if by that we mean engage in the kind of conceptual gobbledygook (*laïus*) that is good for textbooks and which, through an extraordinary misconstrual of the logic of science, passes for Theory in much of Anglo-American social science. I never set out to 'do theory' or to 'construct a theory' *per se*, as the American expression goes. And it is a complete misapprehension of my project to believe that I am attempting some kind of 'synthesis of classical theory'. There is no doubt a theory in my work, or, better, a set of *thinking tools* visible through the results they yield, but it is not built as such. (1989c, p. 50)

In Chapter 2, we also referred to the development of educational research in terms of a move away from a quasi-scientific, semi-experimental approach, which characterized much activity up until the 1950s. Since then, and influenced by wider trends in social science, research in education has increasingly adopted ethnographic, interpretative approaches usually concerned to develop analyses of subjective meanings and interactions. Such studies often involve the researcher going out into the field as a 'participant observer', making detailed observation notes and then analysing them for commonalities and patterns in relation to the research issues addressed. This latter approach leads to data and analysis which is more qualitative and descriptive in comparison to the statistical, quantitative data and analyses characteristic of the scientific, experimental paradigm.

Of course, it is misleading to over-emphasize the opposition between quantitative and qualitative techniques: many researchers make use of a combination of both, and the distinction does not map clearly on to the more abstract one between paradigms. Bourdieu's own work includes a range of data including statistics and more descriptive analyses of his field studies. Nevertheless, there are different ways of conceptualizing the social world, as well as the related differences in the ways we conduct research into it. These differences themselves give rise to distinct forms of knowledge in representing research.

We shall later see how Bourdieu treats various quantitative and qualitative techniques. For the moment, given its widespread appeal in contemporary educational research, it is worth pausing to consider ethnography.

In Chapter 2, we referred to Ethnography as being described as a 'culture studying culture' (Spradley, 1980), which pertains to its anthropological origins. In other words, it is concerned with describing group cultures and activities much as early anthropologists described so-called primitive tribes. These studies may include issues of organization, habit, practice, belief, behaviour, and outcome. It is not initially difficult to think of education in similar terms. Even so, in ethnography, as in its parent anthropology, there is much debate and controversy concerning how to conduct research and the desirable outcome of such activities. The whole point of ethnography is that it gives an authentic picture of the social world. However, in this very strength is its main weakness. It may be that what is represented is a unique event against which very little can be said of a general nature. On the other hand, in an effort to produce generally robust statements about a feature, it may be that a symmetry between theory and practice is constructed in a way that misrepresents what exists in reality. As discussed in Chapter 2, Hammersley has referred to this dichotomy as the tension between 'realism and relativism' (1992, p. 54). This dichotomy is everywhere apparent in books on ethnography in recent decades. For example, the 'grounded theory' approach of Glaser and Strauss (1967) proceeds by saturation of data which aims for the emergence of categories from minihypotheses, which in turn eventually lead to theories which are robust enough to be tested against further data. This approach seems to mimic scientific practices and appears to lead to what Denzin calls 'a pragmaticism which produces a crippling commitment to an interpretive sociology too often caught in the trappings of positivist and post-positivist terms; validity, proposition and theory' (1992, p. 20). Hammersley is also critical of this pseudo-scientificity:

> The crucial question, it seems to me, is: how can the fact that a theory has 'emerged' from data justify our belief that the processes it describes were operative in the case investigated, and (more important still) that they represent universal principles. Unfortunately, today . . . we are left with an appeal to intuition. (*op. cit.*, p. 19)

Unfortunately, this realization sometimes leads to a form of relativism, where data can only speak for itself; without any intention to produce analytic statements at all. The root of this position is in the anthropological attempt to create a 'thick description' (Geertz, 1975) of a culture as a way of capturing and presenting its reality. However, at its post-modernist extremes, ethnographic representation is denounced as merely an expression of the 'politics and poetics' of the researcher themselves (cf. Latour, 1988; Marcus and Fischer, 1986; Clifford and Marcus, 1986). In a similar vein, Tyler (1985, 1986) argues that, from a post-modernist position, the objective of educational research is not how best to represent but how to avoid representing. 'Evocation' is recommended as a suitable alternative, as only here is ethnography freed from mimesis, which he sees as an inappropriate mode of scientific rhetoric that entails 'objects', or facts, descriptions, inductions, generalizations, and concepts of truth.

The scientific, positivist paradigm has long been criticized as an inappropriate approach for understanding the social world, yet as we saw in Chapter 2 some forms of ethnography do seem to attempt to parallel its techniques of analysis and reporting procedures. Yet, the outcome of this approach has not always been so successful; in particular, ethnographers' efforts to form theories which are 'scientifically' robust. Hammersley writes of ethnography's 'dismal performance in the case of theorising' (1986, p. 179). However, a credible alternative does not yet appear to have established itself, and, once the positivist frame is broken, it seems that all manner of relativism and anti-theory and method emerges. Does Bourdieu offer a different course?

Participant observation is often advocated by ethnographers, as intervening in the social world is seen as a means of getting closer to the authenticity of situations. However, this intervention is also a source of heightened anxiety for researchers of a post-modernist persuasion, who see research as only an expression of the researcher themselves. We want to consider how Bourdieu's approach differs in intent and construction from these various ethnographic and qualitative procedures. The role and status of theory and theorizing in research is central to this discussion.

In order to illustrate Bourdieu's approach, we want to again consider his own personal intellectual origins and academic trajectory. He started as a student of philosophy, before embracing anthropology and finally sociology as his guiding academic disciplines. However, it would be wrong to see this as the rejection of one field for another. There is a sense in which his ongoing method and theory are shaped by all three disciplines: philosophical; anthropological; sociological. Indeed, it might be best to understand Bourdieu's mission to be that of a social anthropologist; explaining the processes of groups, cultures and systems within, primarily, French society. He often explains this academic development as the result of his own personal necessity, as a relative outsider, to understand and explain experiences. These include his home region; Algeria; and coming to Paris in the 1950s, to what was at that time the international centre of philosophy and anthropology (see Bourdieu and Grenfell, 1995). These experiences included real, first-hand problems (requiring practical as well as theoretical solutions) which at the same time provided Bourdieu with a way of making sense of his own social environment. His position with respect to these experiences implied an intimate, personal involvement rather than that of the 'disinterested', 'objective' observer. Bourdieu uses 'ethno' words a lot — ethnography, ethnology, ethnomethodology — to refer to approaches which claim to study the authentic processes of social phenomena. However, in many cases, he distinguishes his own approach from other common 'ethno-approaches'. This is not the place to go through these in detail and draw out the various differences. In any case, within our own western educational research culture, there is no single ethnographic approach. Nevertheless, there are perhaps three ways in which Bourdieu's method differs from conventional ethnography in educational research.

Firstly, as already discussed, is the status of theory:

> For me, theory is not a sort of prophetic or programmatic discourse which originates by dissection or by amalgamation of other theories for the sole purpose of confronting other such 'theoretical theories . . . Rather, scientific theory as I conceive it emerges as a program of perception and of action — a scientific habitus if you wish — which is disclosed only in empirical work which actualises it. It is a temporary construct which takes shape for and by empirical work. (1989c, p. 50)

This first difference is problematic. Theory is not something to be gained, 'out there', and, in extreme cases, polished to perfection through a Popperian discourse of falsification. Rather, it is a developed understanding, sometimes grasped empathetically, gained as part of a practical engagement with empirical situations and the problems they present. Bourdieu's theory is one *of* practice and *for* practice. It is not theory developed *ex nihilo*, but one which is founded on a very specific epistemological stance. Practice and theorizing are not regarded as separate activities, displaced in time and place during the research process, but mutually generative of the ways and means of collecting data, analysing it and developing explanations which lead to an understanding of the object being investigated. By contrast, common forms of ethnography and ethnographic theorizing can seem to be quite static and lacking in dynamism in a way that Bourdieu's approach is not.

The second distinction between conventional ethnographic methods and Bourdieu's own relates to philosophical foundations. As previously discussed, Bourdieu's stated objective is to go beyond the problems created by crude forms of objectivism and subjectivism. The basis of this philosophical third way might be termed 'phenomenological structuralism'. The phenomenological tradition, led this century by the likes of Husserl, Schütz and Merleau-Ponty, foregrounds the *relations* between individual human beings and the objects which surround them. There is the sense in which these relations are structural in the way they set up practical intentions and give rise to specific consequences. There is also the sense that these relations are everyday and have a commonsense representation, which has to be 'bracketed' by the researcher as part of the process of establishing the grounding structures and their generating principles. Such a perspective has clear parallels with Bourdieu as it highlights individual experience of the objective world, and the way this world acts on particular subjectivities; except, of course, that in his case the defining principles are always socio-culturally derivative. It is possible to extrapolate this phenomenological approach to the ways in which individuals relate to the generating structures around and within them; in other words, the symbolic capital of the world. This is as true of the research process as it is of any other sphere of activity. Ethnography traditionally provides insider accounts and employs methods of participant observation in order to get information on other people. 'Good' ethnography can make claims to authenticity of representation: that there is a reality to be captured and presented. Phenomenology takes a different philosophical stance, seeing interpretation as a relational event. As we saw in Chapter 8, the element of reflexivity draws attention to the interests of the observer, and their criteria for selecting data sources. In this case, the observer is made visible in the data analysis in a way that is not true of ethnography. No phenomenologist would take the research back to the researched for authentication, and the separation and variety in foci is an essential element in the method: different people produce different accounts in different ways. This essential phenomenological position leads Bourdieu to develop a particular perspective on reflexivity and participant objectification, a theme to which we will return.

The third distinction between Bourdieu's ethnography and other conventional forms involves his terms of analysis. In many ways, Bourdieu offers a very open-ended approach to research: it is guided by a particular philosophical stance but is not methodologically prescriptive. Nevertheless, and consistently over the decades, he makes continuous use of a set of conceptual metaphors: most noticeably those of habitus and field. They are central to his method and practice, and all other considerations seem to flow from them. In particular, they are the pivot on which he constructs his attempted synthesis of subjectivism and objectivism. Nevertheless, they appear as one-word constructs, and, without considering their philosophical roots, might easily be taken to express a rigid schematicism if not an explicit determinism (see criticisms of them mentioned in Chapter 2). Bourdieu characterizes his own work by labelling it 'constructivist structuralism or structuralist constructivism' (1989b, p. 14) and explains:

> By structuralism or structuralist, I mean that there exist, within the social world itself and not only within symbolic systems (language, myth, etc.), objective structures independent of the consciousness and will of agents, which are capable of guiding and constraining their practices or their representations. By constructivism, I mean that there is a twofold social genesis, on the one hand of the schemes of perception, thought, and action which are constitutive of what I call habitus, and on the other hand of social structures, and particularly of what I call field and of groups, notably those we ordinarily call social classes. (*ibid.*)

Most ethnographies would avoid starting with such constructs. Bourdieu calls them 'thinking tools', the value of which we must assess according to the results they give us. Some of the results of researchers' thinking with such tools are reported in Part II of this book. The outcomes are very different, and there are questions about what is concluded, why, and whether this approach gives us a distinctive understanding of the social phenomena which it deals with.

As the accounts in Part II demonstrate, there are different ways of using such 'thinking tools' in the course of carrying out research. In some cases, thinking in terms of *habitus* accentuates the sense of individual disposition in a research area; and *field* allows for a mapping of ongoing organizational and consequential ideational forces at play. However, the commonest error in thinking in these terms is to see habitus responding in a mechanical way to the 'rules' of the field. Such determinism is the very antithesis of Bourdieu's project, which is to show up the underlying logic of practice in operation in particular social activities. This logic is actualized in face-to-face encounters between individuals in fields, the result of which is neither random nor determined. The accounts in Part II show how this outcome is 'negotiated' in terms of the legitimate values of various fields expressed in objectifiable capital: the currency of field discourse. Using terms such as habitus, field and capital can sensitize one to these processes after the research event, as it were. However, they might also be adopted from its outset. In either case, the attempt is to go beyond the sort of strict representations of social theories which have a strong predictive force but risk reifying dynamic processes; what Bourdieu sees as going from a 'model of reality' to the 'reality of the model' (1980a, p. 67). The logic of practice, which is constitutive of and constituted by various fields, is expressed in generating principles which can be identified in the operations and outcomes of the dynamic relationships between habitus and fields. However, to research in this way, is not to discover or apply laws of causality or rules of practice, which presupposes a detached observer and a higher epistemological authority. Rather, it is to engage in the social world in theory and practice in ways which implicate the researched and the researcher in the same theory *of* practice. Wacquant (Bourdieu and Wacquant, 1992b, p. 23) warns against 'searching the productions of habitus for more logic than they actually contain', for, in Bourdieu's words, 'the logic of practice is logical up to the point where to be logical would cease being practical'; in other words, there is always an element of practical free-play beyond strict principles of practice.

In fact, the content and process of habitus can never be fully exposed empirically. Rather, the mission is 'to produce a precise science of an imprecise, fuzzy, woolly reality' (Wacquant, *ibid.*). Research within a Bourdieuian framework entails a shift in thinking where practical problems are thought through relationally in terms which involve habitus and field, which, although originating in a very precise epistemology, should not be regarded as an end in themselves. Their boundaries should be kept soft as we use them to represent the surface structure of the logic of practice governing social processes. Key concepts in any such project are: reciprocality, autonomy, homology, interaction, correspondence, value, interest, legitimacy (we acknowledge Henry Barnard in making this point as part of a Bourdieu Web page discussion).

The distinction between theory and practice becomes much less certain in this approach. One can only theorize in practical terms; and being practical entails a theoretical positioning. This is as much true for the researcher as the researched. The researcher wants to discover and theorize the practice of the researched. The first parts of the next section suggests how they might go about this. At the same time, what the researcher wants entails a theory of practice which itself needs to be objectified. For this reason, the final part of this chapter gives further discussion to the role of reflexivity in this 'objectification of the objectifying subject'. The summation of this undertaking is, in Bourdieu's words 'to be capable of engaging very high "theoretical" stakes by means of very precise and very often mundane empirical objects', and 'for this, one must learn how to translate very abstract problems into very concrete scientific terms' (1989c, p. 51). In the next two sections, we cover the preliminary stages in this process: namely, Constructing the Research Object; and Thinking Relationally.

Constructing the Research Object

At the end of an interview with Bourdieu (1989c) covering a summative statement on his theory of practice, Bourdieu gives a four-point plan to the would-be researcher as a way of avoiding the common traps of 'empty theory' and 'blind research'. In one of these, he warns us to

> beware of words . . . Common language is the repository of the accumulated common sense of past generations, both lay and scientific, as crystallized in occupational taxonomies, names of groups, concepts . . . and so on. The most routine categories . . . (e.g., young and old, 'middle class' and 'upper-middle class') are naturalized pre-constructions, which, when they are ignored as such, function as unconscious and uncontrolled instruments of scholarly construction. (pp. 54–5)

The language we use in research itself should be viewed with suspicion, or seen, itself, as a social construction. Such constructions include a 'common' sense which, much as in the phenomenological method, needs to be 'bracketed' in order to get to a better reality behind it. Only then, as researchers, can we be sure of our attempts not to be 'taken in' by assumed meanings as represented in orthodox definitions of our own terms of reference. The social categories commonly used in social science research are a good example of this.

At this stage, it is worth thinking back to the accounts in Part II and the sort of language used to describe them: Mothers, Schools, Primary Schooling, Language, Classroom, Teaching, Student Experience, Higher Education, Young People, Career, Decision Making. Even in the titles to the separate chapters, we can see a number of representations, which, at first seem rather obvious in meaning, yet with a little reflection appear much less so. We think we know, and readily accept such terms, but, in such easy acceptance, lies the danger to which Bourdieu is alluding. This danger can lead the researcher to invest their own relation to the object of study in the research rather than explain and understand it in its own terms. This happens through language, and because of language, results in a 'misrecognition' on the part of the researcher of what is being described: the processes of the object of research, or the researchers' dispositions inherent in it through the language (and thus underlying epistemological stances, both personal and professional), which is used to describe it. Of course, it is never possible to completely eradicate this effect. It is, however, possible to maintain a constant awareness of it and minimize its influence. Indeed, this objective is central to the research process, and, in constructing an explanation, one must, at every stage, take account of the language which is being used, not only to explain it, but to conceptualize it in the first place.

The use of irony is a common feature of post-modernist discourse in discussing issues in the social sciences. Irony, it is believed, avoids overt constructivism and quasi-scientific reductionism. However, in extreme forms, such irony can lead to a total avoidance of what might be termed an explanatory narrative. In its place, is put evocation and supreme interpretative relativity. Perhaps a more pragmatic use of irony is defined by the American philosopher, Richard Rorty. For him, the post post-modern ironist is always working with a 'final vocabulary', which is the present best they can do. It is contingent and relative and open to continual adjustment; it is presented as such, rather than as a definitive, totalizing narrative. The ironist is someone who fulfils three conditions:

> Firstly, she has radical and continuing doubts about the final vocabulary she currently uses, because she has been impressed by other vocabularies, vocabularies taken as final by people or books she has encountered; secondly, she realises that argument phrased in her present vocabulary can neither underwrite nor dissolve these doubts; thirdly, in so far as she philosophises about her situation, she does not think that her vocabulary is closer to reality than others, that is in touch with a power not herself. (Rorty, 1989, p. 73)

However, Bourdieu goes beyond this kind of liberalism. For him, language is an object of analysis which must go under his epistemological microscope (using his conceptual terms of habitus and field) in order to throw up its diversionary effects and thus avoid being captured by common sense constructs, both within the academic field and without. In other words, the misrecognitions which common discourse leads one to must be kept in mind at the very outset of conducting research:

> We tend too easily to assume that the social or political importance of an object suffices in itself to grant importance to the discourse that deals with it. What counts, in reality, is the rigor of the *construction* of the object. I think that the power of a mode of thinking never manifests itself more clearly than in its capacity to constitute socially insignificant objects into scientific objects . . . or to approach a major socially significant object in an unexpected manner. (1989c, p. 51)

Perhaps the best way to understand this argument in practice is to follow through Bourdieu's own 'linguistic deconstruction' of a common object of education and educational research — that of profession and professionalization. This account is given in the text of his Parisian Workshop (Bourdieu and Wacquant,

1992b). In a section entitled 'A Radical Doubt' (pp. 235–47) he first begins by reiterating the argument given above:

> The construction of a scientific object requires first and foremost a break with common sense, that is, with the representations shared by all, whether they be the mere commonplaces of ordinary existence or official representations, often inscribed in institutions and thus present both in the objectivity of social organizations and in the mind of their participants. *The preconstructed is everywhere.* (*ibid.*, Bourdieu's emphases)

As must now be apparent, Bourdieu is engaged in a constant struggle to break with orthodox, or established, academic positions. In order to effect this 'rupture' with common sense or the preconstructed, one must first think of the object of research as already the product of collective constitution:

> the problem that ordinary positivism . . . takes for granted has been *socially produced*, in and by a *collective work of social reality*; and that it took meetings and committees, associations and leagues, caucuses and movements, demonstrations and petition drives, demands and deliberations, votes and stands, projects, programs, and resolutions to cause what was and could have remained a *private*, particular, single problem to turn into a *social problem*, a public issue that can be publicly addressed . . . or even an official problem that becomes the object of official decisions and policies, laws and decrees. (*ibid.*, Bourdieu's emphases)

Bourdieu cites the construction of phenomena such as the elderly and the fates of homosexuality and abortion. However, the same might be said of a whole range of educational constructs: differentiation, competencies, learners with special needs, the 'gifted', national curriculum, not to mention schools and agencies of management and inspection. Bourdieu takes the concept of 'profession' as an example to show what he means by 'rethinking' it as an object of study in terms which break with the orthodox ways of dealing with it, in both common sense and academic terms. He highlights the common practice of drawing a sample from a field as a representation of its totality, and comments somewhat sceptically:

> If you accept the notion of profession as an instrument, rather than an object, of analysis, none of this creates any difficulty. As long as you take it as it presents itself, the given (the hallowed *data* of positivists) gives itself to you without difficulty. Doors and mouths open wide . . . In short, as long as you remain within the realm of socially constituted and socially sanctioned appearances — and this is the order to which the notion of 'profession' belongs — you will have all the appearances with you and for you, even the appearance of scientificity. On the contrary, as soon as you undertake to work on a genuine constructed object, everything becomes difficult: 'theoretical' progress generates added 'methodological' difficulties. 'Methodologists', for their part, will have no difficulty finding plenty to nit-pick about in the operations that have to be carried out in order to grasp the constructed as best one can. (*ibid.*)

In other words, the type of undertaking advocated is difficult and 'doubtful', yet necessary in order to, in Bourdieu's words, 'wrench scientific reason from the embrace of practical reason' and 'to avoid treating as an instrument of knowledge what ought to be the object of knowledge'.

Terms such as 'profession' and 'professionalization' cannot, then, be taken as a given in the way, for example, that much research does on teacher education:

> The notion of profession is all the more dangerous because it has, as always in such cases, all the appearances of neutrality in its favor . . . (It) is a folk concept which has been uncritically smuggled into scientific language and which imports into it a whole social unconscious . . . This is why this 'concept' works so well, or too well in a way . . . The category of profession refers to realities that are, in a sense, 'too real' to be true, since it grasps at once a mental category and a social category, socially produced only by superseding or obliterating all kinds of economic, social and ethnic differences and contradictions which make the 'profession' . . . a space of competition and struggle. (*ibid.*)

Bourdieu's point is that by employing such concepts as 'profession' in an unproblematic way, by avoiding the difficulties involved in rethinking their definitions, boundaries and actual operations, research is rendered 'quintessentially conservative' and instrumental in maintaining the dominant orthodoxies or 'legitimate' versions of its objects of study. The alternative entails a reconceptualizing of the ways and means of research itself, no less than its object. This undertaking might involve activities which will be heavily criticized by established research paradigms and their representatives. To paraphrase Bourdieu, we must often give up the notion of being 'scientific', at least as conventionally understood, or even run counter to its normal ways of working so that we might challenge ordinary criteria of scientific rigour. Not surprisingly, Bourdieu claims that to practise this 'radical doubt' is akin to becoming 'an outlaw', as it is a method which breaks with the powerful hierarchies of orthodox research. However, it is a necessary means to the end of avoiding the pitfalls of these orthodoxies and gaining an enhanced understanding of the objects of research.

Not surprisingly, this break and radical doubt is expressed in terms of habitus and field. For 'profession' to be understood as *field* is to see it as a structured space of forces and struggles into which individuals along with their habitus-specific dispositions enter. The outcome of this encounter, both for the profession and the processes of professionalization for the individual, is the product of the interaction between them. In order to understand these processes of interaction, it is important to conceptualize the field as a whole structure, along with positions occupied within it. This is quite a different task to the conventional drawing out of a 'representative' sample of individuals (or the choosing of a case study) to investigate thoughts, experiences and activities in order to find commonalities between them or patterns amongst them, as is a common approach in research into teacher education.

Teacher education is also a research field which is awash with schematic metaphors — socialization (Lacey, 1985), craft knowledge (Brown and McIntyre, 1986), teacher thinking (Calderhead, 1987) — which are brought to the research. Such concepts would only be useful in an approach based on Bourdieu's methodology in as much as they can be expressed in terms of their operations between the educational field and the individual habituses located there. Otherwise, they are too utilitarian, more real than the phenomena they seek to represent, and innately conservative. The argument here is that re-thinking such concepts in terms of Bourdieu's approach can reveal a new potential for understanding and reform of the practices to which these concepts allude (See Grenfell, 1996). This rethinking involves the structure of the field and positioning within it at various relational levels. However, before addressing how this might be achieved in practice, it is worth considering just what it means to think relationally.

Thinking Relationally

We have seen how Bourdieu's approach is grounded on a quasi-phenomenological understanding of the relationship between the subject and the object, methodologically expressed in terms of habitus and the field in which objects (both material and ideational) are located or 'positioned' according to identifiable principles. Moreover, this 'relation' is as much a feature of the researcher and the researched, as it is within the research phenomenon itself. The latter part of this chapter will discuss the implications of this relational view for researchers themselves, and we have already seen that one consequence of this argument is that a 'break' is made, not only with common sense views of phenomena, but also with common academic constructs of them. Once this break has been realized in principle, if not yet actualized in practice, the next step is to develop an interpretation of it in relational terms. Moreover, it is necessary to think in terms of the valued products and relations of a particular site of activity; for example, degrees of 'connaissance' and 'reconnaissance', configurations of capital, legitimate ways of thinking and acting. Bourdieu's own work is full of diagrams, constructed conceptually in order to express the relations between these terms of analysis, and a schematic representation is often a helpful way to 'think through' a particular feature.

Here, it is worth thinking through an example by way of illustration. Chapter 5 discussed the operation of language in the classroom, and explored the ways in which the 'legitimate' values represented in the contents of lesson, cognitive processes, and the way of behaving, operated in the pedagogic discourse. We gave samples of pedagogic dialogue between pupils and pupils, and pupils and teachers. Figure 9.1 (adapted from Bourdieu, 1979, p. 191) attempts to represent this interaction; it is based on a two-person exchange. On the left hand side (1), are the 'objective conditions of existence', expressed in structural terms, the positioning of fields within fields. Such conditions act on individual habitus (2): both are structured (thus identifiable) and structuring (thus constituting). In terms of language, the relation between the two gives rise to 'generating language systems' and 'perceptions of language' (3); that is, systems that are productive and differentiating according discernible values. The field (*le champ*) (4) delineates the specific context of activity, which in turn conditions individual thoughts, perceptions and cognitive processes. The site context in Chapter 5 was the classroom. Schematically, in Figure 9.1, the relation between those involved is represented in its simplest form: a dyad. It is drawn in this way to indicate individual persons coming into the field context.

Figure 9.1: Model of a theoretical basis of a 'linguistic market'

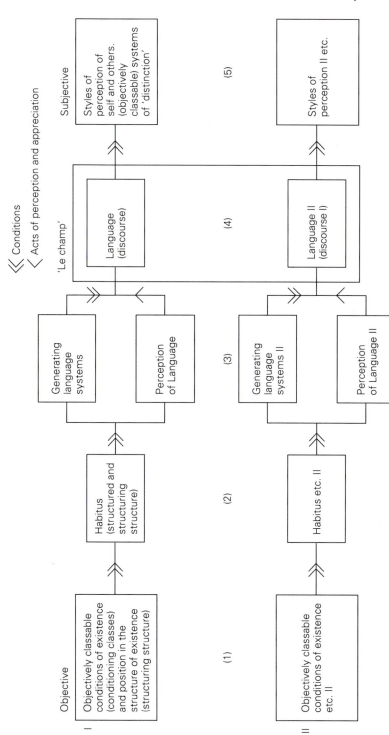

Source: Grenfell, 1993 (based on Bourdieu, 1979, p. 191)

Figure 9.2: A schematic 'linguistic market'

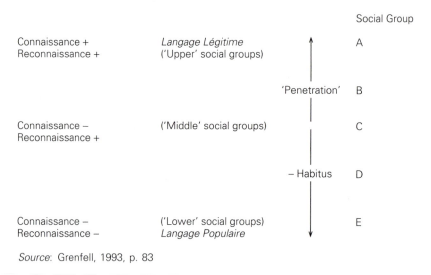

Source: Grenfell, 1993, p. 83

However, they do not, of course, come into the field as identical individuals. Rather, they come with their own particular, objectively derived, habitus. If we replace person I and person II, with teacher and pupil, we can see that a hierarchy is set up and there are questions of match and mismatch between the ways of thinking between them. It is necessary to insist again: we are not claiming that this is not inevitable, and that all forms of education do not involve some degrees of authority — those who know and those who do not. What is at stake in this case, is the quality of that pedagogic relationship and the ways the learner's individual cognition may help the learning process rather than being seen as something which has to be reformed along 'legitimate' lines. We saw in Chapter 5 that this is not always the case, and the production of academic metaphors such as 'scaffolding' may mislead rather than result in a clearer understanding of what constitutes a productive pedagogic exchange.

The habitus of the teacher and pupil in this case is not simply a question of the content of subject curricular areas, but ways of thinking which can be culturally derived as well as socio-economically based in terms of class differences which so preoccupy Bourdieu. The pupil–pupil exchanges in Chapter 5 illustrate these cultural differences. In all cases, however, the exchange operates as a kind of negotiation in terms of recognizable valued products: specific knowledge content, ways of thinking, behaving, etc. Figures 9.2 and 9.3 express this in terms of what were described earlier as processes of 'connaissance' (productive schemes of thought) and 'reconnaissance' (interpretive schemes of thought). Again, in these examples, there is a hierarchy drawn up between legitimate and popular language. The social groups indicated should not be thought of simply in terms of socio-economic classes; indeed, for education, cultural capital is not synonymous with economic capital. What the diagrams do indicate, however, is that those coming from a cultural background

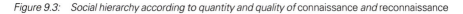

Figure 9.3: *Social hierarchy according to quantity and quality of* connaissance *and* reconnaissance

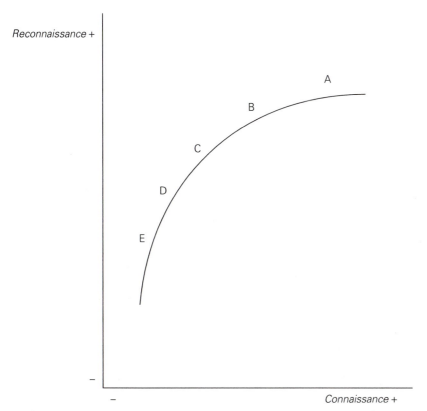

Source: Grenfell, 1993, p. 82

(often expressed in language) which is closest to the orthodox school culture, will have a whole set of productive and receptive schemes of thought and valuing which will render the pedagogic process less problematic. The reverse is also true.

It might be worth thinking through how such diagrams would look and work if we imagined them representing a deviant culture outside of the school. In other words, the 'legitimate' language is now non-orthodox, and is present when an individual enters a deviant field or group. What happens now according to the various social groups an individual may come from?

At the middle level in Figure 9.2, individuals located there are pulled in two different directions. On the one hand, there is the pull to penetrate the more legitimate forms of language and thought; on the other there is the downwards pull of those individual aspects of habitus which run counter to this. The result is that productive and receptive processes do not run in parallel. Those fully inducted in the legitimate ways of doing things have active knowledge and recognition of what is at stake (although one must remember that this is not always the same as conscious know-ledge). The reverse is also true. In between these points, it is possible for individuals to recognize what is at stake, but not to be able to operationalize it in a productive manner. Figure 9.3 expresses this relation: that recognition can run ahead of practical knowledge for various groups. The fact that 'connaissance' and 'reconnaissance' do not run in parallel as two equally proportioned cognitive forms is indicated by the curve of the line expressing the relationship between them.

These diagrams attempt to express the conceptual terms of analysis involved, and it would be possible to work through any number of examples. However, having established something of the conceptual relation between habitus and field in a site context and the processes involving capital and connaissance/reconnaissance, there is another task of relational thinking to be done in terms of the structure of the fields themselves. Our second example does this in terms of teacher education.

An issue of concern in teacher education in many countries is the relationship between the school and training institution. Figure 9.4 takes these two, and again

Figure 9.4:   The basic structure of the training field

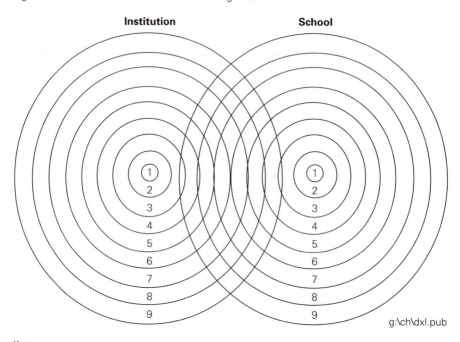

g:\ch\dxl.pub

Key:
1. Trainee / Colleague / Trainer / Mentor Interaction
2. Individual Course Sessions
3. Subject Programme
4. The Training Course
5. University Department of Education
6. University
7. Education Profession
8. Individual Trainee Lives
9. Society

9. Society
8. Individual Trainee Lives
7. The Education Profession
6. Schools
5. Modern Language Department
4. Classrooms
3. Classes
2. Lessons
1. Teacher/Pupil Interaction

Source: Grenfell, 1998, p. 121

attempts to 'rethink' them in relational terms. At the heart of each, there is the face-to-face interaction between teacher and pupil in school and teacher (trainee) and trainer in the training institution. However, outside of these micro-contexts, we can think of the teachers' relations to individual lessons, individual classes, classroom environments, school departments, schools, the education profession, their individual lives and society at large. Similarly, in training, their course sessions, a subject training programme, the training course, training departments, training institutions, the education profession, individual lives and society. The point of thinking it through in these ways, is to see a field such as training as itself made up of a whole lot of organizational structures, some close to the training context, others less so, each with their own knowledge and ways of doing things, which in turn can partly be defined in terms of their relation to the respective dominant (legitimate) forms of knowledge and ways of doing things. The two contexts overlap, and, for example, a trainee will be situated in one or the other site at any particular time, thus distancing the other. Such are the necessities of time and space. However, at any one time and place, the influence from various levels may be felt to a greater or lesser extent. Thus, for example, a teacher may be in a school classroom but operating according to the prescriptions of the government-derived National Curriculum (coming through level 7) or the teaching-method requirements of their training course (level 3).

A phenomenon such as training or professional development can be thought through as a field, which in turn reveals a network of fields within fields. However, the outcome of training is not of course simply a product of the field structure, but also depends on what individuals bring into it; in other words, their backgrounds, schemes of thinking and dispositions — their habitus. Figure 9.5 expresses this in

Figure 9.5: Structural levels of the training field

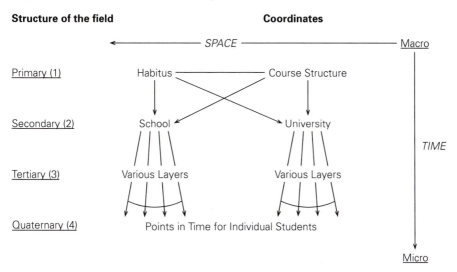

Structure of the field   **Coordinates**

Source: Grenfell, 1996, p. 293

terms of macro (holistic) and micro (site context) structures. There is the training course structure and the individual student habitus. The latter will be located with the trainee in school or the training institution. In either case, the various layers given in Figure 9.4 will apply in terms of their field of operation and/or the determining features acting upon it. Finally at any one point in time, combinations of these various influences will be acting in terms of the generating principles constitutive of how any one thinks and acts. This action, therefore, can be understood as the outcome of individual trainee habitus and the field contexts through which they pass. Both are organized, structured and structuring. Both have ideational representations in the form of personal expressions and formal, for example policy, statements. Thinking in this way allows us to see the individuality of field contexts and those positioned in them, all whilst understanding the outcome in general terms as the interaction between these two. For analytic purposes, we have labelled these various structures: primary; secondary; tertiary; quaternary. This labelling provides a 'mapping of the field', as a way of expressing the positions of individuals at any one time. In theory, at least, it is also possible to collect data at these different sites, and from these different structural sources as a way of illustrating the ongoing operations at particular times and places. It is also possible to relate these to a trainees' habitus-specific dispositions gained from their own educational background and professional experience; for example, their subject knowledge and the practical dispositions these create in a pedagogic context, and their previous careers which may shape how they think about organizing their educational activities. However, it is again necessary to insist that these individual dispositions will only be actualized in accordance with the site contexts in which they find themselves. The product is the outcome of the interaction between the two.

Thinking of educational phenomena as fields, thinking of them relationally, seems to open the door on a complex picture of multitudinal layering and interconnecting links. The use of schematic diagrams can help in thinking in these terms. At the same time, the notion of capturing the totality of even these simplified diagrams is a daunting one, and there seem to be numerous points at which one may come to rest in the process of conducting research into a particular educational phenomenon. On the one hand, there are the micro contexts of person-to-person interaction; on the other, large organizational structures. Bourdieu's theory of practice insists that both should be included, both are mutually constitutive. Next, we see how it is possible to break this complexity down and locate various research activities at different levels of operation.

A Three Level Analysis

Bourdieu does give a very explicit account of what it is to analyse a field (Bourdieu and Wacquant, 1992, pp. 104–7). In effect, the way to proceed is to think of the field in terms of three distinct levels, as follows:

1 Analyse the position of the field *vis-à-vis* the field of power;
2 Map out the objective structure of relations between the positions occupied by agents who compete for the legitimate forms of specific authority of which the field is the site;
3 Analyse the habitus of agents; the systems of dispositions they have acquired by internalizing a determinate type of social and economic condition.

Obviously, Bourdieu has in mind systems of power hierarchies, the way they are organized within society, and the consequent effects on individuals who both are produced by and reproduce them. Nevertheless, it is possible to think of education in similar relational ways. At level 1, there is the relationship between education and the political and economic systems of society. This relationship is crucial in terms of what is expected of education; how it is organized and to what ends — in other words, what is valued and legitimate. Education does not exist as a uniform totality, however, but is made up of a series of institutions and agents, each of which can be defined in terms of their position within the field as a whole: the fields within the field (level 2). Different sectors — primary, secondary, tertiary — have particular areas of activity, which each have specific legitimate terms of governance. Such agents and institutions exist across and within sectors, and their position can be defined ultimately in terms of their relations to each other and the values of the field as a whole. However, there are also intra-institutional structural relations; that is, the way an individual establishment is organized to reflect its competition for legitimate pedagogic products and resources from the field; for example, students and pupils, talented staff, economic and cultural resources, academic achievement, etc. Finally, there is the habitus of the individuals involved (level 3). Such habitus, and the corresponding systems of dispositions, may well be expressed as the organizational ethos of those senior managers who are attempting to apply nationally defined policies; or, the professional activities, thoughts and beliefs of those being organized. It may also include the habitus of students and pupils, and, ultimately, that of their families.

It is important not to consider one level without also taking account of the other two. Nevertheless, it is not always methodologically possible to present analyses on each level simultaneously. They have to be separated to a degree. In an extreme form, it is possible to keep the three levels quite distinct. For example, we have studied the initial professionalization of teachers by considering their 'pedagogic habitus' (Grenfell, 1995); in other words, aspects in trainees' background (professional and cultural) and their education which are pertinent to their preparation as teachers (for example, subject competence, professional training) (level 3). These aspects of habitus were related to the structure of their training at an institutional level and the legitimate ways of acting identifiable there (level 2). The outcome of training could be understood in terms of the interaction between this habitus and field context, which in turn related to the legitimate national policy view of professionalization; in other words, the relation between a field site context and the authority of the education field as a whole which is inscribed in the versions of training found in national prescriptions (level 1).

Ceiriog-Hughes (1997) has also studied teaching as a 'profession' in terms of Bourdieu's three distinct levels. Level 1 covers the way teaching as a profession is defined in relation to other professions and according to what criteria. Level 2 deals with the way professionalism is expressed in a group of individual teaching establishments. Relations to unions, local authorities, government-backed initiatives, and their 'customers' (the pupils) are all examined at this level, as well as internal organization carried out in response to perceived legitimate expectations from each of these, and stress-management of factors threatening such internal forms. Finally, professionalism is examined in terms of the individual habitus of those involved (level 3); how they act 'professionally' and how they define their own professional value and those of others around them.

However, this degree of separation between the three levels is not strictly necessary. In Bourdieu's own work, the three are invariably covered in an integrated fashion. It is important, however, to keep all three of them distinctly in mind, both in conducting research and reading its outcome.

The research projects in Part II can be looked at in terms of these three levels in order to identify the points of the field analysis. In one sense, each account is about encounters between individual habitus and levels of the field. Chapter 4 is concerned with habitus; for example, the differences between mothers' and fathers' gendered habitus expressed in their relationship to their children's education. These are the relations between levels 2 and 3. By the same token, Chapter 5 also looks at the habitus of teachers and pupils and pupils and pupils (level 3) as expressed in dialogues between them. However, the content of their discussion only makes sense in terms of the legitimate cognitive and behavioural norms of the school, and ultimately the education profession beyond (level 1 and 2).

The relationship between the education field and the field of careers (level 1) was the concern of Chapter 6. Again, habitus is central to the process of career decision making, as is the social and cultural capital gained from family contacts and education. However, there are nationally defined legitimate routes for young people's work-seeking activity, and these are crucial in determining the strategies these young people adopt in pursuit of a professional life.

Chapter 7 deals with the academic discourse within a particular university department. The academic habitus of students and lecturers is expressed differentially. The latter have an explicit valuing system which links them differentially to aspects of their job, such as teaching and research. In this case, the authority and power of expectations defined from outside of the institution (level 1) has a determinant effect on what happens within it (level 2). The students do not know of this valuing at first, and respond according to their own habitus specific judgment criteria. However, their own induction into the academic space comes about partly as a result of (and partly results in) a change in this valuing; in other words, an altered relation to teaching and research and thus the taking on of some of the legitimate norms of the academic world (level 3).

As this brief discussion shows, these levels of analysis offer a way of 'mapping' objects of research themselves. There remain questions of how to demonstrate empirically what is happening at these points. What data can be used to demonstrate these relations and processes?

Collecting and Using Data

As we have seen, conventional ethnographies in educational research often mirror scientific procedures when designing a project and the techniques and methods to be used in it. Hence, there is the formulation of 'the' research question, the choice of data collection methods justified on technical grounds, the means of analysis, the formulated theories and hypotheses, which may be developed further, and, finally the answers produced. There is an expectation that researchers should show 'what they have found out', and formulated their conclusions in falsifiable statements supported by empirical exemplification. As a consequence, many qualitative studies tend to be apologetic about the difficulties in generalizing; this is especially so for research students who may already be anxious about the strength of claims in their findings. They may not yet have developed the confidence to see this as a methodological issue rather than as a personal shortcoming. In such an approach, methodology and data techniques often seem to drive the research. This is not the case for Bourdieu, who is scornful both of the sometimes 'gratuitous nature of ethnographical enquiry' (1980a, p. 11) and the pseudo-scientificity to be seen in some researchers' ambitions for transcending positivism. 'I was aware from the outset', he claims 'that my task involved not simply telling the truth of this world . . . but also showing that this world is the site of an ongoing struggle to tell the truth of this world' (1989c, p. 35). However, the means of doing this seem very different to conventional research processes. He does refer to his approach as consisting of 'objectivist methods of observation' (*ibid.*), but these are far from a prescribed sequence or series of technical procedures. Rather, research is seen as an 'epistemological experiment' (*ibid.*, p. 33), a kind of act of exploration, in which, technically, 'it is forbidden to forbid' (Bourdieu and Wacquant, 1992b, p. 227). Bourdieu is critical of 'methodological watchdogs':

> Methodologists . . . will have no difficulty finding plenty to nit-pick about in the operations that have to be carried out in order to grasp the constructed object as best one can . . . Among those difficulties . . . is the question of the boundaries of the field. The most daring positivists solve that question — when they do not purely and simply neglect to pose it by using the preexisting lists — by what they call an 'operational definition' . . . without seeing that the question of the definition is at stake within the object itself. (*ibid.*, p. 244)

Rather than start with methodologies, Bourdieu's point of departure is a theory of practice, which, he claims, if followed to its logical conclusion, avoids the multiple problems of technique, theory and practice, objectivity and subjectivity, which orthodox approaches to research encounter. In Bourdieu's research frame, the data collected and the instruments of analysis are no more important than the way the researcher is conducting themselves in the research in terms of theory and practice. It is probably not surprising, therefore, to find Bourdieu using a whole range of qualitative and quantitative data collecting and analysis techniques in his own research, even while criticizing others' use of them. The issue at stake is not whether a particular method should be used. It is, rather, the intention behind it, and the validity claims laid on it. This principled distinction has been summed up in terms of the underlying philosophy of a particular research paradigm:

> Bourdieu is a realist . . . As against positivists, realists accept that explanation may involve analysis in terms of unobserved entities . . . As against rationalists, realists claim that the unobserved and intransitive relations and objects are not unknowable. Rather . . . realist theories about unobserved entities depend on the generation and testing of hypotheses, within which there is always the possibility of making mistakes. The new realism makes claims about (relatively) invariant relations in social life which go beyond the constant conjunctions of logical positivism. However, its empirical propositions have no absolute status, but are only *claims* to truth, to be tested as adequate through the inter-subjective judgement of the scientific community. (Fowler, 1996, pp. 7–8)

In other words, it is not simply a question of what is used in terms of data collecting and analysis, and how it is used, but rather why it is used and to what ends. A good example of these distinctions can be seen in the use that is made of statistics.

In an early paper (1994), Bourdieu writes of statistics and the way social scientists use them rather like 'magical recipes':

> Statistics ceases to be the instrument of rational research to become an incantation for unveiling hidden reality. Thus what we have to denounce is not the use of statistics but the fetishism of statistics . . . This fetishism leads some people to think that only those things which can be measured are worth consideration instead of attempting to measure what deserves to be known . . . It does not follow that statistics is the measure of all things. It does not follow that things which, in the current state of the methods at out disposal, cannot be measured are not worth being known and that intuitive knowledge or plain description are consigned to irredeemable indignity . . . the fact that behaviours or opinions have a statistical frequency does not mean that they are thereby more intelligible; or the fact that behaviours or opinions are more intelligible equally does not imply that they must occur with more statistical frequency. (pp. 8–9)

Yet, Bourdieu does use statistics extensively throughout his research. In early work on education (e.g., Bourdieu and Passeron, 1964/1979; Bourdieu et al., 1994; Bourdieu and Passeron, 1970/1977), he employs statistics to indicate variations across social class in such areas as language competence, family background, academic orientation, etc. In his later research into his own academic elites, he uses statistics to analyse the structure of the field and the ascribed status of those positioned in it (1984b). In *Distinction* (1979/1984a), statistical tables also show the evolving tastes and leisure activities of a range of social groupings. Many of these statistics are quoted in terms of straight frequency tables for comparative purposes. His intention here is to disclose 'relations which would not have otherwise been considered' (1994, p. 10). This intent to show up relations also extends to his use of 'correspondence analysis'. This technique allows him to illustrate social space graphically in terms of gender, age, class and objectifiable aspects of cultural capital, such as the consumption of art, music and literature (cf. 1979/1984a; Wuggenig and Mnich, 1994). Yet behind this use lies the insistence that 'statistics undoubtedly does not know how to reveal relations other than those it is asked to search for' (1994, p. 10). And in such questions, again arises the issue of the construction and categories which are brought to the research. For example, he questions whether 'public opinion' is anything other than a manufactured product of political scientists (1971b). Moreover, he shows how questionnaires often risk simply reproducing the classificatory schemes of their authors (1979, pp. 625–40).

These sorts of insights are not unique to Bourdieu, and orthodox methodologists have for a long time debated such issues. However, his critique comes from a theory of practice that leads to a certain way of doing things and of thinking. To offer an interim summary, we can say that Bourdieu argues that an alternative exists to oppositions between quantitative and qualitative research, between statistical and logical inferencing. However, this alternative should not be seen as any less objective; indeed, he claims a special kind of pragmatic objectivity for it. Much of Bourdieu's work still makes frequent use of statistical methods, all the while insisting that they are the site of a reciprocal dialogue for the researcher, the source of objectifiable relations and temporary categorizations as part of the engagement with the research object. Here, it is worth again raising the fact that Bourdieu is primarily a sociologist, and, therefore, has sociological preoccupations. Thus, his basic terms of analysis are often based on socio-economic categories. That such social class differences exist, no matter how subtly expressed, is hardly a major discovery. Moreover, it is true that in educational research, not all issues of process and practice can be reduced to socio-economic relations. For example, to understand classroom pedagogic discourse, or young people's career decisions, or students' perceptions of the academic discourse, it is necessary to consider factors other than economic determinants. Often, the processes at play are local and affect local individuals. In order to study these, even if general statements can eventually be made, it requires the employment of more micro methodologies such as individual ethnographies and case studies. The objective behind such studies must be the identification of the principles generating the structures of discourse. Such principles may be socio-economic in the final analysis but manifest themselves in all sorts of systems (including the many contexts of education and pedagogy) along the way.

In many respects, case studies offer an excellent opportunity to research in a Bourdieuian way. Case studies of individuals indicate particular habitus constituents and life trajectories. Individuals are also always positioned in some field or other at any one time and place. There is then the possibility of researching the interaction between habitus and field in empirical terms. The same might be said of institutional case studies, which, in keeping with Bourdieu's theory of practice, can be studied as structured (organizationally, managerially, ideationally) and structuring (in terms of their constitutive effects on local activities) structures. They also have inter- as well as intra-structural relations. They offer the possibility of 'mapping the field' and positions within it. Moreover, it is clear that the conclusions drawn from individual cases are not necessarily of a lower order than more extensive studies. As Platt argues: 'If there is a rich and detailed account of many features of the case(s), it may be a considerable achievement to devise an interpretation which can deal with all of them, and this may pose a greater challenge than the fitting of superficial generalizations to larger numbers' (1988, p. 19).

In Bourdieu's latest published empirical work (1993b), he also uses a case study approach in his cataloguing of the daily lives of a range of French people, including teachers. The methods he used to collect data warrant some consideration. Perhaps unsurprisingly, at the heart of the approach is an objectification of the researcher and the object of research; in this case, represented in a number of one-to-one interviews. The logic of such an encounter is, of course, to see it as the meeting of individuals' habitus within a field designated by the researcher. Such a definition of circumstance risks exerting symbolic violence if the researcher merely imposes their own classificatory schemes. The researcher must not forget that in objectifying the researched, they are in effect objectifying themselves and their own social categories. We have attempted to bring such a process to the surface in the authors' reflexive accounts in Chapter 8. This process is likely to become more or less accentuated depending on the proximity of researchers and the researched. For example, Bourdieu warns that when we use interviews we should avoid accentuating this distance, but rather find a convergence with the interviewee. Questions should never be raised which do not come from the respondent themselves. Instead, the interviewer should attempt to help them 'disclose those aspects of the social determinants of their opinions and their practices, which are most difficult to admit and accept' (1993b, p. 913 own translation). Bourdieu refers to this research encounter as a 'spiritual exercise', and:

> To try to really situate one's mind in the place the interviewee occupies in the social space from necessity by starting to question them from that point, in order to take their part in it in some way, . . . is not to project oneself into others in the way that phenomenologists claim. It is to give oneself a generic and genetic understanding of who they are, based on the (theoretical and practical) command of the social conditions which produced them. (*ibid.*, p. 910 own translation)

Understanding in this sense, does not begin as an analysis of data, or even mean good intentions on the part of the interviewer to be sympathetic with the interviewee. Rather, it is an understanding that emerges out of the structural relationships set up by the interview itself. 'It occurs in the way the interview is presented and conducted — at one and the same time intelligible, reassuring and with commitment — so that the situation and questioning has a sense for the interviewee; especially in the way that problems are raised' (*ibid.*). As a result, the interview is a genuine encounter, where the interviewer can still explore possibilities intuitively and work on provisional hypotheses. The private experiences of individuals are transferred to the public sphere, not out of interest in the individuals themselves but in the general, generative processes which have produced them as social beings. Bourdieu refers to this as a 'realist construction' and gives an example of three secondary school students:

> One cannot really understand what is being said in an apparently quite banal conversation between three secondary school students, unless, . . . one knows how to read, in what they have to say, the structure of present and past objective relations between their trajectory and the structure of the educational establishments they attended, and, by that, see the structure and the history of the educational system to be found there. (*ibid.*, own translation)

We can see the analysis at three levels, discussed earlier, in this statement. Bourdieu continues:

> Contrary to what a naively personalist view might have us believe about the singularity of people, it is the disclosure of the immanent structures in remarks made in a particular interaction which, alone, allows us to grasp the essential of what makes up the idiosyncrasy of each of the young women and all the singular complexity of their actions and reactions. (*ibid.*, own translation)

In contrast to the 'symbolic violence' that, Bourdieu claims, can be done in the name of research, this form of researcher engagement amounts to a kind of 'intellectual love' (p. 914), since it accords with a 'natural order' in the exchange between interviewer and the interviewed.

In each of the accounts in Part II, it is possible to see how commentaries on various educational issues have been constructed from interview data. Much of this involved personal enquiry. In Chapter 4, the researcher herself was a mother with children at one of the schools involved and had been a teacher there as well. Chapter 5 represents less 'hands on' experience in research and is more an exercise in 'thinking in these terms' in order to see what an important academic area of research might look like from a Bourdieuian perspective. Chapter 6 used interview techniques, both structured and semi-structured. In this case, the individuals involved were professional researchers, and it is necessary to ask if the type of interviews described above were achievable in this context. In Chapter 7, the researcher was himself carrying out research for a higher degree, and thus was able to truthfully present himself as a fellow mature student to the people he interviewed. At the same time, he was an academic member of staff, and so was able to present himself as holding a similar position to interviewees who were working as academics.

Some of these accounts might be taken as examples of 'reflective practitioner' research, where the researcher's own situation is the object of enquiry. Similarly, the accounts in Part II do seem to paint a picture of 'participant observation' research, which is common in educational ethnographies. Here, it is felt that closer proximity to the research context allows a closer understanding of the processes at stake there. This assumption itself again raises questions about the relationship between the researcher and the research, which are epistemological in nature. It thus brings us full circle in this chapter in order to consider the form and status and knowledge produced in research conducted from Bourdieuian perspective.

Participant Objectivation

By now it is clear that Bourdieu's whole project is to find a way in which to conduct research which is true to the 'breaks' he has found necessary to make in developing a theory of practice which avoids reifying the dynamic of social processes. His approach rests on a way of thinking or doing things in order 'to find out', but crucially includes a reflexivity which at all times implicates the researcher and the actions they undertake in conducting research and presenting its 'findings'. According to Bourdieu's theory of practice, it is easy to understand why he sees crude forms of 'participant observation' as simply a contradiction in terms. There is no 'value-free', neutral, free-standing objectivity in Bourdieu's method; only individuals (with particular social, scholastic and academic habitus) positioned in fields which structure the representations of their products. Reality is contested. For the social scientist not to recognize this is a supreme act of bad faith. If the method Bourdieu proposes is significantly different from others, it is because of this element of reflexivity which continually turns back on itself, at every stage, the very theory used in the design and carrying out of research in the first place. Such reflexivity is also applied to the theoretical understanding used to interpret findings. Crucial, in this, is the position of the researcher in the social space and the research field, as well as the privilege of being able to objectify a field rather than being subsumed by it. Only a reflexive method guards against an overly constructed interpretaion, where the researchers' conclusions can be regarded as the uncovering of a God-given truth.

Such reflexivity must 'objectify the objectifying subject' (i.e., the researcher) (Bourdieu and Wacquant, 1992a, pp. 175–85) in a process of 'participant objectivation' (Bourdieu, 1978). Such an auto-objectification goes beyond a preoccupation with the construction of the concepts of analysis, but positions the researcher and the objectification in terms of their social origins and trajectory within the academic field. However, such reflexivity eschews the highly subjectivist accounts of researcher introspection common in post-modernist ethnographies.

Earlier in this chapter we referred to Bourdieu's own academic trajectory. However, the reader of his work will not find personal details of his life. This may seem at first paradoxical, but it underlines the point that what must be objectified, first and foremost, is the positioning of the researcher with regard to the object of research in structural, relational and ideational terms. This is not the same thing as objectifying a biography and demonstrating its uniqueness. An example of what we do mean can be seen in the way we located Bourdieu with respect to various academic and intellectual disciplines. This, rather than personal detail, is 'participant objectivation'.

We concluded the previous chapter with a quotation from Bourdieu, where he argues for a systematic critique of the presuppositions used in constructing research. This is achieved through 'participant objectivation', as a means of avoiding treating the social world as distant spectacle. Instead, it is viewed as an amalgam of practical problems, which have to be addressed by individuals within a scientific community. The necessary objectification is as much a responsibility of a particular academic community as of the individual researcher. The project is more than a personal mission, as it is only in the collectivity that this break with what might be termed an 'intellectualist bias' can ultimately occur; by a process through which the personal and scientific habitus are rendered distinct:

> The scientific habitus can be autonomous from the personal empirical habitus . . . it is possible to create a kind of subject that is snatched away from social forces . . . it is possible by work and collective checking to be scientific. Moreover, this subject is in fact a collective subject; not an individual. The subject has more chance of being autonomous the more they are collective; that is to say, the more they accumulate what is available from the field, techniques, methods, concepts. The more they are collective and reflective, the more they are separate from the empirical subject. (Bourdieu and Grenfell, 1995, p. 29 own translation)

Bourdieu here is claiming that it is within the collectivity that the necessary means to the end of reflexivity must be obtained. In effect, it is a radical critique of any academic field that does not institutionalize a profound reflexivity at the heart of its critical evaluations. However, this necessarily assumes a two way process. Individual researchers must be reflexive, but the field must also recognize and reward reflexivity as part of a process of mutual transformation.

Conclusion

From the preceding discussion, it is possible to see how Bourdieu constructs a research practice in his own epistemological terms. This 'theory as method' is predicated on what he might call a 'double refus' in order to indicate his positioning with regard to dominant academic discourses. His own theory of practice is, literally, neither one thing nor the other, but an autonomous third way. The approach involves a certain way of thinking, and a range of tools in order to think with. It also involves procedures and techniques which are not uncommon, although the way they are employed may be. It would be wrong to see Bourdieu as a methodological libertarian or advocating a *laissez-faire* attitude to research practice. In comparison to the oversights of those Bourdieu terms the 'methodological police' (Bourdieu and Wacquant, 1992b, p. 227), his own approach, he claims, is 'doubly rigorous'.

Reflexivity is involved at every stage in the research process: in the construction of the object research; in data collection; and in analyses and presentation of findings. It involves 'participant objectivation', or knowledge of knowledge, as a way to avoid imputing to the object of research the presuppositions of the researcher themselves. This form of 'reflexive objectivity' is quite distinct from the objectivist claims of much social science research, which Bourdieu sees as disguising the common behaviour of researchers to objectify in order to negate other's work and 'crush one's rivals' (1989c, p. 35) in the field of competing academic interpretations. For Bourdieu, aspiring to be 'scientific' does not involve the presentation of hard positivist theories, but an 'understanding and explaining' that is both transformative and liberating. That this science involves a different way of acting and thinking is self evident. However, it results in resistance from established orthodoxies in philosophical, sociological, and educational research. What is promised is a break with the past, together with its false methodological and epistemological dichotomies. It is probably self-evident that the process of working in this way, and with these risks, is demanding. A final word from Bourdieu is appropriate here:

> There is no risk of overestimating difficulty and dangers when it comes to thinking the social world. The force of the preconstructed resides in the fact that, being inscribed both in things and in minds, it presents itself under the cloak of the self-evident which goes unnoticed because it is by definition taken for granted. Rupture in fact demands a *conversion of one's gaze* and one can say of the teaching of sociology that it must first 'give new eyes' as initiatory philosophers sometimes phrased it. The task is to produce, if not a 'new person', then at least a new gaze ... and this cannot be done without a genuine conversion, a *metanoia*, a mental revolution, a transformation of one's whole vision of the social world. (Bourdieu and Wacquant, 1992b, p. 251, emphasis in original)

Chapter 10

Conclusion

We noted in the introduction that this book arose from a conviction that research carried out in terms of Bourdieu's theory of practice offers insights and understandings which show up elements of pedagogic processes which are not easily visible in other approaches. We also outlined two main aims. The first of these was to present the main components of Bourdieu's theoretical position in a way which would highlight its implications for education; the second was to offer practical examples of the ideas in use in educational settings. We have sought to meet these aims in an integrated fashion, through a process of assembly and interconnection of a series of chapters with various theoretical, practical and empirical emphases.

As we near the end of the book, it is worth referring to another aspect of it that was signalled at the very beginning, in our choice of 'Acts of Practical Theory' as a subtitle. This was a deliberate reference to Bourdieu's own research journal *Actes de la Recherche en Sciences Sociales*. 'Actes' in French can, of course, simply refer to research papers or proceedings, yet there are many other connotations, as there are with the English 'acts'. They include enactment, performance, an Act in a play, an Act of Parliament, even a 'deed' (interestingly, a commercial or legal document which gives a symbolic permanence to sets of actions). It is thus a word which calls attention to both *dynamic* and *contextual* matters. We felt that this sense best summed up the spirit of the book. We see the pieces of research reported here as individual 'acts' to understand various educational phenomena in terms of the dynamic processes and surroundings, both material and ideational, which give rise to them and are in turn re-constituted by them. At the same time, we have highlighted the individual contributors' awareness of the conditions of these acts themselves by calling on a level of reflexivity which renders visible important elements of their production and construction. By acting as a researcher, any individual is already taking up a position with respect to the object of study that is distinct from a 'common sense' relation. Moreover, the researcher is connecting with an academic, scientific field with its own structures, values and expectations.

At different points in this book we have acknowledged that the kind of investigation and analysis Bourdieu's work promotes can be uncomfortable to carry out. His own position is opposed to — yet also a synthesis of — a number of orthodoxies in the social sciences, and this makes him a target of attack. It can also feel like a risky endeavour to advocate the extension of a theory of practice outside of its sociological base, but we have done so in various ways to a greater or lesser extent. We do not wish to attempt any totalizing justification for these extensions, but instead would want to leave the practical and theoretical discussion given in each of the chapters to speak for itself. The whole point in producing the book stemmed from a belief that what Bourdieu had to say about understanding and explaining events in the social world (and the methodology necessary to bring this about) had relevance in investigating a wider range of issues and topics in education than those normally studied in sociology. However, by making such a commitment in print, we are aware that the book will come to occupy a position in a research field which is already fragmented, if not factional. Our use of 'acts', then, alludes as well to a situational understanding of this position; that we recognize the space our collective work might occupy in the field of forces made of the relationships between the products of educational research.

It is clear that Bourdieu's work can give rise to some highly productive ideas, and that it can even be inspirational. Some of Bourdieu's staunchest critics find him 'good to think with' (Jenkins, 1992) and 'très amusant' (Alexander, 1995); the latter evoking images of the French 'wit' who is both coquettish and intriguing. Amongst the advice Bourdieu gives to the would-be researcher is included the idea that first and foremost they should have fun (1989c, p. 54). There is indeed humour in Bourdieu's work, and often extreme irony and satire. But none of this should be taken as a sign of superficiality. Bourdieu's work always has serious and practical purposes.

For some audiences, the approach we wish to encourage can seem to give inadequate emphasis to the uniqueness of individuals. Yet if Bourdieu is about anything, he is about researching and investigating the social in a way that takes real account of individuals in their existential reality. His own work is characterized by a respect for the dignity of individual people living their individual lives as best they can. Rather than leading to a fragmented individualism, the approach makes constant connections between individual subjectivities and the generating principles acting on them in the fields through which they pass in their life trajectories. There is a modernist rationality at stake in his attempts to show up the processes and forces operating in these encounters. Such a project must have an implicit 'liberating' intent. Yet, at the same time, the immediate product of such explorations is never the formulation of corrective measures to alleviate the impositions and misrecognitions; for Bourdieu also applies the same critique to the very products of these investigations. The values of researchers and their reasons for intervening are thus also rendered open to scrutiny. In both the field and the field which is studying the field, Bourdieu is suspicious of the language which is used, and, again, draws attention to the inequalities of class, status, gender, race and age which are expressed in it. In this respect, he can be considered post-modern in his 'deconstructions' of terms in which intercommunications operate. However, he never falls into the abyss of self-referential relativity, and sees that resistance to the forces of inequality and misunderstanding amounts to more than simply describing inequalities, naming contradictions or devising policies to overcome them. Such policies are in any case likely to represent the development of further strategies in order to maintain the operational processes of the status quo, albeit in a newer misrecognized form. But do these arguments lead inexorably to a form of disabling pessimism?

How one deals with such a question depends on a number of things, including, perhaps, the faith one may or may not have in an enlightenment project or notions like progress and reform. In Chapter 9, we suggested that Bourdieu's own project starts by thinking in the terms of the theory of practice he offers. No substantive outcome or intent is here preordained when using such concepts as habitus and field as what Bourdieu refers to as 'thinking tools' when addressing a topic of research. What is required, however, is a further willingness to apply the same epistemological critique, both individually and collectively, to the research activities in which we engage. This book represents an attempt to act in this way. In Chapter 2 we discussed paradigms as ways of identifying a collectivity which shared a way of doing things. Whether Bourdieu does offer an alternative paradigm to those dominant in educational research is as yet open to debate. The range of activities of those now working along the lines of Bourdieu's work suggests that this may be the case. We know that some unique insights are fostered by working with his 'tools', but, as yet, we cannot be sure that this should justifiably be termed a paradigm shift. Perhaps, what is more important than whether or not such a shift is taking place, is that an engagement with the ideas be made in the first place. When researchers think in these terms and work in these ways, they by definition transform the structure of the research field itself. New structures and activities give rise to new 'scientific' products, both theoretical and practical. The nature of these products cannot be foreseen in advance. Once they become available, however, they provide new ways of thinking and acting to guide educationalists and researchers. It is in these thoughts and acts, and the ways they act upon us, that our understanding of education is enhanced and our consequent action transformed.

Notes on Contributors

Michael Grenfell presently works in the Centre for Language in Education at the University of Southampton. He was associate researcher at the *Centre de Sociologie Européenne* in Paris and has collaborated with Bourdieu in projects on language and scholastic exclusion. He is the co-founder of an international network of scholars working with Bourdieu's ideas and organizer of a major international conference on Bourdieu: Language, Culture, and Education. He is also joint convenor of symposia on Bourdieu at the conferences of the British and European educational research associations. His research interests include the sociology of language, teacher education and philosophical issues in educational research.

Phil Hodkinson is professor of post-compulsory education and training in the Manchester Metropolitan University. He worked as a teacher for twenty years before entering Higher Education. He has a long-standing interest in the transition from school to work, and in the lives and experiences of young people. His recent research interests include career decision making and the role of careers guidance. He is exploring the value of hermeneutics in understanding the nature of qualitative research.

David James began his teaching career in Further Education. He now works in the Faculty of Education at the University of the West of England, Bristol, where he is Director of the Research Degrees Programme and editor of *The Redland Papers*. He has jointly organized symposia and presented a number of papers at national and international conferences on the significance of Bourdieu's ideas for understanding educational processes. His interests include the study of teaching, learning and assessment across a range of settings in post-compulsory education.

Diane Reay is research fellow working at King's College, London. Prior to moving into Higher Education she worked as a primary school teacher in inner London for twenty years. She researched and published in the areas of children's peer group cultures, parental choice, staff relations in secondary schools, ability groupings, feminist theory and methodology, social mobility and young people's choice of Higher Education. She is currently researching into children as consumers of popular culture and urban space.

Derek Robbins read English at Cambridge and did his doctorate under Raymond Williams. He has taught at what is now the University of East London since 1970.

He was one of the founding members of staff of the School of Independent Study and, in 1988, published an account of this innovation. Since 1986, his research has focussed on the work of Bourdieu. In 1991 he published *The Work of Pierre Bourdieu: Recognizing Society*, and he has completed a book on Bourdieu and culture which will be published in 1998 by Sage. He is now head of the newly established Department of Social Politics, Language and Linguistics at UEL.

Bibliography

ADAMS, B. (1990) *Time and Social Theory*, Cambridge: Polity Press.

ALDERMAN, G. (1996) 'Audit, assessment and academic autonomy', *Higher Education Quarterly*, **50**, 3, pp. 78–192.

ALEXANDER, J. (1995) *Fin de Siècle Social Theory*, London: Verso.

ALHEIT, P. (1994) *Taking the Knocks: Youth Unemployment and Biography — A Qualitative Analysis*, London: Cassell.

ALLATT, P. (1993) 'Becoming privileged: The role of family processes', in BATES, I. and RISEBOROUGH, G. *Youth and Inequality*, Buckingham: Open University Press.

ANTKAINEN, A., HOUTSONEN, J., KAUPPILA, J. and HUOTELIN, H. (1996) *Living in a Learning Society: Life Histories, Identities and Education*, London: Falmer Press.

ARCHER, M. (1983) 'Process without system', *Archives Européennes de Sociologie*, **24**, 1, pp. 196–221.

ASHTON, D.N. and FIELD, D. (1976) *Young Workers*, London: Hutchinson.

AUDIT COMMISSION (1993) *Unfinished Business: Full-time Educational Courses for 16–19 Year Olds*, London: HMSO.

BANKS, M., BATES, I., BREAKWELL, G., BYNNER, J., ELMER, N., JAMIESON, L. and ROBERTS, K. (1992) *Careers and Identities: Adolescent Attitudes to Employment, Training and Education, Their Home Life, Leisure and Politics*, Milton Keynes: Open University Press.

BANKS, O. (1968) *The Sociology of Education*, London: Batsford.

BARNES, D. (1976) *From Communication to Curriculum*, Harmondsworth: Penguin.

BARNES, D. and TODD, F. (1977) *Communication and Learning in Small Groups*, London: Routledge and Kegan Paul.

BARRETT, L.R. (1996) 'On students as customers — Some warnings from America', *Higher Education Review*, **28**, 3, pp. 70–3.

BARRETT, M. (1991) *The Politics of Truth: From Marx to Foucault*, Cambridge: Polity Press.

BARRETT, M. (1992) 'Words and things', in BARRETT, M. and PHILLIPS, A. (eds) *Destabilising Theory*, London: Polity Press.

BASSEY, M. (1990a) 'On the nature of research in education — Part 1', *Research Intelligence*, **36**, pp. 35–8.

BASSEY, M. (1990b) 'On the nature of research in education — Part 2', *Research Intelligence*, **37**, pp. 39–44.

BASSEY, M. (1990c) 'On the nature of research in education — Part 3', *Research Intelligence*, **38**, pp. 16–18.

BASTIANI, J. (1989) *Working with Parents: A Whole School Approach*, Windsor: NFER-Nelson.

BATES, I. (1990) 'No bleeding, whining Minnies: The role of YTS in class and gender reproduction', *British Journal of Education and Work*, **4**, 1, pp. 79–90.

BATES, I. (1993) 'A job which is "right for me"' in BATES, I. and RISEBOROUGH, G. (eds) *Youth and Inequality*, Buckingham: Open University Press.

BATES, I. and RISEBOROUGH, G. (1993) (eds) *Youth and Inequality*, Buckingham: Open University Press.

BECHER, T. (1989) *Academic Tribes and Territories*, Buckingham: Society for Research into Higher Education/Open University Press.

BENNETT, R.J., GLENNESTER, H. and NEVISON, D. (1992) *Learning Should Pay*, Poole: BP Educational Service.

BERGER, P. and LUCKMANN, T. (1967) *The Social Construction of Reality*, Harmondsworth: Penguin.

BERNSTEIN, B. (1986) 'On pedagogic discourse', in RICHARDSON, J. (ed.) *Handbook of Theory and Research in Sociology of Education*, Wesport, CT: Greenwood Press.

BERTAUX, D. (1981) 'From the life-history approach to the transformation of sociological practice', in BERTAUX, D. (ed.) *Biography and Society: The Life History Approach to the Social Sciences*, London: Sage.

BLACKMAN, S. (1987) 'The labour market in school: New vocationalism and issues of socially ascribed discrimination', in BROWN, P. and ASHTON, D.N. (eds) *Education, Unemployment and Labour Markets*, London: Falmer Press.

BOURDIEU, P. (1962) 'Célibat et condition paysanne', *Études Rurales*, **5–6**, pp. 32–136.

BOURDIEU, P. (1963) 'Statistics and sociology', first published as 'Stratégies et Sociologie', pp. 9–12 of BOURDIEU, P., DARBEL, A., RIVET, J.P. and SEIBEL, C. *Travail et Travailleurs en Algérie*, Paris, The Hague: Mouton.

BOURDIEU, P. (1994) ROBBINS, D. (trans.) G.R.A.S.P. Working Paper No. 10, University of East London.

BOURDIEU, P. (1965) *Un Art Moyen: Essai sur les Usages Sociaux de la Photographie*, Paris: Les Éditions de Minuit.

BOURDIEU, P. (1966) *L'Amour de l'Art, les Musées d'Art et leur Public*, Paris: Les Éditions de Minuit.

BOURDIEU, P. (1968) 'Structuralism and theory of sociological knowledge', *Social Research*, **35**, 4, pp. 681–706.

BOURDIEU, P. (1971a) 'The thinkable and the unthinkable', *The Times Literary Supplement*, 15 October, pp. 1255–6.

BOURDIEU, P. (1971b) 'L'opinion publique n'existe pas', *Noroit*, **155**, February, Conference, also in *Les Temps Modernes*, **318**, January, pp. 1292–1309.

BOURDIEU, P. (1972) *Esquisse d'une Théorie de la Pratique, Précédée de Trois Études d'Ethnologie Kabyle*, Geneva: Droz.

BOURDIEU, P. (1973) 'The three forms of theoretical knowledge', *Social Science Information*, **12**, 1, pp. 53–80.

BOURDIEU, P. (1975) 'The specificity of the scientific field and the social conditions of the progress of reason' (NICE, R. trans.), *Social Science Information*, **XIV**, pp. 19–47.

BOURDIEU, P. (1977a) *Outline of a Theory of Practice* (NICE, R. trans.), Cambridge: Cambridge University Press.

BOURDIEU, P. (1977b) 'The economics of linguistic exchanges', *Social Science Information*, **XVI**, 6, pp. 645–68.

BOURDIEU, P. (1978) 'Sur l'objectivation participante: Réponses à quelques objections', *Actes de la Recherche en Sciences Sociales*, **23**, pp. 67–9.

BOURDIEU, P. (1979) *La Distinction*, Paris: Les Éditions de Minuit.

BOURDIEU, P. (1980a) *Le Sens Pratique*, Paris: Les Éditions de Minuit.

BOURDIEU, P. (1980b) 'Le capital social: Notes provisoires', *Actes de la Recherche en Sciences Sociales*, pp. 2–3.

BOURDIEU, P. (1980c) *Questions of Sociology*, Paris: Les Éditions de Minuit.

BOURDIEU, P. (1981a) 'Décrire et prescrire: Notes sur les conditions de possibilité et les limites de l'efficacité politique', *Actes de la Recherche en Sciences Sociales*, **38**, pp. 69–73.

BOURDIEU, P. (1981b) 'Men and machines', in KNORR-CETINA, K. and CICOUREL, A.C. *Advances in Social Theory and Methodology: Towards an Integration of Micro and Macro-Sociologies*, London: Routledge and Kegan Paul.

BOURDIEU, P. (1982a) *Leçon sur la Leçon*, Paris: Les Éditions de Minuit.

BOURDIEU, P. (1982b) *Ce Que Parler Veut Dire: L'Économie des Échanges Linguistiques*, Paris: Fayard.

BOURDIEU, P. (1984a) *Distinction: A Social Critique of the Judgement of Taste* (NICE, R. trans.), Cambridge, MA.: Harvard University Press.

BOURDIEU, P. (1984b) *Homo Academicus*, Paris: Les Éditions de Minuit.

BOURDIEU, P. (1985) 'The genesis of the concepts of "Habitus" and "Field"'', *Sociocriticism*, **2**, 2, pp. 11–24.

BOURDIEU, P. (1986) 'The three forms of capital', in RICHARDSON, J.G. (ed.) *Handbook of Theory and Research for the Sociology of Education*, New York: Greenwood Press.

BOURDIEU, P. (1987) *Choses Dites*, Paris: Les Éditions de Minuit.

BOURDIEU, P. (1988) *Homo Academicus* (COLLIER, P. trans.), Oxford: Polity Press.

BOURDIEU, P. (1989a) *La Noblesse d'État, Grandes Écoles et Esprit de Corps*, Paris: Les Éditions de Minuit.

BOURDIEU, P. (1989b) 'Social space and symbolic power', *Sociological Theory*, **7**, pp. 14–25.

BOURDIEU, P. (1989c) in WACQUANT, L. 'Towards a reflexive sociology: A workshop with Pierre Bourdieu', *Sociological Theory*, **7**, pp. 26–63.

BOURDIEU, P. (1990a) *The Logic of Practice* (NICE, R. trans.), Oxford: Polity Press.

BOURDIEU, P. (1990b) *In Other Words* (ADAMSON, M. trans.), Oxford: Polity Press.

BOURDIEU, P. (1990c) 'La domination masculine', *Actes de la Recherche en Sciences Sociales*, **84**, pp. 2–31.

BOURDIEU, P. (1991) *Language and Symbolic Power* (RAYMOND, G. and ADAMSON, M. trans.), Oxford: Polity Press.

BOURDIEU, P. (1992) 'Thinking about limits', *Theory, Culture and Society*, **9**, pp. 37–49.

BOURDIEU, P. (1993a) *Sociology in Question* (NICE, R. trans.), London: Sage.

BOURDIEU, P. (1993b) *La Misère du Monde*, Paris: Seuil.

BOURDIEU, P. (1996a) *The State Nobility* (CLOUGH, L.C. trans.), Oxford: Polity Press.

BOURDIEU, P. (1996b) 'On the family as a realised category', *Theory, Culture and Society*, **13**, 3, pp. 19–26.

BOURDIEU, P. (1997) *Méditations Pascaliennes*, Paris: Seuil.

BOURDIEU, P. and BOLTANSKI, L. (1975) 'Le fétichisme de la langue', *Actes de la Recherche en Sciences sociales*, **4**, pp. 95–107.

BOURDIEU, P. and COLEMAN, J.S. (eds) (1991) *Social Theory for a Changing Society*, Boulder, San Francisco, Oxford: Westview Press.

BOURDIEU, P. and GRENFELL, M. (1995) *Entretiens*, Centre for Language in Education Occasional Paper: University of Southampton.

BOURDIEU, P. and PASSERON, J.C. (1964) *Les Héritiers*, Paris: Les Éditions de Minuit.

BOURDIEU, P. and PASSERON, J.C. (1967) 'Sociology and Philosophy in France since 1935', *Social Research*, **XXXIV**, pp. 162–212.

BOURDIEU, P. and PASSERON, J.C. (1970) *La Reproduction: Éléments pour une Théorie du Système d'Enseignement*, Paris: Les Éditions de Minuit.

BOURDIEU, P. and PASSERON, J.C. (1977) *Reproduction in Education, Society and Culture* (NICE, R. trans.), London-Beverley Hills: Sage.

BOURDIEU, P. and PASSERON, J.C. (1979) *The Inheritors, French Students and their Relation to Culture* (NICE, R. trans.), Chicago-London: The University of Chicago Press.

BOURDIEU, P. and DE SAINT MARTIN, M. (1975) 'Les catégories de l'entendement professoral', *Actes de la Recherche en Sciences Sociales*, **3**, pp. 194–225.

BOURDIEU, P. and SAYED, A. (1964) *Le Déracinement, la Crise de l'Agriculture Traditionnelle en Algérie*, Paris: Les Éditions de Minuit.

BOURDIEU, P. and WACQUANT, L. (1992a) *Réponses*, Paris: Seuil.

BOURDIEU, P. and WACQUANT, L. (1992b) *An Invitation to Reflexive Sociology*, Oxford: Polity Press.

BOURDIEU, P., BOLTANSKI, L. and DE SAINT MARTIN, M. (1973) 'Les stratégies de reconversion: Les classes sociales et le système d'enseignement', *Information sur les Sciences Sociales*, **XII**, pp. 61–113.

BOURDIEU, P., CHAMBOREDON, J.C. and PASSERON, J.C. (1968) *Le Métier de Sociologue*, Paris: Mouton-Bordas.

BOURDIEU, P., CHAMBOREDON, J.C. and PASSERON, J.C. (1991) *The Craft of Sociology: Epistemological Preliminaries* (KRAIS, B. ed. and NICE, R. trans.), Berlin and New York: de Gruyer.

BOURDIEU, P., PASSERON, J.C. and DE SAINT MARTIN, M. (eds) (1965) 'Langage et rapport au language dans la situation pédagogique', in *Rapport Pédagogique et Communication*, The Hague: Mouton.

BOURDIEU, P., PASSERON, J.C. and DE SAINT MARTIN, M. (1994) *Academic Discourse* (TEESE, R. trans.), Oxford: Polity Press.

BOURNE, J. (1992) 'Inside a multilingual classroom: A teacher, children and theories at work', Unpublished PhD thesis: Southampton University.

BOWLES, S. and GINTIS, H. (1974/1976) *Schooling in Capitalist America*, New York: Basic Books.

BREDO, E. and FEINBERG, W. (1979) 'Meaning, power and pedagogy: Pierre Bourdieu and Jean-Claude Passeron, reproduction in education, society and culture: Essay review', *Journal of Curriculum Studies*, **11**, 4, pp. 315–32.

BRITISH GOVERNMENT (1994) *Competitiveness: Helping Business to Win*, London: HMSO.

BROAD, C.D. (ed.) (1975) *Leibniz: An Introduction*, Cambridge: Cambridge University Press.

BROWN, S. and MCINTYRE, D. (1986) 'How do teachers think about their craft?', in BEN-PERETZ, M., BROMME, R. and HALKES, R. (1986) *Advances of Research on Teacher Thinking*, Lisse: Swets and Zeitlinger, pp. 36–44.

BRUBAKER, R. (1985) 'Rethinking classical theory: The sociological vision of Pierre Bourdieu', *Theory and Society*, **14**, 6, pp. 745–75.

BRUNER, J. (1985) 'Vygotsky: A historical and conceptual perspective', in WERTSCH, J.V. (ed.) *Culture, Communication and Cognition: Vygotskian Perspectives*, Cambridge: Cambridge University Press.

BURGESS, R. (1984) 'Exploring frontiers and settling territory: Shaping the sociology of education' (Review Article), *British Journal of Sociology*, **35**.

CALDERHEAD, J. (ed.) (1987) *Exploring Teachers' Thinking*, London: Cassell.

CALHOUN, C., LIPUMA, E. and POSTONE, M. (1993) *Bourdieu: Critical Perspectives*, Cambridge: Polity Press.

CARR, W. and KEMMIS, S. (1986) *Becoming Critical: Education, Knowledge and Action Research*, Lewes: Falmer Press.

CBI (1993) *Routes for Success — Careership: A Strategy for all 16–19 Year Old Learning*, London: CBI.

CEIRIOG-HUGHES, D. (1997) 'Cultural professionalism: A comparative study of teachers' cultural professionalisation in England and France', PhD Thesis: University of Southampton.

CHOMSKY, N. (1965) *Aspects of the Theory of Syntax*, Cambridge, MA.: MIT.

CLARK, T., LIPSET, S. and REMPEL, M. (1993) 'The declining political significance of social class', *International Sociology*, **8**, 3, pp. 293–316.

CLIFFORD, J. and MARCUS, G. (eds) (1986) *Writing Culture*, Berkley: University of California Press.

COLERIDGE, S.T. (RHYS, E. ed.) (1907) *Coleridge's Lectures on Shakespeare and other Poets and Dramatists*: Everyman.

COLERIDGE, S.T. (WHITE, R.J. ed.) (1972) *Lay Sermons: The Collected Works of Samuel Taylor Coleridge*, London and Princeton: Routledge and Kegan Paul.

COLLINS, J. (1993) 'Determination and contradiction: An application and critique of the work of Pierre Bourdieu on language', in CALHOUN, C., LiPUMA, E. and POSTONE, M. *Bourdieu: Critical Perspectives*, Cambridge: Polity Press.

CONNELL, R.W., ASHENDEN, D.J., KESSLER, S. and DOWSETT, G.W. (1982) *Making the Difference*, Sydney: George Allen and Unwin.

CROSS, M. and WRENCH, J. (1991) 'Racial inequality on YTS: Careers service or disservice?', *British Journal of Education and Work*, **4**, 3, pp. 5–24.

DALE, R., ESLAND, G. and MacDONALD, M. (eds) (1976) *Schooling and Capitalism: A Sociological Reader*, Routledge and Kegan Paul with the Open University Press.

DAVID, M.E. (1993) *Parents, Gender and Education Reform*, Cambridge: Polity Press.

DAVID, M.E., DAVIES, J., EDWARDS, R., REAY, D. and STANDING, K. (1996) 'Mothering and education: Reflexivity and feminist methodology', in MORLEY, L. and WALSH, V. (eds) *Breaking Boundaries: Women in Higher Education*, London: Taylor and Francis.

DAVID, M.E., DAVIES, J., EDWARDS, R., REAY, D. and STANDING, K. (1997) 'Choice within constraints: Mothers and schooling', *Gender and Education*, **9**, 4, (in press).

DAVID, M.E., WEST, A. and RIBBENS, J. (1994) *Mother's Intuition: Choosing Secondary Schools*, London: Falmer Press.

DEARING, R. (1996) *Review of Qualifications for 16–19 Year Olds: Full Report*, London: SCAA.

DENZIN, N. (1989) *Interpretive Biography: Qualitative Research Methods Series, 17*, London: Sage.

DENZIN, N. (1992) *Symbolic Interactionism and Cultural Studies*, Oxford: Basil Blackwell.

EDWARDS, C. (1994) 'Pedagogical knowledge in a mathematics classroom — A stimulated recall exercise', Unpublished Mimeograph: Southampton University.

EDWARDS, D. and MERCER, N. (1987) *Common Knowledge*, London: Routledge.

EGGLESTON, J. (ed.) (1974) *Contemporary Research in the Sociology of Education*, Methuen.

ELSTER, J. (1978) *Logic and Society*, Chichester and New York: Wiley.

ELSTER, J. (1986) *Rational Choice*, Oxford: Basil Blackwell.

ELTON, L. (1992) 'Research, teaching and scholarship in an expanding higher education system', *Higher Education Quarterly*, **46**, 3, pp. 252–68.

ERIKSON, R. and GOLDTHORPE, J.H. (1992) *The Constant Flux: A Study of Class Mobility in Industrial Societies*, Oxford: Clarendon Press.

FEATHERSTONE, M. (ed.) (1992) *Cultural Theory and Cultural Change*, London: Sage.

FLUDE, M. and AHIER, J. (eds) (1974) *Educability, Schools and Ideology*: Croom Helm.

FOWLER, B. (1996) 'An introduction to Pierre Bourdieu's understanding', *Theory, Culture and Society*, **13**, 2, pp. 1–16.

FOX, M.F. (1992) 'Research, teaching and publication productivity: Mutuality versus competition in academia', *Sociology of Education*, **65**, 4, pp. 293–305.

FURLONG, A. (1992) *Growing Up in a Classless Society? School to Work Transition*, Edinburgh: Edinburgh University Press.

GADAMER, H.G. (1979) *Truth and Method*, 2nd, ed., London: Sheed and Ward.

GARNETT, D. and HOLMES, R. (1995) 'Research, teaching and learning: A symbiotic relationship', in SMITH, B. and BROWN, S. (eds) *Research, Teaching and Learning in Higher Education*, London: Kogan Page.

GEERTZ, C. (1975) *The Interpretation of Cultures*, London: Hutchinson.

GENESEE, F. and BOURHIS, R. (1982) 'The social psychological significance of code switching in cross-cultural communication', *Journal of Language and Social Psychology*, **1**, 1, pp. 1–26.

GEWIRTZ, S., BALL, S. and BOWE, R. (1994) 'Parents, privilege and the education market place', *Research Papers in Education*, **9**, 1, pp. 3–29.

GEWIRTZ, S., BALL, S. and BOWE, R. (1995) *Markets, Choice and Equity in Education*, Buckingham: Open University Press.

GEWIRTZ, S., BOWE, R. and BALL, S. (1994) 'Choice, competition and equity: Lessons from research in the UK', Paper presented at The Annual Meeting of the American Educational Research Association. New Orleans 6 April 1994.

GIDDENS, A. (1987) *Social Theory and Modern Sociology*, Cambridge: Polity Press.

GILES, H. and POWESLAND, P. (1975) *Speech Style and Social Evaluation*, London: Academic Press.

GIROUX, H. (1983) 'Theories of reproduction and resistance in the new sociology of education: A critical analysis', *Harvard Educational Review*, **53**, pp. 257–93.

GLASER, B.G. and STRAUSS, A. (1967) *The Discovery of Grounded Theory*, Chicago: Aldine.

GLEESON, D. (ed.) (1977) *Identity and Structure: Issues in the Sociology of Education*, Driffield: Nafferton Books.

GOLDTHORPE, J.H. (1980) *Social Mobility and Class Structure in Modern Britain*, Oxford: Clarendon Press.

GOLDTHORPE, J.H. (1983) 'Women and class analysis', *Sociology*, **17**, 4, pp. 465–88.

GOLDTHORPE, J.H. and MARSHALL, G. (1992) 'The promising future of class analysis: A response to recent critiques', *Sociology*, **26**, 3, pp. 381–400.

GOODLAD, S. (1995) *The Quest for Quality Society for Research into Higher Education*, Buckingham: Society for Research into Higher Education/Open University Press.

GOW, L. and KEMBER, D. (1993) 'Conceptions of teaching and their relationship to student learning', *British Journal of Educational Psychology*, **63**, pp. 20–33.

GRENFELL, M. (1993) 'The linguistic market of Orléans', in KELLY, M. and BÖCK, R. (eds) *France: Nation and State*, Southampton: Associaton for the Study of Modern and Contemporary France.

GRENFELL, M. (1995) 'The initial training of modern language teachers: A social theoretical approach', PhD Thesis: University of Southampton.

GRENFELL, M. (1996) 'Bourdieu and initial teacher education — A post-structuralist approach', *British Journal of Educational Research*, **22**, 3, pp. 287–303.

GRENFELL, M. (1998) *Training Teachers in Practice*, Clevedon: Multilingual Matters, p. 121.

GRIFFIN, C. (1985) *Typical Girls? Young Women from School to the Job Market*, London: Routledge.

GUMPERZ, J. (1982) *Discourse Strategies*, London: Cambridge University Press.

HALSEY, A., HEARTH, A. and RIDGE, J. (1980) *Origins and Destinations: Family, Class and Education in Modern Britain*, London: Clarendon Press.

HAMMERSLEY, M. (1986) 'Some reflections upon the macro-micro problem', in HAMMERSLEY, M. (ed.) *Controversies in Classroom Research*, Milton Keynes: Open University Press, pp. 176–83.

HAMMERSLEY, M. (1992) *What's Wrong with Ethnography?*, London: Routledge.

HAMMERSLEY, M. and ATKINSON, P. (1983) *Ethnography — Principles in Practice*, London: Tavistock.

HARKER, R. (1984) 'On reproduction, habitus and education', *British Journal of Sociology of Education*, **5**, 2, pp. 117–27.

HARKER, R. (1990) 'Bourdieu: Education and reproduction', in HARKER, R., MAHAR, C. and WILKES, C. (eds) *An Introduction to the Work of Pierre Bourdieu*, Basingstoke: Macmillan.

HARKER, R. (1992) 'Cultural capital, education and power in New Zealand: An agenda for research', *New Zealand Sociology*, **7**, 1, pp. 1–19.

HASELGROVE, S. (ed.) (1994) *The Student Experience*, Buckingham: SRHE/Open University Press.

HAUGAARD, M. (1992) *Structures, Restructuration and Social Power*, Aldershot: Avebury.

HAWKES, T. (1977) *Structuralism and Semiotics*, London: Methuen.

HEATH, S.B. (1983) *Ways with Words*, Cambridge: Cambridge University Press.

HENRIQUES, J., HOLLWAY, W., URWIN, C., VENN, C. and WALKERDINE, V. (1984) *Changing the Subject: Psychology, Social Regulation and Subjectivity*, London: Methuen.

HENWOOD, K. and PIDGEON, N. (1993) 'Qualitative research and psychological theorizing', in HAMMERSLEY, M. (ed.) *Social Research — Philosophy, Politics and Practice*, London: Sage, pp. 14–32.

HILLIARD, F.H. (1971) 'Theory and practice in teacher education', in HILLIARD, F.H. (ed.) *Teaching the Teachers*, London: George Allen and Unwin, pp. 33–54.

HINDESS, B. (1988) *Choice, Rationality, and Social Theory*, London: Unwin Hyman.

HIRST, P.H. (1966) 'Educational theory', in TIBBLE, J.W. (ed.) *The Study of Education*, London: Rouledge and Kegan Paul, pp. 29–58.

HIRST, P.Q. (1975) *Durkheim, Bernard and Epistemology*, Boston and London: Routledge and Kegan Paul.

HITCHCOCK, G. and HUGHES, D. (1989) *Research and the Teacher: A qualitative introduction to school-based research*, London: Routledge.

HODKINSON, P. (1995) 'Careership and markets: Structure and agency in the transition to work', PhD Thesis, University of Exeter.

HODKINSON, P. (1996) 'The use of hermeneutics in educational research: A case study into the nature of research truths', *British Educational Research Association Annual Conference Paper*, University of Lancaster, September.

HODKINSON, P. and SPARKES, A.C. (1993) 'Young people's choices and careers guidance action planning: A case study of training credits in action', *British Journal of Guidance and Counselling*, **21**, 3, pp. 246–61.

HODKINSON, P. and SPARKES, A.C. (1994) 'The myth of the market: The negotiation of training in a youth credits pilot scheme', *British Journal of Education and Work*, **7**, 3, pp. 2–20.

HODKINSON, P. and SPARKES, A.C. (1995) 'Markets and vouchers: The inadequacy of individualist policies for vocational education and training in England and Wales', *Journal of Educational Policy*, **10**, 2, pp. 189–207.

HODKINSON, P., SPARKES, A.C. and HODKINSON, H. (1996) *Triumphs and Tears: Young People, Markets and the Transition from School to Work*, London: David Fulton.

HONEY, P. and MUMFORD, A. (1992) *The Manual of Learning Styles (3rd edition)*, Maidstone: P. Honey.

HUSSERL, E. (1960) *Cartesian Meditations* (CAIRNS, D. trans.), The Hague: Marinus Nijhoff.

HUSSERL, E. (1982) *Ideas Pertaining to a Pure Phenomenology and to Phenomenological Philosophy — First Book* (KERSTEN, F. trans.), Dordrecht: Kluwer.

HUTTON, W. (1995) *The State We're In*, London: Jonathan Cape.

JACKSON, B. and MARSDEN, D. (1962) *Education and the Working Class*, London: Routledge and Kegan Paul.

JAMES, D. (1995) 'Mature studentship in higher education: Beyond a "species" approach', *British Journal of Sociology of Education*, **16**, 4, pp. 451–66.

JAMES, D. (1996) 'Mature studentship in higher education', PhD Thesis: University of West of England, Bristol.

JENKINS, R. (1992) *Pierre Bourdieu*, London: Routledge.

JUPP, V. and NORRIS, C. (1993) 'Traditions in documentary analysis', in HAMMERSLEY, M. (ed.) *Social Research — Philosophy, Politics and Practice*, London, Sage, pp. 37–51.

KENNETT, J. (1973) 'The Sociology of Pierre Bourdieu', *Educational Review*, **25**, 3, pp. 237–49.

KERCKHOFF, A.C. (1993) *Diverging Pathways: Social Structure and Career Deflections*, Cambridge: Cambridge University Press.

KERFOOT, D. and KNIGHTS, D. (1994) 'Into the realm of the fearful: Identity and the gender problematic', in RADKE, L.H. and STAM, H.J. (eds) *Power/Gender: Social Relations in Theory and Practice*, London: Sage.

KIDD, J.M. (1984) 'Young people's perceptions of their occupational decision-making', *British Journal of Guidance and Counselling*, **12**, 1, pp. 25–38.

KIERKEGAARD, S. (1941) *Concluding Scientific Postscript* (SWENSON, D.F. trans. and LOWRIE, W.), Princeton: Princeton University Press.

KRAIS, B. (1993) 'Gender and symbolic violence: Female oppression in the light of Pierre Bourdieu's theory of social practice', in CALHOUN, C., LIPUMA, E. and POSTONE, M. *Bourdieu: Critical Perspectives*, Cambridge: Polity Press.

KUHN, T.S. (1962/1970) *The Structure of Scientific Revolutions (Second Edition)*, Chicago: The University of Chicago Press.

LABOV, W. (1972) *Sociolinguistic Patterns*, Oxford: Basil Blackwell.

LABOV, W. (1977) *Language in the Inner City*, Oxford: Basil Blackwell.

LACEY, C. (1985) 'Professional socialisation of teachers', in DUNKIN, M.J. (ed.) *International Encyclopaedia of Teaching and Teacher Education*, Oxford: Pergamon Press. pp. 634–44.

LAMONT, M. and LAREAU, A. (1988) 'Cultural capital: Allusions, gaps and glissandos in recent theoretical developments', *Sociological Theory*, **6**, 1, pp. 153–68.

LAREAU, A. (1989) *Home Advantage*, Lewes: Falmer Press.

LAREAU, A. (1992) 'Gender differences in parent involvement in schooling', in WRIGLEY, J. (ed.) *Education and Gender Equality*, London: Falmer Press.

LATOUR, B. (1988) 'The politics of explanation: An alternative', in WOOLGAR, S. (ed.) *Knowledge and Reflexivity: New Frontiers in the Sociology of Knowledge*, London: Sage. pp. 155–76.

LASH, S. and URRY, J. (1993) *Economies of Signs and Space*, London: Sage.

LAW, B. (1981) 'Community interaction: A 'mid-range' focus for theories of career development in young adults', *British Journal of Guidance and Counselling*, **9**, 2, pp. 142–58.

LAYDER, D. (1993) *New Strategies in Social Research*, Cambridge: Polity Press.

LECOURT, D. (1975) *Marxism and Epistemology. Bachelard, Canguilhem and Foucault* (BREWSTER, B. trans.), London: New Left Books.

MACBETH, A. (1995) 'Partnership between parents and teachers in education', in MACBETH, A., MCCREITH, D. and AITCHISON, J. (eds) *Collaborate or Compete?: Educational Partnerships in a Market Economy*, London: Falmer Press.

MAHAR, C., HARKER, R. and WILKES, C. (1990) 'The basic theoretical position', in HARKER, R., MAHAR, C. and WILKES, C. (eds) *An Introduction to the Work of Pierre Bourdieu — The Practice of Theory*, Basingstoke: Macmillan.

MAHONY, P. and ZMROCZEK, C. (eds) (1997) *Class Matters: Working Class Women's Perspectives on Social Class*, London: Taylor and Francis.

MARCUS, G.E. and FISCHER, M.M.J. (1986) *Anthropology as Cultural Critique*, Chicago: University of Chicago Press.

MAY, S. (1994) *Making Multicultural Education Work*, Clevedon: Multilingual Matters Ltd.

MAYNARD, M. and PURVIS, J. (eds) (1994) *Researching Women's Lives from a Feminist Perspective*, London: Taylor and Francis.

McCALL, L. (1992) 'Does gender fit?: Bourdieu, feminism and conceptions of social order', *Theory and Society*, **21**, 6, pp. 837–68.

McCLELLAND, K. (1990) 'Cumulative disadvantage among the highly ambitious', *Sociology of Education*, **63**, pp. 102–21.

MENNELL, S. (1994) 'The formation of we — images: A process theory', in CALHOUN, C. (ed.) *Social Theory and the Politics of Identity*, Oxford: Basil Blackwell.

MERCER, N. (1995) *The Guided Construction of Knowledge*, Clevedon: Multilingual Matters.

MOUSTAKAS, C. (1990) *Heuristic Research: Design, Methodology, and Applications*, London: Sage.

MUSGRAVE, P. (1966) *The Sociology of Education*, London: Methuen.

NASH, R. (1990) 'Bourdieu on education and social and cultural reproduction', *British Journal of Sociology of Education*, **11**, pp. 431–47.

NOWOTNY, H. (1981) 'Women in public life in Austria', in FUCHS EPSTEIN, C. and COSER, R.L. (eds) *Access to Power: Cross-National Studies of Women and Elites*, London: George Allen and Unwin.

O'CONNOR, D. (1957) *An Introduction to the Philosophy of Education*, London: Routledge and Kegan Paul.

PAHL, R.E. (1989) 'Is the emperor naked? Some comments on the adequacy of sociological theory in urban and regional research', *International Journal of Urban and Regional Research*, **13**, pp. 709–20.

PAPADAKIS, E. (1993) 'Interventions in new social movements', in HAMMERSLEY, M. (ed.) *Social Research — Philosophy, Politics and Practice*, London: Sage, pp. 83–104.

PARSONS, T. and PLATT, G. (1968) 'Considerations of the American academic system', *Minerva*, **6**, pp. 497–523.

PIAGET, J. (1968) *Le Structuralisme*, Paris: PUF.

PHILLIPS, D.C. (1987) *Philosophy, Science and Social Enquiry*, Oxford: Pergamon.

PLATT, J. (1988) 'What can case studies do?', in BURGESS, R. (ed.) *Studies in Qualitative Methodology, Vol 1: Conducting Qualitative Research*, London: Jai Press.

REAY, D. (1995a) 'Using habitus to look at "race" and class in primary school classrooms', in GRIFFITHS, M. and TROYNA, B. (eds) *Anti-racism, Culture and Social Justice in Education*, Stoke-On-Trent: Trentham Books.

REAY, D. (1995b) ' "They employ cleaners to do that": Habitus in the primary classroom', *British Journal of Sociology of Education*, **16**, 3, pp. 353–71.

REAY, D. (1995c) 'A silent majority? Mothers in parental involvement', *Women's Studies International Forum — Special Issue on Women in Families and Households: Qualitative Research*, **18**, 3, pp. 337–48.

REAY, D. (1996a) 'Insider perspectives or stealing the words out of women's mouths: Interpretation in the research process', *Feminist Review: Speaking Out: Researching and representing women*, **53**, pp. 55–71.

REAY, D. (1996b) 'Dealing with difficult differences: Reflexivity and social class in feminist research', in WALKERDINE, V. (ed.) *Feminism and Psychology: Special Issue on Social Class*, **16**, 3, pp. 443–56.

REAY, D. (1997a) 'The double-bind of the "Working-class" feminist academic: The failure of success or the success of failure', in MAHONY, P. and ZMROCZEK, C. (eds) *Class Matters: Working Class Women's Perspectives on Social Class*, London: Taylor and Francis.

REAY, D. (1997b) 'Feminist theory, habitus and social class: Disrupting notions of class-lessness', *Women's Studies International Forum*, **20**, 2, pp. 225–33.

REINHARZ, S. (1992) *Feminist Methods in Social Research*, Oxford: Oxford University Press.

RIBBENS, J. (1993) *Mothers and Their Children: Towards a Feminist Perspective on Childrearing*, London: Sage.

ROBERTS, H. (1993) 'The women and class debate', in MORGAN, D. and STANLEY, L. (eds) *Debates in Sociology*, Manchester: Manchester University Press.

ROBERTS, K. (1968) 'The entry into employment: An approach towards a general theory', *Sociological Review*, **16**, pp. 165–84.

ROBERTS, K. (1975) 'The developmental theory of occupational choice: A critique and an alternative', in ESLAND, G., SALAMAN, G. and SPEAKMAN, M. (eds) *People and Work*, Edinburgh: Holmes McDougall with Open University Press.

ROBERTS, K. (1993) 'Career trajectories and the mirage of increased social mobility', in BATES, I. and RISEBOROUGH, G. (eds) *Youth and Inequality*, Buckingham: Open University Press.

ROBBINS, D. (1991) *The Work of Pierre Bourdieu*, Milton Keynes: Open University Press.

ROBBINS, D. (1993a) 'The practical importance of Bourdieu's analyses of higher education', *Studies in Higher Education*, **18**, 2, pp. 151–63.

ROBBINS, D. (1993b) 'A French accent on league tables', *The Times Higher Education Supplement*, 17 September, p. 19.

ROBBINS, D. (forthcoming) 'Bourdieu on language and education: Conjunction or parallel development?', *Proceedings of a Conference on Pierre Bourdieu. Language, Culture and Education, University of Southampton, April, 1997*.

RORTY, R. (1989) *Contingency, Irony and Solidarity*, Cambridge: Cambridge University Press.

ROWLAND, S. (1987) 'Child in control: Towards an interpretive model of teaching and learning', in POLLARD, A. (ed.) *Children and their Primary Schools*, Lewes: Falmer Press.

ROWLAND, S. (1996) 'Relationships between teaching and research', *Teaching in Higher Education*, **1**, 1, pp. 7–20.

RUBIN, L. (1976) *Worlds of Pain*, New York: Basic Books.

RUMELHART, D.E. (1980) 'Schemata: The building blocks of cognition', in SPIRO, R.J., BRUCE, B.C. and BREWER, W.F. (eds) *Theoretical Issues in Reading Comprehension*, Hillsdale, New Jersey: Lawrence Erlbaum.

RUSSELL, B. (1900) *A Critical Exposition of the Philosophy of Leibniz*, Cambridge: Cambridge University Press.

SAMUELOWICZ, K. and BAIN, J.D. (1992) 'Conceptions of teaching held by academic teachers', *Higher Education*, **24**, pp. 93–111.

SCHUTZ, A. (1962/1982) *The Problem of Social Reality: Collected Papers 1*, The Hague: Martinus Nijhoff.

SCOTT, P. (1993) 'The idea of the University in the 21st Century: A British perspective', *British Journal of Educational Studies*, **41**, 1, pp. 4–25.

SINCLAIR, J. and COULTARD, R. (1975) *Towards an Analysis of Discourse: The English Used by Teachers and Pupils*, London: Oxford University Press.

SKEGGS, B. (1997) *Formations of Class and Gender*, London: Sage.

SMITH, D.E. (1988) *The Everyday World as Problematic: A Feminist Sociology*, Milton Keynes: Open University Press.

SMITH, J.K. (1989) *The Nature of Social and Educational Inquiry: Empiricism versus Interpretation*, Norwood, New Jersey: Ablex.

SMITH, D. and GRIFFITHS, A. (1990) 'Coordinating the uncoordinated: Mothering, schooling and the family wage', *Perspectives on Social Problems*, **2**, 1, pp. 25–43.

SPRADLEY, J. (1980) *Participant Observation*, New York: Holt, Rinehart and Winston.

STRAUSS, A. (1962) 'Transformations of identity', in ROSE, A.M. (ed.) *Human Behaviour and Social Processes: An Interactionist Approach*, London: Routledge and Kegan Paul.

STRAUSS, A. (1987) *Qualitative Analysis for Social Scientists*, Cambridge: Cambridge University Press.

STUBBS, M. (1976) *Language, Schools and Classrooms*, London: Methuen.

SPRADLEY, J. (1980) *Participant Observation*, New York: Holt, Rinehart and Winston.

SWARTZ, D. (1977) 'Pierre Bourdieu: The cultural transmission of social inequality', *Harvard Educational Review*, **47**, 4, pp. 545–55.

SWIFT, D. (1968) *The Sociology of Education*, London: Routledge.

TAJFEL, H. (1982) 'The social psychology of minorities', in HUSBAND, C. (ed.) *Race in Britain: Continuity and Change*: Hutchinson U.L.

TALBOTT, J.E. (1969) *The Politics of Educational Reform in France 1918–1940*: Princeton University Press.

TOPPING, K. and WOLFENDALE, S. (eds) (1986) *Parental Involvement in Children's Reading*, London: Croom Helm.

TYLER, S.A. (1985) 'Ethnography, intertextuality and the end of description', *American Journal of Semiotics*, **3**, 4, pp. 83–98.

TYLER, S.A. (1986) 'Post-modernist ethnography: From document of the occult to occult document', in CLIFFORD, J. and MARCUS, G. (eds) *Writing Culture*, Berkeley: University of California Press, pp. 122–40.

VINCENT, C. (1996) *Parents and Teachers: Power and Participation*, London: Falmer Press.

VYGOTSKY, L. (1962) *Thought and Language*, Cambridge, MA.: MIT Press.

VYGOTSKY, L. (1978) *Mind in Society: The Development of Higher Psychological Processes*, London: Harvard University Press.

WALFORD, G. (1992) 'The reform of higher education', in ARNOT, M. and BARTON, L. (eds) *Voicing Concerns: Sociological Perspectives on Contemporary Educational Reforms*, Wallingford: Triangle Books.

WALKERDINE, V. and LUCEY, H. (1989) *Democracy in the Kitchen: Regulating Mothers and Socialising Daughters*, London: Virago.

WHITEHEAD, J. (1993) *The Growth of Educational Knowledge: Creating Your Own Living Educational Theories*, Bournemouth: Hyde Publications.

WILLIS, P. (1977) *Learning to Labour*, London: Kogan Page.

WOLFENDALE, S. (ed.) (1989) *Parental Involvement — Developing Networks between School, Home and Community*, London: Cassell.

WOOLGAR, S. (ed.) (1988) *Knowledge and Reflexivity: New Frontiers in the Sociology of Knowledge*, London: Sage.

WUGGENIG, U. and MNICH, P. (1994) 'Explorations in social space: Gender, age, class fractions and photographical choices of objects', in GREENACRE, M. and BLASIUS, J. (eds) *Correspondence Analysis in the Social Sciences*, London: Academic Press, pp. 302–23.

YAO, E.L. (1993) 'Strategies for working effectively with Asian immigrant parents', in CHAVKIN, N.F. (ed.) *Families and Schools in a Pluralistic Society*, Albany: State University of New York Press.

YOUNG, M.F.D. (ed.) (1971) *Knowledge and Control*, London: Macmillan.

Index